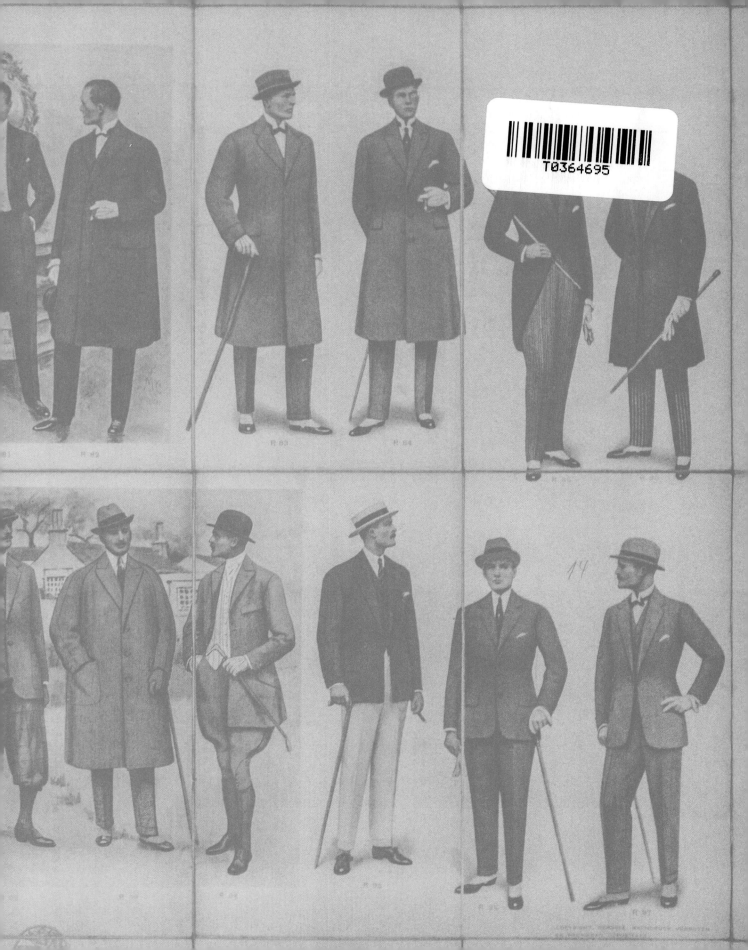

JAMES SHERWOOD

Henry Poole & Co.

THE FIRST TAILOR OF SAVILE ROW

PRINCIPAL PHOTOGRAPHY
ANDY BARNHAM

Thames & Hudson

WITH 150 ILLUSTRATIONS

CONTENTS

FOREWORD

SIMON CUNDEY
JOINT MANAGING DIRECTOR, HENRY POOLE & CO

Henry Poole & Co is proud that the company has remained in family hands for over two centuries. As this book reveals, it has been almost too close to call a number of times in our history, but for the tenacity of my forebears. We also survived thanks to generations of craftspeople and loyal customers who have perpetuated British bespoke tailoring at its finest. We would not still be trading on Savile Row if we did not maintain an international outlook and keep a keen eye on the way our clients – both established and new – want to dress. Poole's may not always follow fashion but neither do we ignore it.

This book is the result of a ten-year period of restoring our historic customer ledgers and building a new archive room at No. 15 Savile Row, instigated by my father, Angus Cundey. Only now, after a decade of cataloguing our Hall of Fame by the book's author, James Sherwood, have we been able to discover how many exceptional men and women who made history over the last 200 years have walked through the door of Poole's. No other tailor globally has such a detailed archive over this extensive timeline.

A new customer may be introduced to us knowing we were the first tailor to cut a dinner jacket. They might pay attention to one of our House Cloths inspired by Winston Churchill, William Randolph Hearst or the Prince of Wales (later King Edward VII). However, I grew up remembering my father Angus saying that a customer is not a customer until he has ordered a second suit.

In the past twenty years, working dress codes have fundamentally changed. Certain cities, such as New York, Washington DC, London and Tokyo, still remain very suit-oriented. But we have noticed that even in Silicon Valley, there is an appreciation of handmade sports jackets, even if they are worn with jeans and trainers. Henry Poole can create a beautiful wardrobe for men who favour casual elegance over formality. We are reassured that the man who has a diverse wardrobe will come to Poole's for tailoring.

It is important for our clients to know that the garments they are measured up for, be that in Atlanta or Zurich, are cut and made on the premises at No. 15 Savile Row. They also like to know the cloth is responsibly sourced because they are, by and large, conscious of sustainability in the modern world. This has very much become a factor that makes clients loyal to Savile Row, as does the knowledge that the garments we make for them are built to last. With designer ready-to-wear, for example, the purchase is made and thus ends your relationship with the brand. With Poole's, a client can and does return to maintain or possibly alter a suit for whatever circumstance. The best compliment a tailor can receive is when the client is told that he looks well rather than that the suit looks good. On hearing this, we know our work is done.

Our international visits to the US, Europe and the Far East are a vital cornerstone of our business. We have a history of trunk shows, where half-completed garments are brought out to cities and returned to be finished on the Row, then collected or shipped. When Poole's was forced to close its shops in Paris, Berlin and Vienna in the first half of the 20th century, we took it upon ourselves to travel. With a strong clientele in the US, this took us across the seas aboard the *Queen Mary* and the *Queen Elizabeth* in the 1950s and '60s. With railway rather than air travel, the US would become a month-long trip. In the 1970s, the jet age shortened the time and allowed us to add cities such as Tokyo, with which we had traded since 1910. As this book demonstrates, Poole's has century-long relationships with Russia, India, South America and China, all of which are potential locations to revisit.

However far we travel, we know our clients love to visit us on Savile Row. They enjoy paying a call on their cutter in the showroom, perhaps placing a new order, and touring the workshops to visit their coat-, vest- or trouser-maker. These key craftspeople are the heart and soul of Henry Poole & Co, together with the apprentices they are training up to continue the tradition and advance the craft.

I was brought up in the family firm. I remember hearing clients' names and then welcoming their grandsons three decades later. Similarly, it is gratifying to see an apprentice join Poole's at nineteen and watch them develop, then spread their wings into a fine cutter who travels the globe and has a passion for the craft. At Poole's we understand that if we do our job correctly and with care, a client will be with us for a lifetime. As managing director, I understand that to cox a crew who row beautifully in time makes a winning team, not an individual. Savile Row has seen many changes over the years, with celebrity tailors coming and going, but I feel optimistic that as long as we maintain the quality, service and skill for which Poole's has always been known, the first tailor of Savile Row will remain where it belongs.

INTRODUCTION

'If you were to go through the pages of *Burke's Peerage* and the
Almanach de Gotha from 1850 to the end of civilization in 1914,
I think we could match you page-by-page with our ledgers.'

SAMUEL CUNDEY, CHAIRMAN OF HENRY POOLE & CO (1960)

It has been the author's privilege to spend the previous decade restoring, cataloguing and researching the illustrious names of famous and infamous men and women listed in the ledger books of Savile Row founding father Henry Poole & Co. This is the most comprehensive and complete set of bespoke tailors' ledgers, dating from 1846, when Henry Poole took over his father's firm, to the present. Allowing for repetition of loyal customers who were Poole's men in their lifetimes – and in the case of the Dukes of Bedford seven generations of continued loyalty to Poole's – I have identified 500 people who significantly contributed to and helped shape world history.

Without the licence to write a book as thick as the *Almanach de Gotha*, it was a challenge to whittle down the list of famous customers to sixty for the purposes of *The First Tailor of Savile Row*. These we have divided into Emperors & Maharajas, Politicians & Statesmen, Financiers & Courtiers, Kings & Queens, Artists & Writers and Heroes & Villains.

The ledgers list in detail every order placed by customers of consequence, so we can definitively locate Henry Poole & Co 18 oz (500 g) tweeds as worn by the 5th Earl of Carnarvon when the tomb of Tutankhamun was unsealed in the Valley of the Kings in 1923, and court dress worn by Prime Minister Benjamin Disraeli when he offered Queen Victoria the title Empress of India. The Henry Poole & Co ledgers offer a perfect sartorial game of six degrees of separation that this book hopes to explore. A fine example is the doomed Crown Prince Rudolf of Austria, whose suicide at Mayerling was the scandal of the late 19th century. His mother, the Empress Elisabeth 'Sisi' of Austria, was a customer, as was her sister-in-law, the Empress Carlota of Mexico, whose husband, the Emperor Maximilian, wore a Poole's frock coat when he was executed by firing squad.

The British royal connection is strong, not least in the uninterrupted roll-call of Royal Warrants from Queen Victoria to Queen Elizabeth II. All of Queen Victoria's nine children held accounts at Poole's, as did their spouses and offspring. Poole's dressed six British prime ministers, fifteen emperors and twenty kings. The tailor of kings can also link all the major players in the 1960s Profumo affair, from Secretary of State for War John Profumo and Lord Astor to Stephen Ward. It is a tantalizing thought that these men met on Savile Row as well as around the pool at Cliveden.

It is thanks to the foresight of present chairman Angus Cundey MBE, the sixth generation of his family to direct Henry Poole, that the ledgers have not only survived but also been expertly rebound and restored for future generations by the Wyvern Bindery. The

Henry Poole & Co archives have also allowed the author to tell the story of the Poole and Cundey families with factual information that had been buried for more than a century in previously unopened tin trunks containing letters, wills, telegrams and legal documents.

As an introduction to our Hall of Fame we begin with extended profiles of two men who deserve our attention and applause as arguably the most important customers to contribute to the success of Henry Poole & Co. HM King Edward VII when Prince of Wales and Prime Minister Winston Churchill were legends in their own lifetimes, with their legacies still having resonance today. Their patronage has brought Henry Poole & Co's ledgers to the attention of cultural creatives today, such as Jane Ridley, who wrote her definitive biography *Bertie: A Life of Edward VII* in 2012, Academy Award-nominated *Darkest Hour* costume designer Jacqueline Durran (2017), Adidas Originals creative director Paul Gaudio (2017), and luxury winter apparel brand Canada Goose (2019).

If this book hopes to achieve one thing it is to demonstrate that Henry Poole & Co's future is informed by its past and that the craft of bespoke tailoring has been passed down the generations and is still holding its own in the increasingly crowded men's tailoring trade, which has enjoyed a renaissance in recent years. Savile Row's story is one of survival of the fittest, and Henry Poole & Co is the only firm on the Row to be owned by direct descendants of the family who founded the company. In addition to the chairman, Angus Cundey, and his son, managing director Simon Cundey (sixth- and seventh-generation guv'nors), the latter's two sons, Henry and Jamie, have already shown a keenness to join the family firm. If the former becomes managing director, he will be Henry the Eighth Generation.

Henry Poole continues to travel to the four corners of the world to showcase the best of British bespoke tailoring, and the diary at present includes representatives being sent to Europe (Paris, Frankfurt, Luxembourg, Geneva and Zurich), America (Atlanta, Boston, Chicago, Los Angeles, Monterey, New York, San Francisco, Washington, New Orleans, Jupiter Island and Palm Beach) and Asia (Tokyo, Beijing, Shanghai, Singapore and Hong Kong). The beauty of the business is that Henry Poole & Co has been trading with all of these territories for well over a century. In this respect Poole's is coming home when it goes abroad.

JAMES SHERWOOD

Page 15: Poole's historic customer ledgers were badly water-damaged in 1941 after an incendiary bomb struck the building at 36–39 Savile Row. They survived in this perilous state until restoration commenced in 2010.

Opposite: The restored collection of more than 120 customer ledgers bound in Henry Poole's house green cloth are housed in the purpose-built new Archive Room at No. 15 Savile Row, opened in 2015.

HENRY POOLE'S
GREATEST CUSTOMERS

HM KING EDWARD VII OF GREAT BRITAIN, EMPEROR OF INDIA

PATRONAGE   1860–1876, then 1901–1910

ROYAL WARRANT   HRH Prince of Wales (1863); HM King Edward VII (1902)

SIGNATURE GARMENT   The short lounging coat – the prototype of
the contemporary suit jacket – that the Prince of Wales favoured as early as
the late 1860s

TOTAL SPEND   £10,940 (£646,870 today)*

CONNECTIONS   Henry Poole dressed King Edward VII's sons, the princes
Albert Victor and George (King George V), under their father's account.
The King's mother, Queen Victoria, held her own account, as did Queen Alexandra,
the King's brothers, Alfred, Duke of Edinburgh, Prince Arthur and Prince Leopold,
and his sisters, the princesses Victoria, Alice, Louisa, Helena and Beatrice.

The eldest son of Queen Victoria and Prince Albert, Prince Albert Edward (1841–1910) – known from birth as Bertie – was an affable, amiable child who seemed to disappoint his parents and was thus excluded from political power for the entirety of Queen Victoria's long reign. Underemployed, the Prince became a notorious playboy with a fondness for the turf, mistresses, cigars, rackety company, gambling and the fine tailoring of his friend Henry Poole.

The Prince was nineteen when he first visited Poole's in 1860. As his grandson the Duke of Windsor wrote in his 1960 memoir, *A Family Album*, 'from that day Poole became the Prince's chief tailor'. Poole's palatial showroom on Savile Row became a de facto gentlemen's club for the Prince and his Marlborough House set, who would meet on the Row to smoke Henry's cigars and drink his brandy en route to the theatre, White's Club or the Café Royal.

The Queen blamed profligate Bertie for her beloved husband's death after Prince Albert had been dispatched to Cambridge in 1861 to admonish his son about a dangerous liaison with actress Nellie Clifden in Dublin. The chill Prince Albert caught allegedly speeded the typhoid fever that killed him. The Queen never recovered from what she

* National Archive calculator, www.nationalarchives.gov.uk

called 'Bertie's Fall', and after the Prince Consort's death she confided to her eldest daughter, Vicky (Crown Princess Frederick of Prussia), that 'I never can, or shall, look at him without a shudder'.

In 1863 the Prince married the exquisite Danish princess Alexandra, who would lead women's fashion just as Bertie led men's. The Prince's sartorial innovations included the Prince of Wales check, the Homburg hat (adopted on his travels to the spa town of Marienbad), the Norfolk jacket, black tie and evening tails. He also wrote the rule that the bottom button of the waistcoat was left undone: a consequence of the corpulence that earned him the nickname 'Tum-Tum'.

With the Prince of Wales's Royal Warrant in 1863 came a royal flush of illustrious royal customers at Henry Poole & Co, such as the Duke of Edinburgh (Bertie's brother), King Christian IX of Denmark (his father-in-law), King George I of the Hellenes (his brother-in-law) and the future Tsar Alexander III of Russia (the Princess of Wales's brother-in-law).

The story of Henry Poole cutting the prototype dinner jacket for the Prince of Wales to wear at private dinners at his country estate, Sandringham, in 1865 is well documented (see page 243). The short smoking jacket in blue silk – an informal alternative to the white tie tailcoat – was indeed the first mention of such a garment in the company's records, and the first dinner jacket tailored on Savile Row.

> Though all of the tailors on Savile Row extended credit to illustrious customers, Henry Poole was particularly vulnerable, being a friend to princes. The company ledgers for Bertie record infrequent payments on account that accumulated over twenty years.

Though all of the tailors on Savile Row extended credit to illustrious customers, Henry Poole was particularly vulnerable, being a friend to princes. The company ledgers for Bertie record infrequent payments on account that accumulated over twenty years. The last surviving letter from Henry in the company archives is written in 1876 and rather sadly reads: 'There will be nothing much to leave behind me. I have worked for a prince and for the public and must die a poor man – and less trouble to the Executor.'

As he predicted, Henry Poole left the firm in dire straits on his death. A bill was sent to Bertie at Marlborough House. He paid the balance, then withdrew his custom for more than twenty years, until, on his accession in 1901, King Edward VII patronized Poole's Livery Department. He would never again give the firm his personal custom, preferring the establishment of his great-uncle King George IV's tailor, Mr Meyer.

The long-suffering Princess Alexandra bore the prince two sons – the princes Albert Victor and George – and three terribly plain daughters. She turned a blind eye to Bertie's infidelities with married ladies Lillie Langtry, Daisy, Countess of Warwick, and Alice Keppel; as well as to his penchant for courtesans such as Catherine 'Skittles' Walters, Cora Pearl and La Barucci, whom he visited in the smarter brothels of Paris and London. Bertie's popularity was dented in 1870 when he became the first British royal to be called

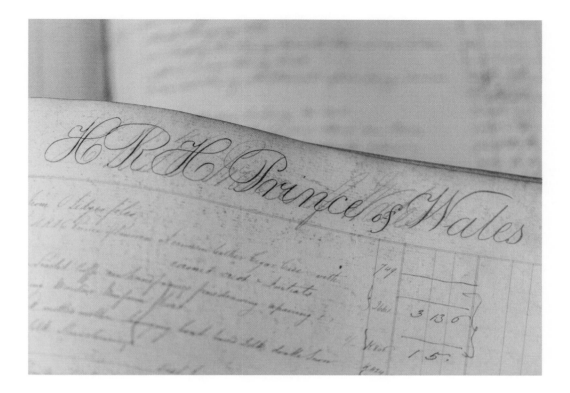

as a witness in an adultery case. His narrow escape from typhoid fever the following year did much to restore him to the affections of the public.

Scandal was never far from Marlborough House, however, and in 1890 the Prince found himself in court once again when it emerged that he had illegally played the card game baccarat at a house party at Tranby Croft, Yorkshire (see page 105). He only narrowly avoided his private affairs being made public again by Sir Charles Beresford and Lord Randolph Churchill thanks to the machinations of his trusted household. The death of his eldest son, Prince Albert Victor, in 1892 once again directed the nation's sympathy towards the Prince and Princess of Wales.

When King Edward VII came to the throne in 1901, he proved a popular and stable monarch, dubbed the 'uncle of Europe' because of his extensive web of relatives among the European monarchies. He famously fostered the Entente Cordiale with the French and held his pugnacious nephew Emperor (Kaiser) Wilhelm II of Germany at bay. Queen Alexandra remained faithful to her husband and even allowed his last *maîtresse-en-titre*, Mrs Keppel, to make her goodbyes on the King's deathbed at Buckingham Palace in 1910. The King's last words were 'I am very glad', on being told that his horse Witch of the Air had romped home at Kempton Park that afternoon.

SIR WINSTON CHURCHILL

PATRONAGE 1906–1965

TOTAL SPEND £1,587 (£80,400 today), a minimum considering four of
Churchill's ledger pages are water-damaged and illegible

SIGNATURE GARMENT Grey chalk-stripe single-breasted Fox flannel suit
seen in the infamous 'Tommy gun' portrait of Churchill as prime minister

CONNECTIONS Churchill's father and mother, Lord and Lady Randolph
Churchill, both held accounts with Henry Poole & Co, as did his first cousin the
9th Duke of Marlborough, the Duke's wife, Consuelo Vanderbilt Balsan, and the
Duke's sons, the future 10th Duke and Lord Ivor Spencer Churchill.

Winston Churchill (1847–1965) was Britain's greatest 20th-century prime minister. He served twice, first from 1940 to 1945, when his fortitude, eloquent speech-making and iron resolve never to surrender to Hitler's Nazi regime steered Britain to victory in World War II. He returned to power between 1951 and 1955, when he had the distinction of being HM Queen Elizabeth II's first prime minister, though his health was ailing and his party hostile. Churchill remains one of the most famous British men in the world, and he had the distinction of being the first person in history to be made an honorary citizen of the USA.

Churchill's father, Lord Randolph Churchill, was the third son of the 7th Duke of Marlborough. He was a charismatic Tory politician and a controversial figure in London high society for his questionable conduct towards his erstwhile friend the Prince of Wales. He was also a Poole's man. Churchill's mother was an American beauty christened Jennie Jerome, who also held an account with Poole's. Neither parent was particularly attentive to young Winston over and above giving him an allowance that was insufficient, thus forcing the young soldier who served in British India, the Sudan and the Second Boer War in Africa to work as a war correspondent to supplement his income.

In his early career as a Tory politician, Winston Churchill was a contentious figure unpopular with the leadership, who questioned his judgment when he opposed Indian Home Rule and supported King Edward VIII during the Abdication Crisis. As Minister for War during World War I, Churchill had authorized the disastrous Gallipoli campaign that saw heavy Australian and British casualties. The 1930s were known as Churchill's 'wilderness years', not only for his support for the King's marriage to twice-divorced American Wallis Simpson but also for his being an isolated voice in the dark criticizing Nazi Germany and urging Britain to arm itself in the face of an impending attack by Adolf Hitler. Churchill's reputation had not recovered from the Gallipoli defeat and he was looked on as a bullish warmonger. Yet history proved Churchill correct and, following the resignation of pro-appeasement Prime Minister Neville 'Peace in our Time' Chamberlain,

Churchill was invited to form a wartime government in 1940. He became known for his rousing speeches to galvanize the British population who stood alone against Nazi Germany but for the Free French Resistance and eventually the USA.

Churchill's words are some of the most powerful ever quoted: 'I have nothing to offer but blood, toil, tears and sweat', for example, or his great call to arms: 'We shall fight in France, we shall fight on the seas and oceans, we shall fight with growing confidence and growing strength in the air, we shall defend our island whatever the cost may be, we shall fight on the beaches, we shall fight on the landing grounds, we shall fight in the fields and streets, we shall fight in the hills. We shall never surrender.'

Churchill ordered from Poole's his formal apparel as Under Secretary of State for the Colonies, Privy Councillor, President of the Board of Trade, Home Secretary, First Lord of the Admiralty, Secretary of State for War, Chancellor of the Exchequer and an Elder Brother of Trinity House.

The Prime Minister famously fought with the 'Black Dog' of depression, which he taught to walk to heel by drinking a silver tankard of Champagne (Pol Roger) every morning, painting and, somewhat bizarrely, bricklaying at his country estate, Chartwell in Kent. He married Clementine Hozier in 1908, a woman Churchill relied upon for her intelligence, intuition and fortitude. Clementine Churchill tolerated her husband's remarkable capacity for alcohol but criticized his excessive fondness for Romeo y Julieta cigars, with which he would burn his Henry Poole & Co uniforms and civilian suits.

It was something of a shock to Churchill that he was voted out of power in 1945, the very year that victory in Europe was declared. Britain had not been brought to its knees in the same way that occupied France had, but whole swathes of cities had been blitzed, and rationing would be imposed until well into the 1950s. He was returned to Downing Street in 1951, but retired owing to increasingly fragile health four years later.

Queen Elizabeth II offered Churchill a dukedom (the Duke of London) but he declined and accepted the Order of the Knights of the Garter instead. When he died in 1965 at the age of ninety, the Queen commanded that Churchill be given a full state funeral at St Paul's Cathedral, an honour previously conferred on national heroes such as Admiral Lord Nelson and the 1st Duke of Wellington.

Churchill's patronage of Henry Poole predated World War I. As *Henry Poole & Co: A History* author Stephen Howard wrote, 'in addition to civilian clothes, Churchill ordered from Poole's his formal apparel as Under Secretary of State for the Colonies, Privy Councillor, President of the Board of Trade, Home Secretary, First Lord of the Admiralty, Secretary of State for War, Chancellor of the Exchequer and an Elder Brother of Trinity House … one of his favourite uniforms that Poole's tailored consecutively as the Prime Minister's waist expanded'. Such was Churchill's devotion to Poole's that he even had white cotton painting smocks for use in his studio at Chartwell bespoken to the firm.

Like King Edward VII, Churchill fell foul of Henry Poole & Co when a bill was sent to No. 10 Downing Street instead of Chartwell. Churchill was notorious for not paying his

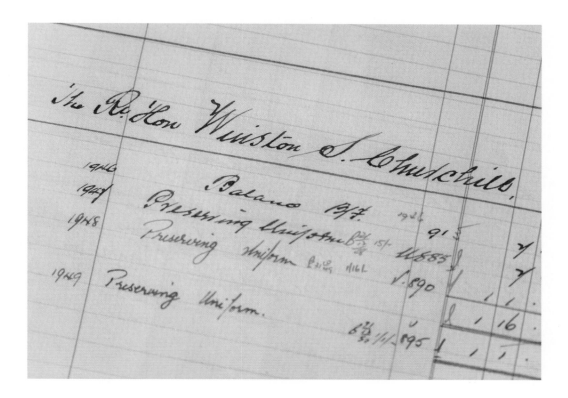

tradesmen's bills. Churchill did pay the final bill for £197 (£7,750 today) in 1940, but did not return to Poole's for his civilian suits after the war. What he did was continue to send his uniforms back to the firm until 1965 to be repaired, taken out, steamed and pressed.

In 2012, managing director Simon Cundey commissioned Somerset cloth merchants Fox Brothers & Co to re-weave a grey wool chalk-stripe cloth that Churchill wore as a three-piece made by the firm for the duration of World War II, as a house special bale of cloth. The Churchill grey flannel was also chosen for one pair of the Adidas Originals trainers made in collaboration with Poole's as a limited edition in 2017, which sold out in a day. In 2016, Oscar-winning costume designer Jacqueline Durran came to Poole's to research Winston Churchill's measurements for the 2017 film *Darkest Hour* starring Gary Oldman.

Star.

EPTEMBER 25, 1816. PRICE SEVEN-PENCE.

CHAPTER ONE
THE BEGINNING
1806–1836

'Gold is not more closely associated by tradition with Golconda
than is tailoring with Savile Row and it is the house of Poole which
founded that association of ideas. Indeed, the two names have
become almost interchangeable. Men say, "he always looks
as though he is dressed in Savile Row" or "as though Poole
dressed him" meaning the same thing.'

TAILOR & CUTTER (6 SEPTEMBER 1946)

The story of Henry Poole & Co begins in Bloomsbury, a modest borough of London,
in 1806. King George III is on the throne but already showing signs of the madness
that will see him forcibly incarcerated in Windsor Castle until his death in 1820.
Though not named regent until 1811, the King's eldest son, the Prince of Wales,
already rules London society and leads fashion by following his sartorial master
George 'Beau' Brummell, a commoner.

France was indirectly the making of the British tailoring industry. The French Revolution
of 1789 not only toppled the monarchy but rendered the elaborate silk court dress worn
at the Palace of Versailles extinct. Practically overnight the French silk industry in Lyon
collapsed and the focus shifted to English tailoring in honest wool. At the turn of the 19th
century Brummell popularized the understated but expertly cut clothing of the English
landed gentry, thereby consigning the foppish French court fashion to the previous century.

It was to London's wealthy, gaudy metropolis that Shropshire lad James Poole and
his wife, Mary, both born in 1781, came to seek their fortune. Mary was a widow of considerable means, who might well have financed James Poole's escape from the village of
Baschurch. A lease preserved in the Henry Poole archive records that James Poole set
up shop as a draper at No. 7 Everett Street in Bloomsbury.

Everett Street was equidistant between Russell Square and Brunswick Square, neither
as fashionable as they had been when first laid out. According to the Survey of London, the
houses neighbouring James Poole's drapers shop were populated by barristers, physicians,
surgeons, solicitors and dentists. Bloomsbury was also nose-to-tail with a less savoury
London district. We have a gang of thieves on the Holborn/Clerkenwell border – where,
incidentally, Charles Dickens located Fagin's den in *Oliver Twist* (1838) – to thank for the
little we know about James Poole's business in Bloomsbury. In the missing years leading
up to the crime in question, Mary gave birth to James (1809), Mary Ann (1912) and Henry
George Poole (1814), all of whom were born and raised at the Everett Street address.

Opposite: An 1816 edition of the *Star* kept in Poole's archive reporting the hanging of three men
convicted of theft from James Poole's Everett Street shop.

A *c.* 1822 etching of Nash's magnificent Regent Street façade of Henry Poole's first West End shop.

The crime was perpetrated in 1815 and recorded in detail in the oldest newspaper cutting in the Poole archive, dated 12 January 1816. Reporting from the Old Bailey, the *Star* newspaper relates that three housebreakers, Thomas Batts, Robert Rawley and John Farthing, 'were indicted for burglariously [sic] breaking and entering the dwelling house of James Poole, a tailor in Everett Street, Brunswick Square, and stealing therein six yards of brown cloth value £5'.

From Old Bailey records, we learn that James Poole was a thrifty man, because he refused counsel and decided to tell 'the plain honest truth' himself. The trial transcript also confirms that by 1815 James Poole was a working tailor and cutter. Of the day of the burglary, James testified that 'it was about twenty minutes before five; it was darkish. I had left my work of cutting out as I could not see to cut out.' Old Bailey Online confirms that Batts, Rawley and Farthing, all twenty-four years old, were hanged.

Company lore passed down the centuries propounds the theory that James was not a tailor until 1815, when he, like many London civilians, enlisted as a volunteer in the British Army. The Emperor Napoleon had escaped from exile on the isle of Elba and mounted his last push against Allied forces. The story, as told in a 1925 edition of *Tailor & Cutter*, goes that James – like all volunteers – was expected to tailor his own tunic.

'It was such a beautiful production that it caught the eye of one of the officers. On being asked if he were a tailor, Poole said he was and then came the further question "could you make me a tunic like that?" He made one and then another. One officer recommended him to a brother officer and so it went on. That was the origin of the business of which the trade is proud.'

It is highly unlikely that James and/or Mary had never threaded a needle before being asked to tailor a military tunic in 1815 … particularly one that won the admiration of the officer class. A far more plausible scenario would be that James had seen the advantage of tailoring military uniform soon after his arrival in London, when the Napoleonic Wars were already three years fought. His subsequent years practising the craft would indeed have made him a master tailor who could cut an exceptional military tunic.

In 1822, James's trade was sufficiently bullish for him to take the leap into the fashionable West End. He not only moved to Mayfair but chose the most ambitious development in Central London since the Great Fire of 1666: architect John Nash's Regent Street.

Regent Street carved a grand boulevard between aristocratic Mayfair and the slum dwellings and sweatshops of Soho. Approved by royal charter in 1813, Regent Street was designed to link the Prince Regent's residence Carlton House with Piccadilly Circus, then progress onward, curving gently up to Regent's Circus (now Oxford Circus) and on towards All Souls Church. The sinuous promenade of stucco-façade buildings was available on ninety-nine-year leases to shopkeepers, restaurateurs and tavern-keepers.

James Poole took No. 171 Regent Street, a five-storey Corinthian-columned façade next to the White Horse Tavern on the corner of New Burlington Street. Though the shop was small, the Poole family lived in some luxury on the three floors above, with a first-floor balcony on the piano nobile looking out over the passing show beneath. Poole's sub-let Regent Street in 1828 and, incidentally, the ninety-nine-year lease on the property would prove to be the firm's salvation after Henry Poole's death.

In 1927 *Tailor & Cutter* wrote an appreciation of Henry Poole & Co to mark the death of company chairman Howard Cundey. Within it are quoted 'some of James Poole's rules for the conduct of business':

(1) That no matter what a customer asked for, every effort should be made to give it to him, however unreasonable it may seem.
(2) That his cutters were not to dictate their opinions to customers, but rather consult their wishes, and attempt to satisfy them.
(3) That all accounts, accurately kept, should be punctually rendered.
(4) Always write an autograph letter thanking a customer for a recommendation.
(5) Among other things, to give comfort in clothes.

Give or take the willingness to meet a customer's demands however unreasonable – what being the point of sending a gentleman out in a Poole's garment that does not reflect well on the house? – James's rules are still adhered to at Henry Poole & Co today.

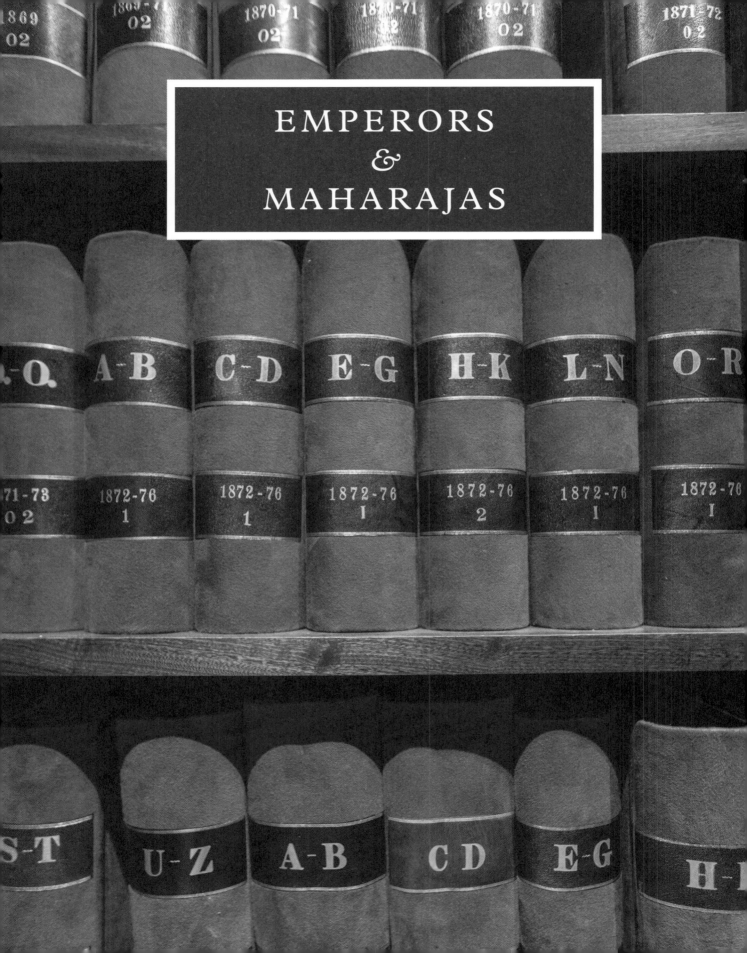

EMPERORS
&
MAHARAJAS

HIM EMPEROR NAPOLEON III OF THE FRENCH

PATRONAGE 1846–1871

ROYAL WARRANT HIM Emperor Napoleon III of the French (1858)

SIGNATURE GARMENT When not in uniform as Emperor of the French,
Napoleon III wore Henry Poole & Co black frock coats with silk facings

TOTAL SPEND £311 (£82,080 today)

CONNECTIONS Napoleon III's consort, the Empress Eugénie, held her
own account with Poole's livery department, and his son, the Prince Imperial,
was dressed by Poole's until his death by Zulu spear in 1879.

Prince Louis-Napoleon Bonaparte (1808–1873) was the nephew and heir of the first Emperor Napoleon, and fulfilled his dynastic ambitions in 1852 by ascending the French throne as Emperor Napoleon III on the forty-eighth anniversary of his uncle's coronation. He holds the unique position as the first titular president of France and the nation's last absolute monarch.

As pretender to the throne, Prince Louis-Napoleon repeatedly instigated uprisings and coup attempts from his exile in London but was unsuccessful largely through lack of funds and a disinclination by the French people to accept another dictatorship in lieu of a republic. In 1840, the Prince was incarcerated in a fortress in the Somme department of northern France ostensibly to serve a life sentence. He escaped in 1846 using the time-honoured trick of exchanging clothes with a peasant, and returned to London. The fate of the peasant is unrecorded.

It was in 1846 – the year Henry Poole inherited his family firm – that the Prince first patronized the tailor and made friends with its affable eponymous owner. Billeted at the Brunswick Hotel in Mayfair while plotting in the cellars of the St James's wine merchant Berry Bros & Rudd, Prince Louis-Napoleon was to become Henry Poole's first royal customer, and in 1858 would give the firm the first of its forty Royal Warrants.

According to company lore, Henry Poole contributed to a war chest that would finance Prince Louis-Napoleon's successful coup d'état that saw him proclaimed emperor in 1852. A more likely story is that Louis-Napoleon met Baron Meyer de Rothschild at Poole's Savile Row showroom and it was he who financed the coup, with additional funds raised by the Prince's mistress Harriet Howard.

The Second Empire under Napoleon III was ostensibly a golden era for Paris. The medieval city was practically razed to the ground and rebuilt as a series of grand boulevards and elegant aristocratic townhouses in the Rococo revival style as designed by Baron Haussmann. The Emperor married Spanish aristocrat Countess Eugénie de Montijo, who in 1856 gave him a son and heir, styled the Prince Imperial.

We know that Henry Poole was a guest of the Emperor at Saint-Cloud and Compiègne, where it was said the Empress – who had a personal account with Poole's – was most entertained by his skill as a pianist. One wonders if fellow guests knew that Mr Poole was the tailor of the liveries designed by the Emperor and Empress for each of their châteaux?

In the early years of his reign, Napoleon III stabilized the French economy, tempered colonial ambitions and refused to engage in costly foreign wars. 'The Empire means peace,' he declared. By forming an alliance with England against the Russians in the Crimean War, Napoleon scored a diplomatic success not achieved by his pugnacious uncle.

In the latter half of Napoleon's reign, France became increasingly hubristic and acquisitive. New Caledonia and Senegal became French territories and troops were sent to China, Korea, Japan, Indochina, Lebanon, Algeria and Mexico, with varying degrees of success. In China, French and British troops infamously burned the Chinese emperor's Summer Palace to the ground and looted priceless contents.

The Second Empire collapsed when the Emperor failed in his attempt to defend the Austrian Empire against Prussia. The Emperor was captured at the Battle of Sedan in 1870 and deposed by the newly elected Third Republic of France. Napoleon and Eugénie fled Paris separately and re-united in England to live out their days in exile. The former emperor died in 1873.

HM EMPEROR MAXIMILIAN I OF MEXICO

PATRONAGE 1861–1866

SIGNATURE GARMENT Emperor Maximilian's imagined coronation portrait
(1863) depicts him in an Austrian regulation uniform tailored by Poole's.
The Emperor was never crowned.

TOTAL SPEND £158 (£9,320 today)

CONNECTIONS Though she herself never held an account with Poole's,
between 1861 and 1865 the Emperor ordered twelve riding habits for his Empress
Carlota, to be worn with matching trousers beneath and detachable white linen
collars and cuffs.

Born in the Schönbrunn Palace in Vienna, son of Archduke Franz Karl of Austria and Princess Sophie of Wittelsbach and grandson of the Holy Roman Emperor Franz II, Austrian Archduke Maximilian (1832–1867) was plagued from birth by rumours that he was the illegitimate child of Napoleon II of the French. Maximilian was highly educated by tutors and learned to speak English, French, Italian, Spanish, Hungarian and Slovak as well as his native German. He far surpassed his elder brother, the future Emperor Franz Joseph of Austria, in every endeavour, be it academic, sporting or military.

The Archduke was old enough to understand the volatile political climate that exploded in 1848: a year of revolution. Austria rioted, suppressed rebels were executed, Maximilian's uncle, Emperor Ferdinand I, abdicated, and Franz Joseph was chosen to succeed. The sixteen-year-old Maximilian said of the year his uncle and King Louis Philippe of France were deposed: 'We call ours the Age of Enlightenment but there are cities in Europe where, in future, men will look back in horror and amazement at the injustice of tribunals.'

Maximilian entered military service in the Austrian Navy, taking office as commander-in-chief in 1854 aged only twenty-one. It was on his watch that the naval ports of Trieste and Pula were established and that frigate SMS *Novara* became the first Austrian warship to circumnavigate the globe. Politically, Maximilian was of liberal persuasion. His moral and social codes were decidedly progressive for the notoriously stiff, formal and draconian Austrian court.

In 1857 the Archduke married his second cousin, Princess Charlotte of Belgium, who was first cousin to both Queen Victoria and her husband, Prince Albert. Installed as Austrian viceroys of Lombardy-Venetia, the couple were popular and provoked the ire of a jealous Emperor Franz Joseph, who dismissed Maximilian from his post. The Archduke retired to Trieste and built the magical castle he christened Miramare.

In 1859 Maximilian was approached by the Mexican monarchist party to restore the throne of the Central American republic. The cause was bolstered by Emperor Napoleon III of the French, whose troops had captured Mexico City. Despite Franz Joseph's

disapproval, Maximilian accepted the throne and set sail on board SMS *Novara* bound for Veracruz. Queen Victoria commanded that her garrison on Gibraltar fire a gun salute as the new emperor's ship sailed past.

The Emperor and his Empress Carlota landed at Veracruz in 1864, though liberal President Benito Juárez refused to acknowledge their presence and the public reception was lukewarm at best. Despite choosing Chapultepec Castle in Mexico City as their primary palace, the couple would never be crowned. Emperor Maximilian's first acts as absolute ruler were undermined by liberal reform.

The end of the American Civil War shifted the axis of power and doomed the adopted dynasty. Arms were sent over the border to support Juárez and the Emperor was deserted by Napoleon III's troops. The Empress was sent to Europe to rally support at the courts of Austria and France. She also appealed to Pope Pius IX with a personal visit to Vatican City. Carlota's mission failed and she suffered a catastrophic mental collapse from which she never recovered.

With the support of the United States, Juárez staged a coup against the Emperor, who was deposed in 1867, court martialled and sentenced to death by firing squad. He went to his death in a drab serge Henry Poole & Co frock coat and trousers. Maximilian's last request was that the executioners did not shoot him in the face so that his mother, Princess Sophie, would recognize the corpse. His last words were: 'I forgive everyone and ask everyone to forgive me. May my blood, about to be shed, be for the good of the country. Viva Mexico! Viva la independencia!'

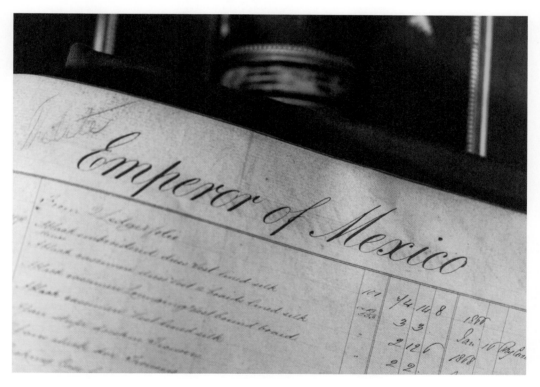

HIM TSAR ALEXANDER II OF RUSSIA

PATRONAGE 1864–1874

ROYAL WARRANT HIM Tsar Alexander II of Russia (1875)

SIGNATURE GARMENT The dark-green wool coat with red collar and cuffs
with state emblem gilt buttons, gilt collar embroidery and epaulettes tailored for
Alexander's coronation as Tsar

TOTAL SPEND £98 (£5,790)

CONNECTIONS Tsar Alexander's father, Emperor Nicholas I, had an account
with Poole's, as did his sons the grand dukes Alexander, Vladimir, Alexei, Sergei
and Paul

In three centuries of Romanov rule, Tsar Alexander II of Russia (1818–1881) was the best-prepared heir to the imperial throne. His father, the 'Soldier Tsar' Nicholas I, was a pugnacious emperor who sought to expand the Russian Empire and rule his subjects with an iron fist. By contrast, Grand Duke Alexander's education was placed in the hands of poet and literary critic Vasily Zhukovsky, who told the Tsar that he would educate the Tsesarevich (heir apparent) as 'a future enlightened monarch'. Tsesarevich Alexander would also distinguish himself at the first Military Academy and serve in the Caucasian War.

Aged nineteen, Alexander was sent on a tour of Russia and Europe. In 1839, the twenty-one-year-old paid court to Queen Victoria, who reported in her diary: 'I really am quite in love with the Grand Duke. He is a dear, delightful young man.' Tsar Nicholas I crushed all hope of a union that would have demanded Alexander's being removed from the line of succession. He continued to tour Europe and fell in love with Prussian princess Marie of Hesse-Darmstadt, who converted to Russian Orthodoxy, became Maria Alexandrovna and married Alexander in 1841.

In 1855, Tsar Nicholas I died, leaving the new emperor, Alexander II, to galvanize his people in the aftermath of the disastrous Crimean War, which had seen monumental loss of life among the Russian peasant class, who were forced to enlist and die as cannon fodder. Tsar Alexander inherited a Russia humiliated by the Crimean defeat. The Russian Empire was essentially ruled like an 18th-century autocracy in a mid-19th-century world.

We know that Henry Poole & Co tailored the new Tsar's coronation uniform in 1856 because the garments were returned to the Victoria & Albert Museum in 2008 as part of the 'Magnificence of the Tsars' exhibition. The catalogue goes into detail about the dark-green wool short coat with red collar and cuffs being a simplified and more comfortable cut of the uniform of the Guards, of which Alexander was colonel-in-chief. The tunic is plain but for gilt embroidery, buttons, epaulettes and the orders of Saint Andrew

and Saint Vladimir. The overalls are scarlet wool with gold trim and the helmet is black leather with a bronze gilt decoration and a plume of cock feathers.

Alexander would go down in Russian history as the greatest reformer since Peter the Great. He prophetically said that 'it is better to abolish serfdom from above than wait for the time when it will begin to abolish itself from below' … a lesson his grandson Nicholas II failed to heed, hence the Russian Revolution of 1917. In 1861 Alexander commanded that Russia's 22 million serfs be freed, under the Emancipation Reform.

In 1876 Alexander embarked on his most distinguished military campaign when he came to the aid of Bulgaria, a country annexed by the Ottoman Empire for 500 years. The Tsar was a champion of oppressed Orthodox Christians and, though 200,000 Russian soldiers were killed, Bulgaria was liberated, earning the Tsar the title 'Il Liberator'. Despite his liberalism, Alexander was the target of numerous assassination attempts.

In the last years of his life, Alexander contemplated giving up his 'divine right' to rule and making Russia a constitutional monarchy. The fate of the Romanov dynasty might have been very different had he done so. On 13 March 1881, a trio of assassins from the People's Will faction ambushed the Tsar's carriage with a bomb that killed the Cossack guards but left Alexander unharmed. The Tsar got out of his carriage to tend to the wounded but a second assassin hurled a bomb at his feet. The assassin described the scene thus: 'Through the snow, debris and blood, you could see fragments of clothing, epaulettes, sabres and bloody chunks of human flesh.' Alexander bled to death with his beloved Irish setter, Milord, and his family by his side.

HH SAYAJIRAO GAEKWAD III, MAHARAJA OF BARODA

PATRONAGE 1900–1911

SIGNATURE GARMENT The Maharaja was a regular visitor to Europe for the
season. Poole's tailored a blue chalk-stripe double-breasted short lounging coat,
single-breasted vest and trousers for his European sojourns.

TOTAL SPEND £491 (£38,580 today)

CONNECTIONS The Maharaja's eldest son and heir, Fatehsinrao, ordered
Western dress on his father's account. On 15 September 1908 the Poole's clerks
posted a Reuters notice that Fatehsinrao had died.

Maharaja Sayajirao Gaekwad III of Baroda (1863–1939) was one of the longest-serving and most controversial Indian princes to reign during the British Raj. He was the product of the morganatic marriage of his father, the first Raja of Baroda, which technically disqualified him and his brothers from the line of succession. He was born in the reign of Maharaja Khanderao Gaekwad II, who was a popular ruler of the third wealthiest Indian princely state.

Upon the death of Khanderao, his brother Malharrao ascended the throne. The new maharaja was a tyrant and a spendthrift. He commissioned the fabled jewel-encrusted Pearl Carpet of Baroda and two cannons cast in solid gold. He also plotted to have the British Resident poisoned with a compound of arsenic, for which the Secretary of State for India, Lord Salisbury, had him removed from the throne in 1875.

Dowager Maharani Jamnabai was tasked with choosing a new heir from cadet branches of the Gaekwad dynasty, including twelve-year-old Sayajirao and his brothers. Legend has it that when Sayajirao was asked why he had come to Baroda's capital, he replied: 'I have come to rule.' Sayajirao was adopted by Maharani Jamnabai and, being a minor, ruled under a council of regency led by the British Resident and the Dowager Maharani.

The Maharaja's education was placed in the hands of tutor Raja Sir Madhava Rao and an Englishman, F. A. H. Elliot. Elliot gave the Maharaja a British public school education. He rose at 6.00 a.m., undertook Indian strength-building exercises and rode his horses before breakfast, then spent the day being schooled in languages, history and Baroda's constitution. He was taught to sword-fight and to play cricket, football and hockey. When the Prince of Wales (later King Edward VII) visited Baroda in 1875, he reported of Sayajirao that 'he is really a very intelligent youth though only six months ago he was running about in the streets adorned with the most limited wardrobe'.

When the Maharaja reached the age of majority in 1881, he began a programme of reform in Baroda inspired by the British masters. He was a passionate advocate of

education, social mobility and judicial and agricultural reform. He developed Baroda's textile industry, banned child marriage, legalized divorce, removed the stigma of the 'untouchable' class, and developed Sanskrit, education and the arts. He also built railways and, in 1908, founded the Bank of Baroda. His collection of books became the nucleus of today's Central Library of Baroda and he opened schools and libraries across the state.

The Maharaja could afford to be magnanimous. Such was the Baroda state wealth at his disposal that he built the 170-room Laxmi Vilas palace – four times the size of Buckingham Palace – as the primary residence for himself and his wife, Maharani Chimnabai I, whom he married in 1880. B7 1908, *Time* magazine rated him as the sixth richest man in the world

The Maharaja was unpopular with the British Raj overlords because he consistently if not always intentionally slighted the British monarchy. A teetotaller, the Maharaja was criticized for drinking Queen Victoria's health with a glass of water. Though he attended the Delhi Durbars (assemblies to celebrate the proclamation of a new emperor or empress of India) of 1877, 1903 and 1911, he caused serious offence at the latter. The 1911 Durbar was the first time a British monarch – King George V and Queen Mary – had attended in person. The Maharaja presented himself without a single jewel, wearing a plain white tunic, and bowed just once instead of three times before turning his back on the King. The British never trusted the Maharaja again.

On each visit to London the Maharaja would order Western-style tailoring from Henry Poole & Co. In England he favoured frock coats, much to the disappointment of Queen Victoria when he was received at Windsor Castle not wearing the fabulous Baroda jewels. All of the Maharaja's dissolute sons were educated in England, though his prophecy that 'rich children have their own dangers' proved correct. His eldest son, Fatehsinhrao, was sent down from Balliol for dissipated behaviour and his second son, Shivajirao, died aged thirty in a clinic while being treated for alcoholism.

When Maharani Chimnabai I died of tuberculosis in 1885 Sayajirao married a second consort, known as Chimnabai II, who was a great advocate for the rights of women in Baroda. The marriage lasted for fifty-three years. When Maharaja Sayajirao died in 1939 he was one month shy of his seventy-sixth birthday. He had celebrated his diamond jubilee and had made Baroda one of the most advanced princely states in India.

HIM EMPEROR FREDERICK III OF GERMANY

PATRONAGE 1868–1887

ROYAL WARRANT HRH The Crown Prince of Prussia (1868)

SIGNATURE GARMENT White general's tunic made to Prussian Regulations by Henry Poole & Co

TOTAL SPEND £1,842 (£121,910 today)

CONNECTIONS Emperor Frederick's consort, the Empress Frederick (Princess Victoria, eldest daughter of Queen Victoria), held a personal account with Poole's, as did his eldest son, the future Emperor Wilhelm II.

Prince Frederick Wilhelm of Prussia (1831–1888) reigned as Emperor Frederick III of Germany for only ninety-nine days in 1888. His premature death from cancer of the larynx serves as one of the great 'what if?' moments of European history. Had he lived, the pacifist constitutional monarch could perhaps have prevented the catastrophic world war that was declared by his son Kaiser (Emperor) Wilhelm II and which led to the fall of the Prussian Hohenzollern dynasty.

Prince Frederick was the oldest son of the future Emperor Wilhelm I of Germany and Princess Augusta of Saxe-Weimar. Like all Prussian princes, Frederick underwent a strict military education. But with the encouragement of his uncle King Frederick Wilhelm IV of Prussia, he broke with tradition and became the first Hohenzollern prince to attend university in Bonn, where he studied history, politics and law.

In 1851 Fritz, as the Prince was known in royal circles, accompanied his mother and father on a visit to London to view the Great Exhibition in the Crystal Palace erected in Hyde Park. He met Vicky, eldest daughter of Queen Victoria and Princess Royal, in the Chinese drawing room at Buckingham Palace, and love appeared to blossom. In 1855 Fritz paid a private visit to Balmoral Castle and won the hand of the Princess Royal. He said of the love match: 'It is not politics. It is not ambition. It is my heart.'

Fritz married Vicky in 1858. Theirs was the first royal nuptials at which Felix Mendelssohn's *Wedding March* was played. They would have eight children, the eldest, Wilhelm, being born with a withered arm following a breech birth that gave rise to a life-long hatred of his mother. Prince Frederick suffered from depression all his life, and his British princess found the German royal court in Berlin hostile to her and her perceived Anglophile influence on her husband.

Vicky and Fritz became Crown Prince and Princess in 1861 on the accession of Emperor Wilhelm I. The Emperor's queen, Augusta, proved to be a malign influence who seemed to take pleasure in isolating Vicky and taking a controlling influence over her grandchildren's education. The death of Vicky's beloved father, Prince Albert, made

an already prolific private correspondence between Vicky and her mother an almost daily ritual that led to suggestions that the Crown Princess was a British spy.

It soon became obvious that Emperor Wilhelm and his chancellor, Otto von Bismarck, intended to marginalize the Crown Prince and Princess and starve the heir of political influence. Underemployed, Fritz and Vicky spent an inordinate amount of time in England. Fritz first visited Henry Poole in 1865 and ordered a wardrobe suitable for Queen Victoria's country residences Osborne House and Balmoral, where he and Vicky were entertained on relatively low-key private visits.

Among other conflicts, Fritz fought in the Second Schleswig War in 1864 and the Franco-Prussian War of 1870 and was much lauded by the *Times*, which said of him that 'the Prince has won as much honour for his gentleness as for his prowess in war'. Fritz was quoted as saying: 'I do not like war, gentlemen. If I should reign, I would never make it.' His words did not please his father, who, after the unification of Germany in 1871, was declared Emperor of Germany.

Emperor Wilhelm would live until his ninetieth birthday, by which time his heir had already been diagnosed with the cancer that would kill him. With their son, the young Prince Wilhelm, waiting in the wings, Emperor Frederick III and his Empress Victoria were crowned. On his deathbed, the Emperor wrote: 'I cannot die. What would happen to Germany?' What indeed?

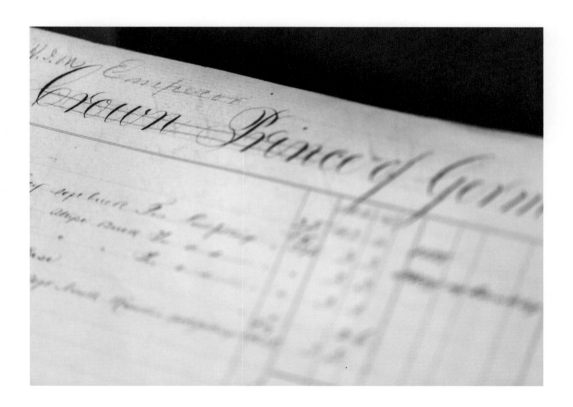

HIM EMPEROR PEDRO II OF BRAZIL

PATRONAGE 1871–1874

ROYAL WARRANT HIM Emperor Pedro II of Brazil (1874)

SIGNATURE GARMENT The Emperor was a parsimonious monarch who always dressed in black, save for two state occasions per year when he wore uniform. Poole's tailored for him black superfine frock coats ordered with a black double-breasted 'cassimir' (cashmere) vest.

TOTAL SPEND £2,379 (£148,950 today)

CONNECTIONS A number of garments tailored for Emperor Pedro II by Henry Poole & Co survive in the Imperial Museum Petropolis housed in the Emperor's former summer palace built in 1845.

Dom Pedro II, second and last emperor of Brazil (1825–1891), succeeded his father aged five in 1831, when Dom Pedro I abdicated and returned to Europe whence the Brazilian branch of the House of Braganza hailed. Unlike the ill-fated Emperor Maximilian of Mexico, Dom Pedro II was born in the country he was to rule, in Rio de Janeiro.

Brazil was the largest and wealthiest colony belonging to Portugal. It had thus been an obvious destination for Dom Pedro I to flee to when Portugal was invaded by Napoleon's troops in 1807 and the House of Braganza was overthrown. With Napoleon's defeat, Dom Pedro I's sister Maria was declared Queen of Portugal, and it was to secure her throne that he returned to Europe and ceded Brazil to a five-year-old. The young Pedro's mother died when he was an infant so he was effectively an orphan, and a regency council controlled the early years of his reign.

Pedro was a studious, shy child who, according to his beloved governess, 'saw books as a refuge and retreat from the real world'. He was declared fit to rule at the age of fourteen and was crowned in 1841, two years before being forced into an arranged marriage with Princess Teresa Cristina of the Kingdom of the Two Sicilies. When the youth first saw Princess Teresa he declared, 'they have deceived me' – for the lady was short, stout and plain.

The boy grew into a 1.9 m (6 ft 3 in) tall Adonis with blue eyes and blond hair. His childhood being ruled by faction and the regency council, he learned to mask his emotions and devote his time to study. He later said, 'I was born to devote myself to culture and sciences.'

The young man had inherited a nation on the verge of chaos. He earned his title 'Pedro the Magnanimous' by championing civil rights, freedom of speech, economic prosperity for all strata of Brazilian society and the abolition of slavery. The latter was the most controversial of the Emperor's crusades because Brazil's was a plantation-based economy that relied on slave labour.

The Emperor woke at 7.00 a.m. and did not sleep again before 2.00 a.m. In idle hours, he read or studied. The records at Henry Poole & Co bear out his reputation for sobriety in all things. Pedro ordered frugally and modestly, preferring black frock or tailcoats that were practically monastic in their lack of embellishment. He wore the royal regalia only twice a year, to open and close Brazil's General Assembly. As he said, 'I understand that useless expenditure is the same as stealing from the nation'.

The darkest hour for Brazil's last emperor was the War of the Triple Alliance (1864–1870), which saw the nations of Brazil, Argentina, Paraguay and Uruguay fighting each other singularly and in faction, even though Brazil was never defeated. Personal disappointments for the Emperor included the death in infancy of both his male progeny and the disintegration of his marriage to the Empress. From 1850, Dom Pedro II conducted a number of affairs, most notably with the Countess of Barral, who was governess to his daughters, Isabel and Leopoldina.

The reputation of Brazil's emperor as a scholar and philosopher was famed throughout the courts of Europe, and he corresponded with Charles Darwin, Victor Hugo, Richard Wagner, Louis Pasteur, Henry Wadsworth Longfellow and Friedrich Nietzsche. Darwin said of him: 'The Emperor does so much for science that every scientific man is bound to show him the utmost respect.'

Dom Pedro II was deposed in a military coup at the height of his popularity. Had he fought, it is believed his people would have supported him. But he merely declared: 'Rarely has a revolution been so minor. If it is so, it will be my retirement. I have worked too hard and I am tired. I will go rest then.' The Emperor went into exile in Europe on 17 November 1889. His last words were: 'May God grant me this last wish – peace and prosperity for Brazil.'

HIM EMPEROR ALEXANDER III OF RUSSIA

PATRONAGE 1873–1881

ROYAL WARRANT HIM Tsar Alexander III of Russia (1881)

SIGNATURE GARMENT The Emperor first visited Poole's in 1873 as
Tsesarevich (heir apparent). He is recorded as ordering a black frock coat lined
with silk. Unfortunately, the ledger for his orders as emperor is lost.

TOTAL SPEND £883 (£55,280 today)

CONNECTIONS Tsar Alexander's wife, the Empress Maria Feodorovna,
held a personal account with Henry Poole, as did her sister,
Queen Alexandra of Great Britain.

Emperor Alexander III (1845–1894) was the penultimate Emperor of All the Russias. 'Sasha', as he was known to his family, was a relatively simple man and a second son, who had no expectations of becoming Russian Tsar, King of Poland and Grand Prince of Finland, until his elder brother Nicholas died in 1865. As was the custom, Sasha was obliged by his father, Tsar Alexander II, to marry his late brother's intended bride, Princess Dagmar of Denmark, in 1866.

Alexander was haunted by the assassination of his father in 1881. The imperial family held vigil over the body mutilated by an anarchist's bomb and watched the old Tsar slowly bleed to death on the marble floor of the Winter Palace. In Miranda Carter's book *The Three Emperors* (2009), Alexander is described thus: 'Like his ancestor Peter the Great, he stood well over six feet tall and was enormously strong; built like a butcher. A Russian to his boots, he was not too highly polished in his manners and had a touch of brutality. He was deliberately provincial, wore sack-like Russian peasant shirts and was famously brusque, taciturn and deeply mistrustful of almost anybody.'

As heir apparent, Sasha disagreed bitterly with his father's liberal politics and despised the court of St Petersburg's admiration for European fashion and culture. Art, ballet, French cuisine and fine wines did not interest him, but he was fortunate to have Grand Duchess Maria Feodorovna as his wife: arguably the most popular foreign consort to marry into the Romanov family for centuries, 'Minnie' was said to have charmed St Petersburg so that Alexander did not have to.

In 1873 Sasha and Minnie visited Bertie (the Prince of Wales) and Alexandra at Marlborough House, their official London residence. Sasha took the opportunity to visit Henry Poole & Co and is listed as HIH the Grand Duke Cesarevich de Russie. He ordered a grey Angola pea coat lined with silk, two white imperial drill lounge vests, a black twill Angola frock coat lined with silk and a double-breasted Angola pea coat possibly for the Royal Regatta at Cowes on the Isle of Wight.

On his accession in 1881, Tsar Alexander III used his father's assassination as an excuse to move the imperial family away from St Petersburg to a place of greater safety. He chose the remote Gatchina Palace, with its 900 rooms, most of which were rat-infested and abandoned. Alexander allowed his father's morganatic wife, Princess Catherine Dolgorukov, to remain in her rooms at the Winter Palace and retain the old Tsar's blood-stained uniform as a keepsake.

Wherever they went, the imperial family was shadowed by the Okhrana, Russia's secret police, and for good reason. Assassination attempts were legion. And yet the Tsar was popular with his people, because he kept Russia out of costly foreign wars, stating: 'We have just two allies in this world: our armies and our navy. Everybody else will turn on us at a second's notice.'

Somewhat ironically, it was an accidental train derailment in 1888 that almost killed the entire imperial family. The man-mountain of a tsar was said to have lifted the crushed roof of the train single-handedly to release his family. Coryne Hall's book *Little Mother Russia* (2009) surmises that the Tsarina may have suffered a nervous breakdown after the event and intimates that the Tsar drank heavily after it.

It was to the Prince and Princess of Wales that the Tsarina turned when the Tsar's health failed during a stay at Livadia Palace in the Crimea. Two days before the Prince and Princess of Wales arrived, Alexander died of kidney failure. Twenty-four years later the Bolsheviks murdered his son Tsar Nicholas II.

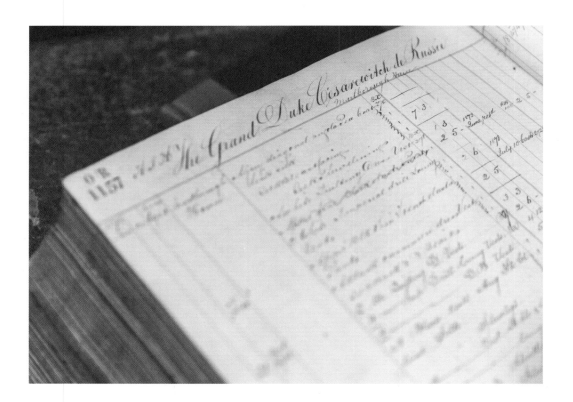

HM SHAH NASER AL-DIN SHAH OF PERSIA

PATRONAGE 1872–1873

ROYAL WARRANT HIM The Shah of Persia (1873)

SIGNATURE GARMENT A scarlet superfine general's tunic lined with silk
with gold lace, gold shoulder cords and stars and crowns on the collar made to
English uniform regulations. The Shah also ordered dress regulations for Austria
and Prussia for his tour of European courts.

TOTAL SPEND £14,134 (£884,910 today)

CONNECTIONS In 1873 Madame Tussauds waxworks commissioned Henry
Poole & Co to replicate the Shah of Persia's general's tunic for a wax model
displayed in its Baker Street premises.

The rise to power of His Imperial Majesty Naser al-Din Shah of Persia (1831–1896) was largely thanks to his mother, who championed the cause of her second son as heir apparent. When his father, Mohammad Shah, died in 1848, the new shah's path to power was smoothed by Amir Kabir, who would become prime minister of Persia (Iran) before being executed on the new monarch's instruction in 1852. Though a moderate reformist, the Shah was an absolute sovereign and held the reins of power tightly until his assassination in 1896.

The Shah was distinguished as the first ruler of his nation to visit Europe. *The Tour Diary of HM The Shah of Persia*, ostensibly written in his own words, chronicles the Iranian monarch's visit to England in 1873 and paints a detailed miniature of British royal circles. He was celebrated in *Vanity Fair* with a 'Spy' cartoon depicting the Shah wearing European clothing tailored by Henry Poole & Co, from whom he ordered prodigiously while his entourage was billeted at Buckingham Palace. The most disturbing rumour of the many that circulated concerned servants who displeased the Shah being strangled and buried in the gardens behind the palace.

Various slips in etiquette were gleefully reported by the press, such as the night at the Royal Albert Hall when the Shah draped an arm over the shoulders of the Princess of Wales and her sister the Grand Duchess Marie of Russia and attempted to feed them bonbons.

Of his many excursions in the capital city, the Shah appeared most enthralled by the Crown Jewels in the Tower of London. His own dress tunics were embellished with magnificent diamonds and rubies. He was most taken by the legendary Koh-i-Noor diamond that had been in the Persian treasury in the 18th century. He witnessed Queen Victoria wearing it as a brooch.

One of the most oft-repeated anecdotes about the Shah involved a comment he made to the Prince of Wales while attending a house party at the invitation of the Duke of Sutherland. The Shah thought the Duke was 'too grand a subject', and announced: 'You'll have to have his head off when you come to the throne.'

Mention is made in the Shah's *Tour Diary* of a visit to Regent Street that rendered him 'bewildered and stupefied by the concourse of people and throng of carriages'. It was perhaps on the same day he visited Henry Poole and placed an order totalling £804 (£50,340 today). Outstanding pieces include a black dress beaver Persian frock coat lined with satin and laced with gold, a pair of black doeskin trousers with scarlet piping and silk fittings and a black Alexandra cloth greatcoat lined with fur. The most elaborate military order was a scarlet superfine general's tunic that was lined with silk, embellished with gold lace, gold shoulder cords, stars and crowns on the collar with mounted gilt buttons and a gold sash with bullion tassels, made to French Regulations with crimson overalls, silk pockets and two gold stripes.

The Shah's sybaritic taste was underwritten by the sale of Persian national assets to foreign investors, whose proceeds he would pocket. Of his numerous trade agreements, the most unpopular was the Shah's attempt to sell Persia's tobacco concession in 1890, which led to a national boycott of tobacco and the withdrawal of the concession. A follower of nationalist agitator Jamal al-Din al-Afghani, who was highly critical of the tobacco scandal, murdered the Shah in Tehran in 1896.

MAHARAJA SIR BHUPINDER SINGH OF PATIALA

PATRONAGE 1953–1974

SIGNATURE GARMENT Patiala state full dress frock coat, British Army
Regulations major general's uniform

TOTAL SPEND £10,075 (£292,756 today)

CONNECTIONS The Maharaja had an estimated eighty-eight children with
numerous consorts and concubines. His eldest son, Yadavindra Singh I – the last
reigning Maharaja of Patiala – had Western clothing tailored by Poole's on his
father's account.

During the sunset years of the Indian princely states and the British Raj, Maharaja Sir Bhupinder Singh of Patiala (1891–1938) was the last of the big spenders. His extravagance was the stuff of legend in the capital cities of Europe, where he embraced the dynamism of aviation, motoring and Art Deco jewellery design, while living like a 16th-century potentate in Patiala.

A brief sketch of the Maharaja of Patiala's character can be given in numbers: 350 concubines in his purpose-built seraglio, forty-four Rolls-Royce cars in the palace garages, 1,001 blue and white diamonds in the breastplate that he wore naked once a year before his court to demonstrate his potency, and eighty-eight children – of whom fifty-two survived to adulthood – born to his five wives and many concubines. In her 2004 book *Maharanis*, Lucy Moore repeats an infamous anecdote: 'We all have different ways of beginning the day. The Englishman begins on bacon and eggs, the German on sausages, the Americans on grape nuts. His Highness prefers a virgin.'

Bhupinder Singh was born in the Moti Bagh Palace in Patiala and educated at Aitchison College in Lahore, where he developed a passion for cricket and polo. He acceded to the throne aged nine after his father died in a riding accident. A regency council ruled until 1910, when the Viceroy of India, the 4th Earl of Minto, invested the eighteen-year-old Maharaja with full powers. The Maharaja's loyalty towards Britain was demonstrated in 1911 when he attended the Coronation Durbar for King George V and Queen Mary in Delhi bejewelled like a peacock.

Later in 2011 the Maharaja captained the Indian cricket team on tour in England. He would go on to play twenty-seven first-class cricket matches between 1915 and 1937 and was made a member of the prestigious Marylebone Cricket Club. When the Maharaja built his summer retreat, Chail View Palace, he laid out the world's highest cricket pitch, as well as a polo field for his team the Patiala Tigers, who were said to be the best in India.

In Patiala it was said that the Maharaja would position naked favourites from his harem around his iced swimming pool so he could steal a caress or a sip of whisky while he swam. His bedroom ceiling was a swirl of erotic sculptures taken from Indian temples, and a wide silk hammock was suspended between two pillars. In the royal harem, a wing was built for perfumers, hairdressers, beauticians, dressmakers and, allegedly, plastic surgeons to transform his seraglio into the London fashion magazine models after whom the Maharaja lusted. Instead of Exalted Highness, he was known as Exhausted Highness.

However debauched the Maharaja's life was in Patiala, it did not prevent him from taking offices of state; he represented India at the League of Nations in 1925 and served as Chancellor of the Indian Chamber of Princes between 1926 and 1938. In 1922 he entertained the Prince of Wales (the future King Edward VII), for whom he ordered a 1,400-piece silver gilt dinner service that was later auctioned by Christie's for £1.5 million.

In 1935 the Maharaja of Patiala had an audience with Adolf Hitler in Berlin. According to *The Automobiles of the Maharajas* written by the Maharaja's grandson, 'the Führer asked grandfather to stay on for lunch and then asked him to come back the next day and then a third day. On the third day he gave him German weapons ... and a magnificent Maybach.' Within three years of meeting Hitler, Maharaja Sir Bhupinder Singh of Patiala was dead. The excesses bred in the bone failed the flesh.

HIM EMPEROR HAILE SELASSIE I OF ETHIOPIA

PATRONAGE   1911–1935

ROYAL WARRANT   HIM Emperor Haile Selassie (1959)

SIGNATURE GARMENT   Dark blue superfine field marshal's tunic, overalls,
six gold stars, gold sash with solid gold buckle and gold bullion tassels, sword knot

TOTAL SPEND   £18,589 (£443,630 today)

CONNECTIONS   The Empress of Ethiopia, Menen Asfaw, and Crown Prince
Asfaw Wossen both had separate Henry Poole & Co accounts.

Haile Selassie (1892–1975), Emperor of Ethiopia from 1930 to 1974, could trace his ancestry back to King Solomon and the legendary Queen of Sheba. The Rastafari movement (named after Selassie's birth name Ras [Prince] Tafari) reveres Selassie as the messiah, though the Emperor was an Ethiopian Orthodox Christian. Selassie rose to power as co-regent of Ethiopia when the corrupt and licentious Emperor Lij Iyasu was deposed in 1916 and his aunt Zewditu acceded to the throne as empress.

Selassie travelled extensively in Europe and the Middle East observing other cultures and political systems that could benefit Ethiopia. Dressed in exotic court costumes when visiting King George V in England, he caused a sensation. He travelled with a pride of lions and gave two to the British king. The Empress, somewhat jealous of Selassie's international profile, attempted to have him arrested and tried for treason on his return to Addis Ababa. But the plot backfired; her husband, Gugsa Welle, raised an army against Selassie but was defeated and killed. The Empress died days later, with rumours of poison rumbling around the vacant throne.

Selassie was declared emperor in 1930 and invited foreign dignitaries from around the world to witness his spectacular coronation. In 1931, he introduced Ethiopia's first written constitution and promised a transition to democratic rule. But in 1934 Italian Fascist leader Benito Mussolini invaded Ethiopia and deployed chemical weapons to defeat the Emperor, in a move that shocked the civilized world. Selassie was forced into exile in 1936, admonishing the League of Nations in Geneva with a speech that concluded: 'God and history will remember your judgment.' *Time* magazine named Selassie its Man of the Year and he became a role model for the anti-Fascist movement.

Selassie lived out his exile in England at Fairfield House in Bath until 1941, when British and Commonwealth troops, supported by the Ethiopian resistance movement, defeated Mussolini and restored him to the throne. Selassie led his troops under the standard of the Lion of Judah. Though a constitutional and religious reformer in spirit, Selassie was an absolute ruler. He celebrated his silver jubilee in 1955 and survived an attempted coup by his Imperial Guard in 1960. While pursuing his policy of decoloni-zation in Africa, Selassie retained strong bonds with Western democracies. By the 1970s he was the longest-serving head of state in power in the world.

The famine of 1972–74 felled 80,000 people in Ethiopia and shone a less than compli-mentary light on the Selassie regime, undermining the Emperor's image as a progressive dictator. In 1974, riots in Addis Ababa eventually resulted in a military-led mutiny against Selassie. The Emperor was deposed on 12 September 1974 and placed under house arrest in the Grand Palace. The imperial family was later moved to Addis Ababa's notorious Kerchele Prison, which was nicknamed 'Alem Bekagne', or 'Goodbye, cruel world'.

Sixty high officials were executed without trial, including Selassie's grandson and two former prime ministers. On 28 August 1975, it was announced that ex-monarch Haile Selassie had died of respiratory failure, though in all likelihood he was strangled to death.

Henry Poole: Founders of Savile Row tells the story of head cutter Edward Mitchell and director Hugh Cundey paying court to Haile Selassie in Addis Ababa in 1953. The Emperor had commissioned a lounge suit and a field marshal's uniform that he expected to be made in a specially kitted-out work-shop in the capital on Churchill Boulevard. The firm thus earned the Emperor's Royal Warrant in 1959. The company ledgers list Haile Selassie as a customer as early as 1948, with orders including a blue superfine field marshal's tunic, overalls, six gold stars, a gold sash with solid gold buckle and gold bullion tassels with accompanying sword, sword knot and case, all engraved with the Lion of Judah.

Left and opposite: Poole's tailored military and civilian dress for Emperor Haile Selassie from 1955, the year of his silver jubilee, until his deposition in 1974. The St George and the Dragon epaulettes in the company archive were undelivered after the Emperor's fall.

Hughes Esq London

CHAPTER TWO
TAILOR OF KINGS
1836–1876

'I have shown the letter you left with me this morning to the Prince of Wales who desires me to assure you how much touched he feels at the messages which were left for him by Mr Poole. His Royal Highness as you are aware had a great regard for him, and looked upon him more in the light of a friend than any other point of view.'

LETTER FROM MARLBOROUGH HOUSE ON THE DEATH OF HENRY POOLE DATED 26 MAY 1876

Like those of showman P. T. Barnum and entrepreneur Gordon Selfridge, the life of Henry Poole has largely been told in anecdotes embroidered over time. More than a few myths about the man London society affectionately called 'Old Pooley' have been smuggled into the history of Henry Poole & Co. Not in dispute is Henry Poole's remarkable achievement in befriending princes, maintaining their loyalty and making his tailoring house the measure of excellence in the courts of Europe and Russia.

Bespoke tailoring was bred in the bones of Henry Poole. We know he was taken out of school in 1829 aged fifteen to apprentice at his father's firm on Old Burlington Street. Henry learned the rudiments of the trade as he progressed through the cutting, sewing and trimming rooms. But his charm made Henry Poole a natural to work front-of-shop and deal directly with eminent customers. This position demanded the instincts of a born couturier to walk the tightrope between subservience and over-familiarity.

According to a typed unpublished manuscript, *Henry Poole: The Prince of Tailors*, written by Donald MacAndrew in the 1950s, 'not until he (Henry) himself was head fitter did his true genius emerge … he knew by instinct how to be at once urbane and deferential; easy without being familiar, ingratiating but not obsequious and to maintain this at dead level till the client was smiled out of the shop'. For a socially ambitious young man, James Poole's customers, largely made up of the military and white-collar workers in the professions, acted as a nursery slope upon which to find his form.

In addition to his duties in the Old Burlington Street showroom, Henry Poole was sent out to the provinces to visit customers, take orders and collect debts. His professional life from 1829 to 1839 appears to have been rather grim, as an undated letter in the company archive suggests. Writing from Newcastle-upon-Tyne, Henry professes to be 'heartily sick of this place as I am unlucky and can get neither orders nor money such as I expected'. He ends his letter: 'I am miserably tired of here. I shall be sorely glad to get home again.'

Opposite: Dated 1846, this is the first company letterhead naming Henry Poole as proprietor and No. 32 Savile Row as the address.

Social mobility between trade and gentry in the early years of Queen Victoria's reign was practically nonexistent, and the only places kings and commoners could meet on equal footing were the East End bordello or the racetrack. Equestrian sport proved to be Henry's introduction to a higher class of customer. His father furnished him with the trappings of wealth and by 1834, the twenty-one-year-old was driving a phaeton (an open carriage pulled by two horses) on Hyde Park's Rotten Row. The modern equivalent would be a Hedge Fund Alpha roaring around Knightsbridge in a custom-made Lamborghini.

Tailored by James Poole, Henry was bandbox-smart and served as a model advertisement for his father's firm. Foremost among Henry's equestrian friends was James 'Jem' Mason, the celebrated twenty-three-year-old steeplechase jockey who won the inaugural Grand National at Aintree in 1839 on a mount called Lottery: a horse that Jem said could jump from ''ell to 'ackney'. The Frankie Dettori of his day, Jem Mason dressed like a swell. His *Times* obituary said of him that 'with his smart figure, gentlemanlike appearance and neat style of dress, he for years led the fashions in certain coteries'.

At the business end of Poole's, 1837 is an important date because it was the year Henry's fourteen-year-old cousin Samuel Cundey joined the business as a junior clerk in the counting house. It became Sam's job to balance the books over thirty years, while Henry played Lord Bountiful dressing prestige customers such as the Prince of Wales at a preferential if not ruinous rate for the firm.

As an exquisitely dressed double act, Poole and Mason were fixtures on the equestrian and social scene; hunting with Baron Meyer de Rothschild's pack, attending Royal Ascot and peacocking in the crush bar at the Royal Opera House. In recognition of Henry's increasing influence on the business, his father renamed the firm James Poole & Son in 1843. James Poole's death in 1846 made Henry head of the family as well as of the family firm. None of the James Poole ledgers survive, suggesting that Henry began with a bonfire and a clean slate.

James Poole did not live to see the firm's first quasi-royal customer, Prince Louis Napoleon, nephew of the great Emperor Napoleon I. Like Henry, Prince Louis Napoleon was not accepted by the upper echelons of society in the 1840s. He was, however, a favourite of the notorious Lady Blessington who, according to Fenton Bresler's 1999 biography of Napoleon III, 'had for years scandalised respectable people by living openly with her tall, handsome, hazel-eyed French lover Alfred, Comte d'Orsay, who had during Lord Blessington's lifetime happily been the lover of both husband and wife'.

One of Henry's first directives on inheriting the firm was to make No. 4 Old Burlington Street the staff entrance, pull down the stable block behind the property and build a grand ground-floor showroom with its customer entrance on No. 32 Savile Row. According to the Survey of London (1963), No. 32 Savile Row had served as a postal address for the Henry Poole counting house as far back as 1832, in tandem with No. 4 Old Burlington Street as the shop front. But it was Henry who first put Savile Row on the letterhead intended for customers, having commissioned Thomas Cubitt, master builder of Eton Square, to design Poole's new showroom.

The Savile Row façade of Henry Poole & Co was a flat-roofed Italianate design flanked by two-storey properties on either side topped by balustrades. The Survey of London likened Poole's grand interior, with its pink marble Ionic columns supposed to have come from the Mount Edgcumbe estate in Cornwall, to the atrium of a Roman villa. Bronzes, statues and mirrors acquired from the Great Exhibition in 1851 decorated the interior and a parlour was installed for friends of Henry's to gather, smoke his cigars and drink his brandy at the appointed hour of 5.00 p.m.

Henry Poole was the first tailor to make it the form for exalted customers to meet on the premises rather than the tailor waiting on the aristocracy at their London mansions. Henry laid down a blueprint for bespoke houses that Savile Row tailors followed until well into the 1970s. 'The exterior of each tailoring house should proclaim the good manners within. A man's tailor should be to him as his family solicitor, or his doctor, he should drop in casually as into his club. Eschew, therefore, all the advertisement, gold letters and window displays. For a bespoke tailor the correct form is opaque glass windows [and] dimness.'

Inside the showroom at No. 32 Savile Row, the customer would observe that military uniforms had been relegated to the shadows to make way for sporting attire such as hunting pinks, shooting coats, Inverness capes and doeskin breeches made in white, buff and lavender. Town coats of every variety – dress, morning, tails, reefer, raglan and Chesterfield – advertised Poole's preference for sober cloths in a Beau Brummelesque palette for gentlemen, while the livery department originally in the basement produced garishly coloured uniforms trimmed with gold lace for house and stable servants.

Henry's affable manner and social success holds the key to why the firm's order books swiftly filled with names from the Court Circular. He knew every introduction could lead to bigger prizes. In the late 1840s, Jem Mason introduced the 7th Earl of Strathmore to Poole's, who in turn recommended Viscount Dupplin (the 12th Earl of Kinnoul). Dupplin then introduced the 6th Earl of Chesterfield, who brought with him the Earl of Mount Charles (the 3rd Earl Coyningham), and so forth. A love of horseflesh united the titled new customers of Henry Poole & Co, proving that dressing Jem was a sound investment.

By the 1850s, Henry Poole was a favourite guest on the country house party calendar, where titled members of the sporting fraternity could entertain commoners such as Henry. He was a regular visitor to Bradgate House, the Earl of Stamford's country mansion. The Earl was persona non grata in Queen Victoria's drawing rooms because his second countess, Kitty Cocks, had before her marriage been a bareback circus rider. When asked to describe the guests at one of Stamford's parties, Henry was said to have replied 'a mixed lot, a very mixed lot', to which one wag replied, 'Come, come, Pooley. We can't all be tailors.'

Henry Poole was clearly not lacking in social swagger or confidence in the company of his 'betters'. Another story places him at a house party where an arrogant young pup in the billiard room complained that his Poole's suit was ill-fitting. Henry reached for the billiard chalk, marked the pup's coat with lines and crosses and told the young man to take it to Savile Row next time he was in town and 'they will put you right'.

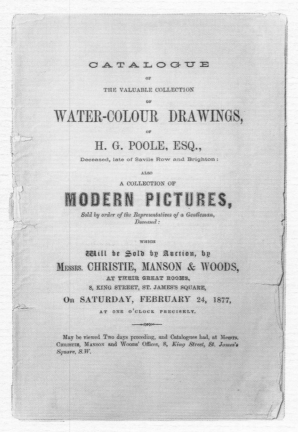

Left: Christie's catalogue from the company archive dated 1877, listing Henry Poole's art collection sold to defray debts a year after his death. **Right:** The only extant carte-de-visite portrait of Henry Poole, dated *c.* 1870, showing him towards the end of his life.

Poole's reputation as a sporting and equestrian tailor would make the firm the pre-eminent bespoke house for ladies as well as gentlemen. The firm had been tailoring for ladies since 1847, but in 1857 Henry installed a wooden horse christened Bucephalus – the name of Alexander the Great's steed – upon which ladies were measured and fitted for riding habits that would drape elegantly as they rode side-saddle. Bucephalus was mounted by courtesans and queens alike, including notorious courtesan Skittles Walters, Countess Kitty Stamford, Lady Randolph Churchill, the Empress Elisabeth 'Sisi' of Austria and her sister Maria Sophia, Queen of the Two Sicilies.

Propriety alone dictated that Henry Poole & Co did not send ladies' riding habits to the firm's workshops at No. 6 King Street in Soho, where 300 tailors worked. Instead, Henry employed a dozen seamstresses who worked exclusively on ladies' attire, led by forewoman Emma Walker. In 1859, Emma Walker would become Mrs Henry Poole, when the couple were both in their forties. The Ladies' Department orders were listed in the Livery Ledgers, suggesting that they shared space on Clifford Street with the aforementioned department.

By the end of the 1860s Poole's also owned Nos 23 to 39 Savile Row and had extended Old Burlington Street from Nos 3 to 5. Gargantuan personal orders placed by the Emperor Napoleon III, who granted Henry Poole his first Royal Warrant in 1858, as well as his wife, the Empress Eugénie, and son, the Prince Imperial, were supplemented by unique liveries for each of the Emperor's many palaces and châteaux. The thriving Livery Department at Nos 20 and 21 Clifford Street had opened in 1875.

However, the last years of Henry Poole's life matched every previous triumph with disaster. Emperor Napoleon III was deposed in 1870, robbing Poole's of its third highest rolling customer after the Khedive of Egypt and the Earl of Dudley. In the same year, newly installed gas fittings in the King Street workshops set the property on fire, destroying all the orders in hand and necessitating an emergency move to temporary space on Heddon Street behind the Row. The Royal Warrants of the emperors Alexander II of Russia and Nicholas I of Prussia in 1875 provided cold comfort for Henry, who had extended unlimited credit to his illustrious customers and, as a consequence, found himself staring down the barrel of a gun.

A financial review in 1872 revealed that Henry Poole's business premises on Savile Row were mortgaged to the tune of £16,000 (£1,001,700). According to the National Archive, this was the equivalent of 80,000 days of skilled labour. He had spent more on his Fulham residence, Dorset Cottage, than it was valued at, and his Brighton home at No. 118 Marine Parade was leased. Poole's London properties, including King Street, were on short leases that could rise incrementally with every rent review.

The outstanding payments on account totalled £23,000 (£1,440,000). Henry's response was to take out a loan of £22,000 (£1,377,400) at 5 per cent interest. He also attempted to settle outstanding accounts, but ruffled the feathers of valuable customers, including future prime minister Archibald Primrose, 5th Earl of Rosebery, who would return only in 1878, as a customer of the Poole Livery Department.

It was reported in Henry Poole's *Vanity Fair* obituary that 'for some time past he had been subject to apoplectic fits and had become much depressed'. The cause of his death in 1876 was said to be the last of a series of strokes, a second violent attack lasting ten hours, complicated by a contracted (shrunken) kidney. The latter is commonly caused by high blood pressure, diabetes, excessive alcohol or all of the above.

The last extant letter from Henry to his friend and executor Charles Bingley in 1876 is rather pitiful when one considers this was a man who dined with the Prince of Wales and played piano at the express command of Empress Eugénie of the French. It ends with the admission: 'The trouble will not be what you thought – there will be nothing much to leave behind me. I have worked for a prince and for the public and must die a poor man.'

POLITICIANS
&
STATESMEN

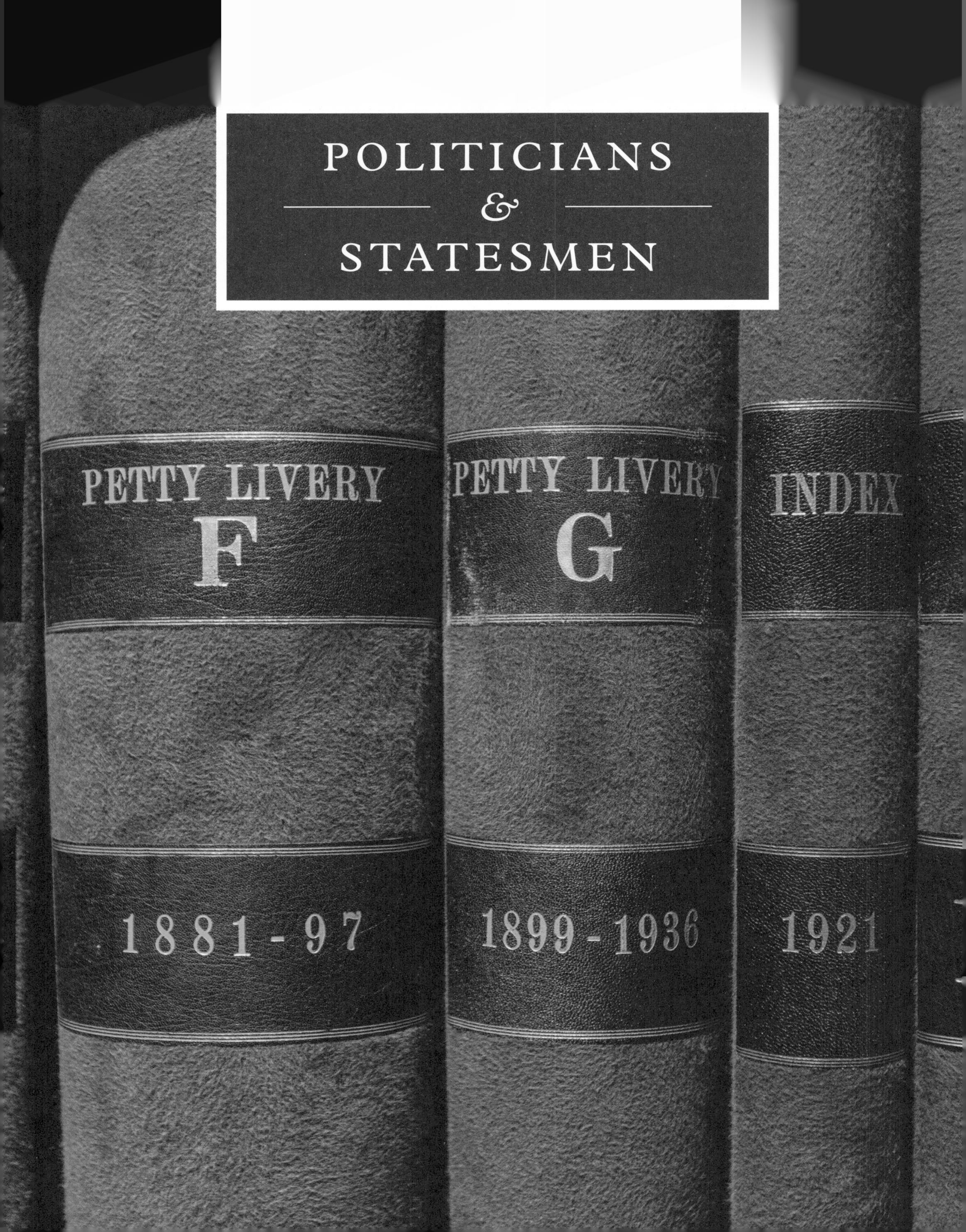

PETTY LIVERY
F

PETTY LIVERY
G

INDEX

1881-97

1899-1936

1921

BENJAMIN DISRAELI, 1ST EARL OF BEACONSFIELD

PATRONAGE 1860

SIGNATURE GARMENT A black Melton short lounging jacket lined with silk

TOTAL SPEND £33 (£1,950 today)

CONNECTIONS Disraeli was the first of six prime ministers dressed by Poole's:
the 3rd Marquess of Salisbury, the 5th Earl of Rosebery, Henry Herbert Asquith,
Neville Chamberlain and Winston Churchill.

Benjamin Disraeli (1804–1881) was a statesman and prime minister credited with introducing 'one nation' Conservatism to British politics. Also a novelist, and a great orator, Disraeli introduced numerous memorable aphorisms to the language, such as 'never complain and never explain', 'I am prepared for the worst, but hope for the best' and 'there are three kinds of lies: lies, damn lies and statistics'. Disraeli's rivalry with Liberal opposition leader William Ewart Gladstone was one of the most robust in parliamentary history.

Born to Italian-Jewish parents, Disraeli was baptised a Christian, hence his eligibility to enter Parliament; in 1837, at his fourth election attempt, he was returned as the Tory MP for Maidstone in Kent. Despite his Anglican upbringing, Disraeli defended the faith into which he was born, replying to an attack in the Commons: 'Yes, I am a Jew and when the ancestors of the right honourable gentleman were brutal savages in an unknown land, mine were priests in the Temple of Solomon.'

Disraeli's path to power as British prime minister was anything but smooth. Aged twenty, he lost his capital speculating on the stock exchange. He then attempted to launch a rival newspaper to the *Times* with publisher John Murray entitled the *Representative*. This endeavour foundered and Disraeli turned his attentions to a satirical novel called *Vivian Grey*, published in 1826 under the pseudonym 'A Man of Fashion'. Unmasked, Disraeli was threatened with defamation, leading to an apparent nervous collapse. For the next decade Disraeli wrote a series of novels and stood repeatedly for Parliament until elected in 1837. His maiden speech was mocked and Disraeli replied prophetically: 'The time will come when you will hear me.'

Lord Derby appointed Disraeli Chancellor of the Exchequer in 1852 during his minority government and, on Derby's retirement in 1868, after several periods in government, Disraeli – dubbed 'Dizzy' by the tabloids – was appointed prime minister. Disraeli struck up an unlikely 'knight and fair lady' relationship with Queen Victoria, telling his cabinet, 'first of all remember she is a woman'. The Queen was not amused when the Conservative government fell and Gladstone – whom she loathed as a pompous windbag – became prime minister for the next six years.

Disraeli's marriage was unconventional. He married a widow, Mary Anne, in 1839, a year after the death of her husband, the MP Wyndham Lewis. She was twelve years older than he and, in later years, said that 'Dizzy married me for my money but if he had the chance again, he would marry me for love'. Despite her eccentricities, Mary Anne Disraeli was equally popular with the Queen. Victoria was amused when Mary Anne said to her at a Windsor Castle dine-and-sleep: 'I wish you could see my Dizzy in his bath.' She also told the Queen that she slept with her arms around her husband's neck.

In 1874, Disraeli's Conservatives were returned with a substantial majority, and he pursued legislation that would lead the Liberal-Labour MP Alexander McDonald to declare in 1879: 'The Conservative party has done more for the working classes in five years than the Liberals have in fifty.'

In 1876 Disraeli cemented his friendship with Queen Victoria by passing the Royal Titles Act that proclaimed her Empress of India. He was rewarded with the title Earl of Beaconsfield in 1879. Disraeli's most successful gamble on the international stage was to persuade Baron Lionel de Rothschild to loan the British government the funds to acquire a 44 per cent stake in the Suez Canal venture. Disraeli died in 1881 and is remembered as one of the great 19th-century prime ministers. When asked if Queen Victoria could visit him on his deathbed, he quipped: 'She'd only want me to pass a message to Albert.'

PRINCE OTTO VON BISMARCK

PATRONAGE 1876

SIGNATURE GARMENT Though Bismarck's name survives in the Poole measure books (recommended by Count Peter Schouvaloff, Russian Ambassador to the Court of St James's) his ledger entries do not survive.

TOTAL SPEND Lost

CONNECTIONS Prince von Bismarck's namesake and grandson, Prince Otto Christian Archibald von Bismarck, was a Poole's customer in 1935 when he was attached to the German Foreign Office in London.

Otto Eduard Leopold, Prince von Bismarck (1815–1898) was prime minister of Prussia, architect of the unified Germany and its first Imperial Chancellor. 'Iron Chancellor' Bismarck is acknowledged as the supreme chess master of European politics in the second half of the 19th century: analytical, persuasive and utterly ruthless. He described politics as the 'art of the possible' and predicted World War I with the words 'some damned foolish thing in the Balkans will set it off'.

Bismarck is remembered as a grim, humourless tactician who transformed Prussia and its surrounding duchies into a united world power. His upbringing was rather more colourful. He was born into the Prussian Junker class – the landed aristocracy – and educated at Berlin's progressive Plamann Institute; he later read law at the University of Göttingen, where he developed a reputation for drinking, womanizing and pugilism.

Bismarck aligned himself with the indecisive King Frederick Wilhelm IV on the brink of abdication, declaring: 'I would rather perish with the King than forsake your majesty in the contest with parliamentary government.' In 1858 Frederick Wilhelm suffered a stroke that left him paralysed, and his brother Wilhelm was named regent. The Regent appointed Bismarck ambassador to Russia in 1859, and acceded to the throne as Kaiser (Emperor) Wilhelm I in 1861. Instead of recalling Bismarck to Berlin, the new emperor posted him to Paris as ambassador to the court of Emperor Napoleon III. On a visit to London, Bismarck met future prime minister Benjamin Disraeli, who said of him: 'Be careful of that man – he means what he says.'

In 1862 Emperor Wilhelm appointed Bismarck minister president (prime minister) of Prussia. It was the year that Bismarck gave his most famous speech, declaring that 'the great question of the time will not be resolved by speeches and majority decisions … but by iron and blood'. Bismarck persuaded Emperor Wilhelm not to abdicate, earning the lifelong enmity of Crown Prince Frederick and the British-born Crown Princess Victoria.

In 1870 Bismarck – by now Chancellor of the North German Federation – lured Napoleon III into the Franco-Prussian War on the premise that Wilhelm supported

a German prince's rights to the vacant Spanish throne. Napoleon III was deposed, Paris was besieged, and Wilhelm of Prussia was declared Emperor of Germany in the Hall of Mirrors at the Palace of Versailles in 1871. Bismarck was elevated to the rank of prince and named Imperial Chancellor of the German Empire.

The cost of eight years of war earned Germany two further decades of peace, during which Bismarck ruled in all but name. He placed colonial ambitions second to the strengthening of Germany's army and economy. He cemented the League of the Three Emperors between the German, Russian and Austro-Hungarian empires. When the German Parliament pushed for a pre-emptive strike against Russia, Bismarck replied that 'preventative war is like committing suicide for fear of death'.

Prince von Bismarck held power until 1888, when Emperor Wilhelm died and was succeeded by his son the Crown Prince Frederick. The liberal, reformist Emperor Frederick III, as he became, was already in the later stages of cancer and died ninety-nine days after his accession. His son, Emperor Wilhelm II, precious, aggressive and rather unhinged in his desire for absolute power, forced Bismarck to resign in 1890. Sir John Tenniel commented on the catastrophic dismissal of the elder statesman with his famous *Punch* cartoon titled 'Dropping the Pilot'.

GENERAL ULYSSES S. GRANT

PATRONAGE 1877

SIGNATURE GARMENT A black superfine frock coat and herringbone trousers

TOTAL SPEND £23 (£1,440 today)

CONNECTIONS Grant was one of the earliest American customers of Henry Poole & Co. His contemporary Junius S. Morgan – founder of the eponymous bank – was also a customer in the 1870s, as was his son, J. P. Morgan.

As evoked by his Greek mythological first name, President Ulysses S. Grant (1822– 1885) was a heroic figure in the birth of modern America. The eighteenth president of the United States served two terms from 1869 to 1877, having previously served as Commanding General of the US Army reporting to the revered President Abraham Lincoln. It was on his watch that the first African-Americans were elected to Congress and the Battle of the Little Bighorn was lost.

Grant was one of the great Unionists who fought in the American Civil War to defeat the Confederacy, which supported the supremacy of a white, landowning social and economic elite at the cost of a white farming underclass and the enslaved black race. In the Confederate worldview, women were at best ornamental and at worst childbearing stock, while the concept of equal rights among white males was anathema – let alone equality between the sexes.

In 1843 Ulysses. S. Grant graduated from the US Military Academy at West Point and later fought in the Mexican Civil War that toppled the Austrian puppet emperor Maximilian I, another Henry Poole & Co customer. Grant had already retired from active service by 1854, but was financially embarrassed by civilian life so re-enlisted when the Civil War broke out in 1861. Within a year his troops had recaptured Kentucky and most of Tennessee and led the Unionist forces to victory in the Battle of Shiloh.

Grant's style as a commander was aggressive to the point of recklessness. As the Confederate states toppled like ninepins, he enlisted the emancipated slaves to serve the Union, often raising them through the ranks as an example of the new world order. By gaining control of the Mississippi River, General Grant split the Confederacy. He was victorious in the Chattanooga Campaign, and Lincoln promoted him to Commanding General of the US Army in March 1864.

The crowning glory of Grant's military career was a series of dogfights with General Robert E. Lee, which he won when he surrounded Lee's army in Richmond, Virginia, and demanded their surrender in 1865. Lee's defeat signified the de facto end of the American Civil War and Grant was elected president three years later in 1868. His primary agenda was to stabilize a nation severely traumatized by the rift between the Confederates and the

Unionists, haunted by the Ku Klux Klan. He championed the freedom of slaves and the ratification of the 15th Amendment giving black men the vote in 1870. The Republican Party to which he belonged was made up of new black voters, northern newcomers, known as 'carpetbaggers', and native Southern white supporters dubbed 'scalawags'.

Like those of many US presidents elected on a ticket of hope and change, Grant's administration unravelled in his second term. The Great Sioux War of 1876 culminated in the massacre of General Custer and his troops in the Battle of the Little Bighorn. Captain William Cooke, a Poole's man, was scalped twice: once for the hair on his head and once for his whiskers. Charges of corruption thundering around the Grant administration only compounded the defeat at the hands of the Native Americans. Grant's attempt to annex the Dominican Republic was rejected by the Senate before a shot had been fired.

Among his practical contributions to stabilizing the United States, Grant could list the implementation of the Gold Standard. However, his administration panicked along with the stock markets in 1873 in the aftermath of the fall of Emperor Napoleon III and the subsequent turbulence in European politics. Grant left the political stage and spent the next two years on a laudatory world tour largely garnering praise for his war record. His tour began in Liverpool in 1877, and he was invited to dine with Queen Victoria at Windsor Castle.

President Grant travelled throughout Europe meeting worthies such as Pope Leo XVIII and German Iron Chancellor Bismarck. He refused to meet the Emperor of China, though he did meet with the influential Prince Gong, and he met the Japanese Emperor Meiji of the Chrysanthemum Throne. It was on the 1877 visit to London that President Grant paid his only visit to Poole's, for civilian clothing including a black frock coat and herringbone trousers.

It is long forgotten that Grant considered standing for a third term of the presidency in 1880 and that he died relatively ignominiously of throat cancer, having completed memoirs that were a great commercial and critical success. His reputation as president was largely rehabilitated in the 1980s during President Ronald Reagan's administration, a tribute from one Western hero to another.

HIS HIGHNESS THE KHEDIVE OF EGYPT

PATRONAGE 1884–1887

SIGNATURE GARMENT A black Angola frock coat

TOTAL SPEND £27,746 (£1,836,360 today)

CONNECTIONS Poole's would wait sixty years after the profligate Khedive of
Egypt for another Egyptian royal prince to patronize the firm. This was playboy Prince
Mohammed Ali Ibrahim of Egypt, nephew of King Fuad I and lover
of silent movie queen Mabel Normand.

Ismail Pasha, Khedive (Viceroy) of Egypt and Sudan (1830–1895) was responsible for
the industrialization of his nation, the expansion of its borders and the complete dis-
sipation of Egypt's wealth. The Khedive's grandfather, Muhammad Ali Pasha, laid down
the foundation of modern Egypt, but it was Ismail Pasha who forged enduring links with
Europe, declaring: 'My country is no longer Africa; we are now part of Europe.'

Ismail Pasha was born in Cairo at the Musafir Khana Palace and was educated in
Paris. On the death of his older brother, Ismail Pasha was appointed heir to his uncle,
Said I. It was Said's strategy to keep his nephew out of Egypt by sending him on diplomatic missions to the courts of the Pope, Emperor Napoleon III of the French and the
Sultan of the Ottoman Empire. Said's exclusion policy only honed the future Khedive's
diplomatic skills and opened his eyes to a rich and diverse cultural knowledge that would
serve him well as ruler.

On the death of his uncle in 1863, Ismail Pasha was proclaimed Khedive of Egypt.
Taking his cue from Napoleon III, the Khedive expanded Cairo with a new quarter based
on the architectural style of Second Empire Paris, built a railway system, inaugurated a
postal service, reduced the trade in slaves and patronized the opera and theatre. In 1874
the Khedive successfully annexed Darfur, but was repeatedly rebuffed from invading and
annexing Ethiopia by its emperor, Yohannes IV.

The Khedive first visited Henry Poole & Co in 1867 and returned in person again in
1869, when he was received at court by Queen Victoria. However, his livery orders for
1868 demonstrate the extravagance that would end his reign. The Henry Poole & Co
livery ledgers record more than twenty pages of orders for the Khedive's stables, making
him the most prolific customer of the 1860s.

Livery for 1868 comprised scarlet state livery frock coats laced with gold and trimmed
with gold aiguilettes and a crown, wigs, white 'cassimir' (cashmere) state waistcoats laced
with gold, white cassimir breeches with gold garters and tassels and black state cocked
hats with feathers laced with gold for his two coachmen and three postilions. He also
ordered two fancy satin racing jackets for his jockeys and one scarlet and one blue racing

cap. The total cost was £1,155 (£72,310). Still not content, the Khedive made three further livery orders for his stables costing £1,331 (£83,330), £1,465 (£91,720) and £1,678 (£105,060), not counting tin trunks, freight to Alexandria, insurance, dock duties and a Poole's man, Foreman, to accompany the deliveries to Egypt at a cost of £96 (£6,010). The total bill for 1868 was £6,963 (£435,950).

The crowning achievement of the Khedive's reign was the opening of the Suez Canal in 1869. But Ismail the Magnificent was a profligate spendthrift and his ambitious building projects and personal spending on a sybaritic existence eventually caused his downfall. Towards the end of his reign, Egypt's national debt had risen to £100 million. The Khedive sold Egypt's shares in the Suez Canal to the British for almost £4 million and ceded control over his nation's finances to an Anglo-French cabal.

The Khedive was pressured to abdicate in favour of his eldest son, Tewfik Pasha. This he did, and in 1879 left Egypt for exile in Naples. In 1885 the ex-Khedive was allowed to return to his Palace of Emirgan on the Bosporus, where he lived as a state prisoner under house arrest until his death in 1895.

ARCHIBALD PRIMROSE, 5TH EARL OF ROSEBERY

PATRONAGE 1869–1928

SIGNATURE GARMENT A scarlet superfine lord lieutenant's coatee trimmed
with silver lace

TOTAL SPEND £16,721 (£1,307,120 today)

CONNECTIONS Lord Rosebery was one of Poole's longest-patronizing
customers and highest rollers. He dressed his grooms, coachmen, jockeys and
household servants from drawers to Mackintosh overcoats. A constant in his sixty
years as a customer were striped primrose-yellow and rose satin racing jackets and
rose satin caps for his jockeys.

When Archibald Primrose, 5th Earl of Rosebery (1847–1929), was a boy he declared that he had three aims in life: to win the Derby, to marry an heiress and to become prime minister. Primrose was only four when his father died and he inherited the title Lord Dalmeny as heir to his grandfather, the 4th Earl of Rosebery. Educated at Eton and Christ Church, Oxford, Rosebery bought his first horse, Ladas, in 1868, when he acceded to the earldom. Owning a horse was against college rules; told by Christ Church to choose between his studies and Ladas, Rosebery chose the racehorse. Ladas was the first of Rosebery's three Derby winners and eleven British Classic race winners.

On his accession, Rosebery took his seat in the Lords and served in Whig Prime Minister Gladstone's cabinet as foreign secretary. In 1878 Rosebery fulfilled his ambition

to wed an heiress. Hannah de Rothschild was the only child of Jewish banker Baron Meyer de Rothschild and was the richest woman in Britain. The Prince of Wales and the Duke of Cambridge attended the society wedding, and Rosebery duly became the master of the Rothschilds' stately home Mentmore Towers in Buckinghamshire and of No. 40 Piccadilly in London, as well as being a landowner in his own right, with properties such as The Durdans in Epsom, Dalmeny House in Scotland and the Villa Delahante in the Bay of Naples, Italy.

When Gladstone retired in 1894, Rosebery was invited by Queen Victoria to form a government, he being her preferred choice of a

A swatch of the Earl's primrose-yellow and pink jockey silks in the archive's Racing Colours ledger.

rather bad bunch of Liberal politicians. However, apart from installing electric light in No. 10 Downing Street, Rosebery was undistinguished as prime minister.

Rosebery never returned to high office, choosing instead to write biographies of William Pitt the Younger, Emperor Napoleon I and Lord Randolph Churchill. Lord Randolph's son, Winston Churchill, wrote Rosebery's political obituary, saying pithily 'he would not stoop, he did not conquer'. Lord Rosebery was implicated in the Oscar Wilde scandal in 1895 when it emerged that the Marquess of Queensbury (father of Wilde's lover Lord Alfred Douglas) had accused him of having unnatural relations with his eldest son, Viscount Drumlanrig, who had allegedly committed suicide on a shooting party in 1894.

The Earl of Rosebery's first livery order is recorded in 1878 – the year he married Hannah de Rothschild – and lists his address at No. 2 Berkeley Square.

The Earl's personal orders are vast. He is first recorded at Poole in 1882 bespeaking a check Angola straight-leg trouser and a grey check Angola shooting coat with matching knickerbockers and hood. In 1885 he ordered the then fashionable long double-breasted greatcoat lined in best mink fur throughout with Russian sable collar. By 1899, the Poole's clerk records payment quarterly after 'less 15%' as an incentive for a rare prompt and regular settlement on account.

Shortly before the end of World War I, the Earl of Rosebery suffered a stroke that seriously curtailed his activities as an owner/trainer. His sister Constance said of his final years that Rosebery endured 'a life of weariness, of total inactivity and in his last year of almost blindness'. He died at The Durdans in 1929.

H. H. ASQUITH, 1ST EARL OF OXFORD

PATRONAGE   1897–1925

SIGNATURE GARMENT   A blue superfine Elder Brother of Trinity
uniform coatee

TOTAL SPEND   £412 (£32,200 today)

CONNECTIONS   The Earl's son, film director Anthony Asquith, was a Poole's
customer. His most notable films include *Pygmalion* (1938), *Fanny by Gaslight*
(1944), *The Winslow Boy* (1948), *The Importance of Being Earnest* (1952) and *The
Yellow Rolls-Royce* (1964).

Herbert Henry Asquith, 1st Earl of Oxford (1852–1928), was Liberal prime minister
between 1908 and 1916, a turbulent period when the suffragettes fought for the
women's vote, and the outbreak of World War I would cost Britain a generation of young
men and Asquith his office. The son of a Yorkshire cloth merchant, Asquith attended the
City of London School and was awarded a scholarship to Balliol College, Oxford, where
he became president of the Oxford Union (debating society). He was called to the bar
in 1876, married his first wife, Helen Melland, in 1877, and took silk (was appointed a
Queen's Counsel) in 1890.

Rarely referred to in public by his first name, H. H. Asquith stood for Parliament in
1886 and was elected as MP for East Fife. Tragedy struck when Helen Asquith lost her
life in the typhoid epidemic of 1891, leaving Asquith the widowed father of five children.
His second wife, Margot Tennant, would become a political hostess and diarist of distinction, of whom Asquith's daughter Violet said that 'she flashed into our lives in 1894
like some dazzling bird of paradise, filling us with amazement, amusement, excitement,
sometimes with a vague uneasiness as to what she might do next'.

Asquith served as Home Secretary to Gladstone's fourth and last government in 1892
and held the same post under Lord Rosebery before the Liberals were thrown out of
office for a decade in 1895. In response, Asquith returned to the bar. The Liberals were
returned to office in 1905 and Asquith was appointed Chancellor of the Exchequer under
Sir Henry Campbell-Bannerman, who referred to him as 'the sledge hammer'.

King Edward VII was convalescing in Biarritz when Asquith was appointed prime
minister and refused to return to London, making Asquith the only prime minister
to kiss the hand of the monarch on foreign shores. His first battle as PM was with the
House of Lords, which had rejected Chancellor David Lloyd George's 1909 'People's
Budget' that advocated unemployment benefit and health insurance. Asquith would
hold the Lords to ransom and threatened to flood the chamber with hundreds of newly
appointed Liberal life peers.

In cabinet, concerns were voiced about Asquith's drinking and his infatuation with a young lady called Venetia Stanley. In the Palace of Westminster, Asquith was nicknamed 'Squiff' or 'Squiffy' by his peers. His love for Miss Stanley manifested itself in his sending her more than 560 letters – often written during cabinet meetings – discussing affairs of state. Churchill called the relationship 'England's greatest security risk'.

History has judged H. H. Asquith as an effective peacetime prime minister but a disaster when war was declared in 1914. He was criticized for not mobilizing British troops until Germany invaded Belgium and blamed for the tragic loss of life in the Battle of the Somme. When Asquith fell ill in 1915, Field Marshal Kitchener said, 'I thought he had exhausted all possible sources of delay. I never thought of the diarrhoea.'

In 1916 a rift with Lloyd George forced Asquith to resign as prime minister, although he remained the party leader; he lost his parliamentary seat in the postwar election of 1918. The elder statesman struck a rather tragicomic pose in his dotage. The writer Aldous Huxley lampooned him in his novel *Chrome Yellow* (1921) as Mr Callamy: 'a *ci devant* Prime Minister feebly toddling across the lawn after a pretty girl'. In 1925 Asquith was made 1st Earl of Oxford and elevated to the House of Lords, but in 1926 and 1927 he suffered three strokes and became confined to a wheelchair. He died at his country home in Berkshire in 1928, and is commemorated in Westminster Abbey.

MUHAMMAD ALI JINNAH

PATRONAGE   1929–1936

SIGNATURE GARMENT   White linen double-breasted jacket with peak lapels

TOTAL SPEND   £870 (£34,230 today)

CONNECTIONS   In 1905 Henry Poole dressed Motilal Nehru, father of the
Indian independence movement, whose son, Jawaharlal Nehru, would become the
first prime minister of independent India in 1947.

The founder and first governor-general of Pakistan, Muhammad Ali Jinnah (1876–1948), was known to the nation he created as Quaid-e Azam (Great Leader). He was the leader of the All-India Muslim League from 1913 until Partition was accomplished in 1947. He has most recently been depicted by Denzil Smith in the 2017 film *Viceroy's House* about the negotiations between Jinnah, Nehru and India's last viceroy, Earl Mountbatten of Burma.

Born into a mercantile family who settled in Karachi, Muhammad Ali Jinnah attended Karachi's Christian Missionary High School, and graduated from Bombay University aged sixteen. In 1892 Sir Frederick Leigh Croft offered Jinnah an apprenticeship in London with Graham's Shipping and Trading Company. Before he left, he entered into an arranged marriage with the fourteen-year-old Emibai Jinnah – a distant cousin – who died while Jinnah was still in London. Much to his father's disapproval, Jinnah gave up his business apprenticeship to study law, joining Lincoln's Inn as an aspiring barrister.

Jinnah's political ambitions were fired when he witnessed the maiden speech of Dadabhai Naoroji, Britain's first Asian MP, from the Visitors' Gallery in the House of Commons. Aged nineteen, he became the youngest Indian to be called to the bar, and abandoned Indian dress for Western tailoring. He would come to own more than 200 bespoke suits, though he did not patronize Henry Poole & Co until his second sojourn in London, in 1929. Jinnah returned to India to practise as a barrister in Bombay (now Mumbai). A fellow pleader described him as having 'a sixth sense: he could see around corners. He was a very clear thinker [and] drove his points home with exquisite selection and slow delivery, word by word.'

By 1916 Jinnah had risen through the ranks of the All-India Muslim League to become president, firm in his belief that 'Hindus and Muslims can never evolve a common nationality'. By 1920 he resigned from the Indian National Congress (the political party that was the leader of the independence movement), which had launched a movement of non-cooperation to undermine British rule that Jinnah fiercely opposed. The Savile Row-suited Jinnah, who spoke English as his preferred language, profoundly disagreed with Hindu Mohandas Gandhi's Indian peasant garb and his whipping-up of what Jinnah

saw as mob rule. He fought with Jawaharlal Nehru (who would become independent India's first prime minister) to place the Muslim League as an equal partner with the Indian National Congress and the British Raj.

A British general's wife who observed Jinnah at a viceregal dinner in Simla wrote of him: 'He is a great personality. He talks the most beautiful English. He models his manners and clothes on (Gerald) du Maurier, the actor, and his English on Burke's speeches. He is a future Viceroy if the present system of gradually Indianizing the service continues.' In 1929 Jinnah returned to England, having separated from his second wife. He would be joined there by his daughter Dina (from whom he would become estranged when she married a Christian) and his sister Fatimah, who would become his lifelong companion.

Jinnah's biographer Hector Bolitho described his tenure in London as 'his years of order and contemplation wedged between the time of early struggle and the final storm of conquest'. Practising law, Jinnah became rich. He lived in a large house in Hampstead, employed an English chauffeur to drive his Bentley, and maintained an Indian and a British chef; in India, he kept houses in Bombay's exclusive Malabar Hill district and in New Delhi designed by Edwin Lutyens. Jinnah's tailor was Henry Poole, and he was said never to wear the same silk tie twice.

In 1935 Jinnah returned to India. A fifty Craven A cigarettes a day man, he was already suffering from poor health owing to tuberculosis, but this was hidden from the public as Jinnah took charge of the Muslim League and began the fight for an independent homeland for India's Muslim community. The battle cry was 'India divided or India destroyed'. The Lahore Resolution, signed in 1940, formally demanded the formation of an independent Pakistan after the British withdrawal from India. Nehru called it 'Jinnah's fantastic proposal', but British wartime prime minister Winston Churchill bargained independence for India and Pakistan for their support during World War II. 'Pakistan is life or death for us,' Jinnah declared.

Pakistan's independence from India was achieved in 1947 at the cost of hundreds of thousands of lives during mass migration and sectarian violence as India was divided along religious lines. The Viceroy of India, Earl Mountbatten, disliked Jinnah, commenting that 'until I had met Jinnah, I would not have thought it possible that a man with such a complete lack of sense of responsibility could hold down so powerful a position'. He also stated that had he known Jinnah was dying in 1947, he would have delayed negotiations. The last viceroy was equally nonplussed that Jinnah was appointed governor-general of Pakistan rather than he.

In power, Jinnah was described thus: 'Here indeed is Pakistan's King-Emperor, Archbishop of Canterbury, Speaker and Prime Minister concentrated into one formidable Quaid-e-Azam.' Governor-General Jinnah did not live long enough to stabilize the world's largest Islamic state, dying in 1948. His adversary, Nehru, first prime minister of India, wrote: 'How shall we judge him? He succeeded in his quest and gained his objective, but at what cost and with what a difference from what he had imagined.'

WALDORF ASTOR, 2ND VISCOUNT ASTOR

PATRONAGE 1898–1941

SIGNATURE GARMENT A lord lieutenant's uniform, greatcoat, cocked hat,
a viscount's crimson velvet coronation robe trimmed with real ermine and a
viscount's coronet for the 1937 coronation of King George VI

TOTAL SPEND £682 (£19,820 today)

CONNECTIONS The 2nd Viscount's father, the 1st Viscount, and the 3rd
Viscount of Profumo affair fame were customers of Henry Poole & Co.

Waldorf Astor, 2nd Viscount Astor (1879–1952), was a press baron and politician born in New York City, whose father, William Waldorf Astor, was proclaimed the richest man in America when he inherited his fortune in 1890. The latter had already moved his family to England in 1889, having tired of the warring Astor clan, and settled briefly in Lansdowne House off Berkeley Square before buying the magnificent Cliveden estate from the Duke of Westminster. Waldorf Astor was educated at Eton and New College, Oxford, where he learned little more than an appreciation of horseflesh, playing polo in varsity matches.

A chance meeting with divorcee Nancy Langhorne on a transatlantic crossing was the making of Waldorf Astor. After a six-month whirlwind romance, they married in 1906. William Waldorf Astor gave the newlyweds Cliveden and relocated to Hever Castle in Kent. Christopher Sykes, author of *Nancy: The Life of Lady Astor* (1972) writes that 'from the day when she married Waldorf Astor, Nancy's legendary life began … within just a few years, she was among the five or six most famous women in the world – loved and hated, admired and deplored'. Astor was elected MP for Plymouth in 1910.

In addition to his public service, Astor was proprietor of the *Observer* newspaper, which he had persuaded his father to buy from Lord Northcliffe. He also served as chairman of the *Pall Mall Gazette*, another of his father's holdings, until 1915. Astor and his wife stayed in their townhouse on the corner of St James's Square (now the In & Out Club) when Parliament was in session, and established a salon known as the 'Cliveden Set' at their country estate.

Suffering from a weak heart, Astor was not fit for active service during World War I so worked instead in munitions. In 1916, Prime Minister H. H. Asquith was forced to resign and was replaced by Astor's friend David Lloyd George, who appointed Astor his parliamentary private secretary. He would also serve as secretary to the Ministry of Food and the Ministry of Health. But in 1919, William Waldorf Astor died and his son reluctantly inherited the title 2nd Viscount Astor, meaning that he had to resign as an MP to take his seat in the House of Lords.

In an unprecedented move, Nancy – now Lady Astor – contested and won her husband's former seat, becoming the first woman to take a seat in the House of Commons. Lady Astor bears the brunt of one of Winston Churchill's most quoted *bons mots*. To Lady Astor's comment 'if you were my husband, I'd poison your tea', Churchill replied: 'Madame, if you were my wife, I'd drink it.'

In the late 1930s, Lord and Lady Astor were the subject of criticism for siding with Prime Minister Neville Chamberlain, who supported appeasement with Hitler's Nazi regime. Lord Astor was accused of antisemitic bias when he allegedly said that 'newspapers are influenced by those firms which advertise so largely in the press and are frequently under Jewish control'. In 1936, the journalist Claud Cockburn coined the term 'Cliveden Set' in a story printed in his anti-fascist newsletter the *Week*.

According to Cockburn, Lord and Lady Astor were at the centre of a cabal of influential people including the editor of the *Times*, Geoffrey Dawson, Lord Halifax, the 9th Duke of Manchester, Lord Lothian, and Samuel Hoare, who met at Cliveden and No 4. St James's Square. When Churchill spoke against the Munich Pact in 1938, Lady Astor was said to have interrupted him, repeatedly crying 'Rude! Rude!', and in 1939, a fellow MP referred to Lady Astor as the Member for Berlin. The Astors did not recover their social standing after World War II and lived apart until the 2nd Viscount Astor died at Cliveden in 1952. Lady Astor lived for another twelve years, never acknowledging her reversal of fortune.

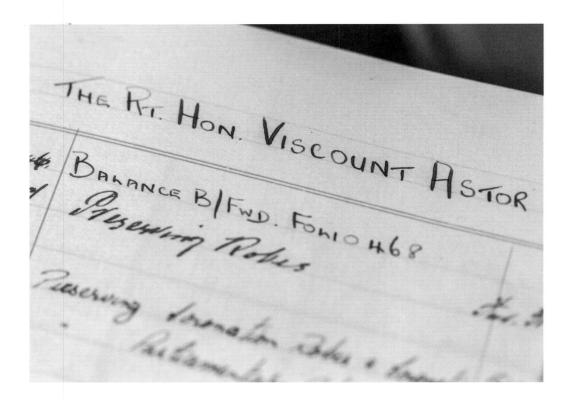

GENERAL DE GAULLE

PATRONAGE 1942–1946

SIGNATURE GARMENT A khaki Melton greatcoat and khaki whipcord
service jacket

TOTAL SPEND £225 (£8,850 today)

CONNECTIONS Famed French politicians to follow de Gaulle to Henry Poole
& Co include Prime Minister Edouard Balladur and President of France Valéry
Giscard d'Estang.

Charles de Gaulle (1890–1970) was the leader of the Free French forces during World War II and founding president of the Fifth Republic between 1958 and 1969. His political manifesto 'Gaullism' – 'the politics of grandeur' – shaped French postwar nationalism and steered his country to the centre of European power. Born into a devout Catholic family of historians, de Gaulle was educated in Paris and would from an early age believe it was his destiny to achieve greatness.

De Gaulle entered Saint-Cyr military academy in 1908 and was commissioned into the French Army in 1911. Like Winston Churchill in Britain, he was a vocal critic of his government for failing to acknowledge the threat of German armament and the lack of preparation for war in France. De Gaulle joined the 33rd Infantry Regiment and was mentioned in dispatches for his bravery in the early years of the Great War.

In 1916, de Gaulle led a charge at the Battle of Verdun that left him stunned by shellfire and unconscious from the effects of poison gas. He was captured and, while in captivity, wrote *The Enemy's House Divided* (published in 1924). Between the wars de Gaulle served in Poland and in occupied Germany, and wrote several books on mechanized warfare and military tactics – including, in 1934, *The Army of the Future*, a book that was largely ignored in France but read by Adolf Hitler. On the outbreak of World War II, he was put in command of a tank brigade and in 1940 was promoted to brigadier general. Prime Minister Paul Reynaud made him Under Secretary of State for National Defence and War. His duties included liaising with British forces, paving the way for his rise to greatness.

After Reynaud was replaced as prime minister by Marshal Pétain, who aimed to seek an armistice with the Germans, on 17 June 1940 de Gaulle and a group of senior French officers flew to Britain. On 18 June, Prime Minister Winston Churchill allowed de Gaulle to deliver a radio address on the BBC rallying occupied France to the cause of resistance and liberation. De Gaulle and his generals established their HQ in Carlton House Terrace in London, though the French House pub on Soho's Dean Street was their de facto home in exile and, allegedly, where de Gaulle drafted his famous 'France has lost the battle. But France will win the war' address.

From London, de Gaulle directed the French Resistance movement and in 1941 he was named president of the Free French National Council, France's government in exile. Writing in retrospect, Churchill said that 'he felt it was essential to his position before the French people that he should maintain a proud and haughty demeanour towards Perfidious Albion although in exile, dependent upon our protection and dwelling in our midst'.

De Gaulle himself declared that 'France has no friends, only interests'. Though he called Churchill a gangster, the Prime Minister recognized that General de Gaulle was 'the spirit of the French army'. When Paris was liberated in August 1944, de Gaulle led Free French troops into the capital. In his speech to the people of Paris from the Hotel de Ville, de Gaulle eulogized: 'Paris outraged, Paris broken, Paris martyred, but Paris liberated.'

The France de Gaulle inherited was on its knees. The country's transport system was shattered, industries sabotaged and the populace engaged in a witchhunt for collaborators. In Paris alone, 4,500 people were executed for treason, though de Gaulle was an advocate for leniency, commuting many death sentences to imprisonment. On the world stage the British ambassador to France, Alfred Duff Cooper, judged that de Gaulle 'was looking for trouble and insults where there were none'.

Having led the Provisional Government of the French Republic from 1944 to 1946, de Gaulle resigned two months after the formation of the Fourth Republic in 1946, whose constitution he campaigned against. His wilderness years between 1946 and 1958 were spent writing his mighty war memoirs.

De Gaulle's third administration, after he was elected President of the Republic in 1958, was characterized by a robust independent foreign policy and the dismantling of France's colonies, taking place in the context of a bullish French economy and a strong European Economic Community (EEC). In April 1969 de Gaulle called a referendum fully expecting the fickle French electorate to support him: he lost. General de Gaulle died two weeks short of his eightieth birthday at his country estate La Boisserie. On his death his successor, Georges Pompidou, declared: 'France is a widow.'

JIRO SHIRASU

PATRONAGE 1953

SIGNATURE GARMENT A chalk-stripe grey worsted double-breasted jacket and trousers

TOTAL SPEND £203 (£6,340 today)

CONNECTIONS Prince Hirohito (the future Emperor of Japan) was a customer of Poole's as early as 1921 and his son Emperor Akihito followed in 1953, when the house tailored a frock coat for his attendance at the coronation of Queen Elizabeth II.

Jiro Shirasu (1902–1985) was one of the cornerstones of Japan's economic development after the country's defeat in World War II. An anglophile, Shirasu graduated from Cambridge University in 1928, where he had cut a dash for his good looks, height (he was 1.8 metres [6 foot] tall and stood head and shoulders above many of his countrymen), his obsession with Bentleys, which he would drive through Europe when down from university, his fluency in the English language and his aristocratic manner.

When he returned to Tokyo in 1928, Shirasu worked as a journalist for the *Japan Times*. He married another overseas student, Masako Kabayama, an art historian, and through his father-in-law was introduced to the political world. Before the onset of World War II in 1939, Shisaru worked as an adviser to the Japanese government, which was keen to scotch the power-grabbing tactics of the Japanese military. Though not an elected politician, he was astute in reading international politics. He predicted the aerial bombing of Tokyo by the Allies and the extreme food shortages that would bring the city to its knees.

When Japan was defeated, Shirasu was appointed by Foreign Minister Shigeru Yoshida (a future prime minister and Henry Poole & Co customer) to work with the Central Liaison Officer to negotiate with the Occupation forces. He was the key liaison officer for US General Douglas MacArthur, Supreme Commander of the Allied Powers. His fluency in English, his honourable character and his pride in the Japanese nation made him something of a national hero. When it emerged that he tore a strip off MacArthur for not giving sufficient respect to a Christmas present sent by the Emperor Hirohito (another Henry Poole & Co man), Shirasu was lauded as the ideal modern Japanese man of principle.

Shirasu was rewarded for his negotiations by being made head of the government's Trade Ministry and he played a key role in establishing the Ministry of Economy, Trade and Industry. A letter dated 1946 from Shirasu to General Whitney gives an indication of his craft as a statesman and negotiator. It begins 'My dear General' and subtly points out the cultural differences between the Allies and the Japanese. 'Your way is so American in the way that it is straight and direct. Their way must be Japanese in the way that it is round about, twisted and narrow.' He signs off with the characteristically self-deprecating sentence: 'I am afraid I have already accelerated the paper shortage by writing this mumble but I know you will forgive me for my shortcomings for which my late father is also partly responsible.'

Shirasu is first recorded in the Henry Poole & Co ledgers in March 1953. Unusually, he settles his £203 bill in cash. His orders include a midnight-blue double-breasted dining jacket and trousers, a fawn- and red-check single-breasted jacket, a fawn dogsteeth [sic] single-breasted jacket, a chalk-stripe brown worsted flannel double-breasted jacket and trousers, a chalk-stripe grey worsted flannel double-breasted jacket and trousers, and a chalk-stripe brown flannel double-breasted jacket and trousers. The air shipping charge to Tokyo was a supplementary £10.

In later life, Shirasu retained his reputation as a maverick. He was one of the first Japanese men in public life to be photographed wearing Western jeans and drove a Porsche well into his eighties. In 2009, a TV film starring Yusuke Iseya about Jiro Shirasu's remarkable life was released, introducing him to a new generation of Japanese men for whom he is a sartorial and national hero.

CHAPTER THREE

THE AGE OF EMPIRE

1876–1916

'The name of Cundey is well known to persons connected with
Henry Poole & Co and I believe the business would suffer very
much if the name of Cundey was no longer connected with it.'

ELIZA CUNDEY'S AFFIDAVIT TO THE ROYAL COURTS
OF JUSTICE, LONDON (1887)

**The *Sporting Life* obituary for Henry Poole noted that 'it is not given to many public
men to create such a sincere regret in high circles by their deaths as, I fancy, it has
been to Mr Poole'. In more immediate circles, Poole's divisive fourteen-page will
would cause his heirs the Cundey family sincere regret and thirty years of legal fees
contesting the document through the Chancery Division of the Royal Courts of Justice.**

The terms of Henry Poole's will were catastrophic for his Cundey family. The business and
residuary personal estate was split into quarters. Sam Cundey was willed two quarters,
another quarter was settled on Henry's step-niece Fanny Cutler and her husband, Edwin,
and the last quarter went to Charles Bentley Bingley, who was appointed Sole Trustee.

Court papers dated 1887 record 'for some years before Mr Poole's death until the
20th of March 1887, the business was personally managed by the late Charles Bentley
Bingley. The services of the late Mr Samuel Cundey were no doubt of value but he was
never solely responsible for the management of the business … it was Mr Bingley alone
who saved the business from being wound up on the testator's credit by pledging his
personal credit for a very large sum.'

According to Henry Poole's will, Bingley was named Trustee 'in recognition and acknowl-
edgement of his kindness in undertaking the management of my business at considerable
personal sacrifice at a time when, from indisposition, I became unable to attend the management thereof myself and of the benefits which have resulted and as I trust and anticipate
will yet result to my estate from his prudent and skilful management of the said business'.

It was in Bingley's power as Sole Trustee to decide whether to sell Henry Poole &
Co, as we are told in court papers filed in 1890. 'On the death of Mr Poole, Mr Bingley
had considerable hesitation about carrying on the business having regard to the state in
which it was left. He frequently spoke in reference to the charge which he proposed to
make of £1,500 a year [£93,900 today] for himself if he continued the management, as

Opposite: Letter in Howard Cundey's handwriting (1907) to his banker Coutts & Co. Poole's first
banked with Coutts in 1819 and continues to do so today.

Deed box containing documents relating to Henry Poole's will and the ensuing thirty-year war for control of the company after his death in 1876.

he intimated that unless that were agreed he should not undertake the management.' Bingley's subsequent actions display ruthless brinkmanship. Sam Cundey had the largest share in the business but no veto, so would have to pay 50 per cent of Bingley's salary while still managing Poole's as he had done for decades, until the very end of Henry's life, when Bingley's shadow loomed large. If Bingley had been a competent solo manager in the last years of Henry's life, surely he was as culpable for the parlous state of the business as his ailing friend Henry's large expenditure.

Charles Bentley Bingley's disinclination to allow Henry's widow, Emma, and his sister, Mary-Anne, to keep personal furniture and art belonging to the deceased borders on the despicable and raises the question as to where the ladies were when Henry expired. Edwin Cutler was the only one present at the deathbed. The contents of Henry Poole's houses were auctioned, leaving Emma with little more than her husband's watch (now in the safekeeping of MD Simon Cundey) and personal effects such as a nest of snuffboxes, now in the showroom at No. 15 Savile Row.

Furthermore, Bingley knew that the £2,500 annuity (£156,500) that Henry willed to Emma and Mary-Anne Poole could not be met by his virtually bankrupt estate. Henry also added a clause in his will instructing the estate not to pay back £3,000 (£187,800) that Mary-Anne had loaned Henry to prop up the firm's ailing fortunes after she had given her brother her share in the annual rent of No. 171 Regent Street.

Emma and Mary-Anne moved into No. 71 Onslow Gardens in Kensington. The terrace with its pillared stucco porticos still stands and appears quite smart by present standards, but was cramped and suburban in comparison to Dorset Cottage. An 1845 print depicting Dorset Cottage reveals a charming Thames-side villa with conservatories on all sides, surrounded by pleasure gardens, mature trees and wide promenades. It is reasonable to conclude that reduced circumstances may have hastened the deaths of Emma in 1877 and Mary-Anne in 1879.

Sam Cundey's death in 1883 left his resourceful, formidable widow, Eliza, in possession of the half share in Poole's and an estate worth £61,000 (£187,800), making her a wealthy woman and Sam a better businessman than cousin Henry. Eliza proved to be a more indomitable widow than Emma Poole. Court papers dated 1890 confirm that Eliza Cundey 'was employed and took part of the management of some divisions in the business', so she had witnessed firsthand her husband being sidelined by Bingley.

To the dismay of the Cundey family, the Royal Courts of Justice ruled that the egregious Bingley was entitled by law to transfer Sole Trusteeship to his son-in-law Sir Reginald Hanson, a former Lord Mayor of London and Master of the Merchant Taylors' Company. An affidavit filed by Eliza Cundey in 1887 contested the decision. 'The testator (Henry Poole's) business has for some time past, under the personal superintendence of my son the above mentioned Howard Cundey, produced large profits.' She concludes: 'Sir Reginald Hanson … knows nothing of the business of a tailor. Having regard to the divided ownership of the property, there is in my opinion a serious danger that the business may not be kept up to its present profitable condition.'

As a stalemate solution, Howard Cundey was named receiver/manager of Poole's on the proviso that an accountant, Henry Leslie (formerly in the employ of Charles Bentley Bingley), work alongside him on Sir Reginald Hanson's advice. The impoverished Cutlers were the immediate losers in the arrangement of 1887. In a pitiful witness statement, Edwin Cutler writes that 'unfortunately, Mr Leslie was able to obtain control of my affairs by inducing Mrs Cundey to place my debt into his hands without giving me notice'.

Howard was making such a success of the business that it was in the Cutlers' best interests to retain the shares, from which they obtained an income. According to his *Tailor & Cutter* obituary, 'Mr Cundey's position at the head of the tailoring trade was unique. He held it not merely by virtue of being the proprietor of the best-known business in the world, but by reason of his infinite charm and ability. It was a position unquestioned and un-grudged; and the craft was fortunate in having as its leader one who stood in the forefront, wherever charity and benevolence was concerned.'

It is to Howard Cundey's credit that while privately he was deadlocked in a thirty-year court case with Sir Reginald Hanson, he was captaining a ship that won the Royal Warrants of King George I of the Hellenes (1877), King Umberto I of Italy (1879), Emperor Wilhelm I of Prussia (1879), Tsar Alexander III of Russia (1881), the Shah of Persia (1892), King Christian IX of Denmark (1893) and, most gratifyingly, King Edward VII in 1902, nearly thirty years after Henry had fallen foul of the then Prince of Wales.

However, in 1887 a sweating scandal threatened to destroy the reputation of London's bespoke tailoring trade. Newspapers such as the *Pall Mall Gazette* exposed the practice whereby eminent Row tailors outsourced work to sweatshops in Soho and Oxford Street where conditions were appalling, pay was a pittance and diseases such as scarlet fever were rife. Though not implicated themselves, Howard Cundey and Poole's led reforms that ended sweatshop labour.

Poole's, which employed 300 tailors in its King Street premises by 1890, was compromised by the London Tailoring Strike of 1891. But Howard Cundey emerged as 'the paladin of the tailoring trade' when he chaired a meeting of master tailors at the Cannon Street Hotel. As *Tailor & Cutter* reported, 'the meeting was large and enthusiastic, practical and business-like. Not only did he [Howard] represent the chief trade in the West End, but by his bearing, manner and business capacity, he imparted dignity to the proceedings.' *Tailor & Cutter* concluded: 'Mr Cundey, who does not appear to have much turned thirty, is a fine specimen of a West End gentleman; he has a light moustache and a fine head of jet-black hair.'

Howard Cundey was also the life and soul of the Master Tailors' Benevolent Association for more than forty years and, following the 1891 strike, was responsible for the formation of the Tailors' Log, a system still loosely used today, ensuring standard pay for a standard number of hours' work. Howard Cundey's own copy of the log in the Henry Poole Archive lists stitch-by-stitch the time taken to make anything from a postilion's jacket (twenty-five hours) to a tweed morning coat (twenty-three-and-a-half hours).

Unlike Uncle Henry, Howard did not socialize outside the trade and assumed the role of *pater familias* to Savile Row. His wedding to thirty-one-year-old Mabel Houle in 1903 was a tailoring state occasion in all but name. The reception was held in the Whitehall Rooms of the Hotel Metropole, now the Corinthia. The *Master Tailor & Cutters' Gazette* described the wedding presents as 'more than ducal'. Mabel would satisfy Howard's dynastic ambitions by bearing him two sons, Sam and Hugh, and two daughters, Rosamond and Olive.

In 1903 Howard's letters were musing on the eventuality of Sir Reginald's death. When the latter obliged and expired in 1905, Howard acted with brisk efficiency. The trustees of Sir Reginald's will applied to the Royal Courts of Justice for the continuance of the Solo Trustee arrangement but Mr Cundey out-manoeuvred them in a letter written from his Sussex Square mansion.

Howard threatens: 'I have come to the conclusion that I will not continue to act as manager of Henry Poole & Co in the event of a new Trustee being appointed. The probability is that I shall start in a business on my own account somewhere in the immediate neighbourhood of Savile Row and as Mrs Cundey, my Mother, with who I have discussed the question, entirely approves of my decision, she will require her capital paid out in order to support me in this course. Here you have my programme in a nutshell.'

After nearly thirty years of a Chancery Court case that was beginning to resemble Dickens's *Jarndyce & Jarndyce*, Howard Cundey thus brought the impasse to an end.

In 1906 Poole's Paris branch moved to No. 10, Rue Tronchet, where it remained until 1940.

Without his leadership and Eliza Cundey's capital, Henry Poole would have been worthless to Sir Reginald's trustees and to the Cutlers.

Despite nearly two more years of negotiation, the Cutlers finally agreed to sell their share to Howard. In a letter to Coutts dated 7 February 1907, Howard writes: 'Negotiations are in progress for the purchase of the business of Henry Poole & Co by myself as sole executor of the will of my mother Mrs Eliza Cundey who died on the 17th of December last. It was my mother's intention had she lived long enough to acquire the whole concern.'

Howard's letters from the first decade of the 20th century show a man secure in his role as father of Henry Poole & Co. Even before Sir Reginald's death, he had made the momentous decision to open showrooms in the great capital cities of Europe. He swats away Sir Reginald's request for a financial report on Poole's Paris branch, opened in the Rue Glück in 1904, by writing that he had already moved the business to larger premises on the Rue Tronchet without Sir Reginald's blessing. A Viennese Poole's opened in 1905 and a Berlin branch in 1906. There is evidence in a recently opened minutes book that Poole's also briefly opened a showroom in Budapest.

As it transpired, the Great War of 1914 would sweep the emperors of Austria and Germany from their thrones and thus close the branches of Poole's in Vienna, Berlin and Budapest. Though it was not the end of the lucrative trade in court and ceremonial dress that Pooles was famed for, the cessation of World War I in 1918 saw the old world order end. It would be Howard Cundey's role once again to steer Henry Poole & Co to safety.

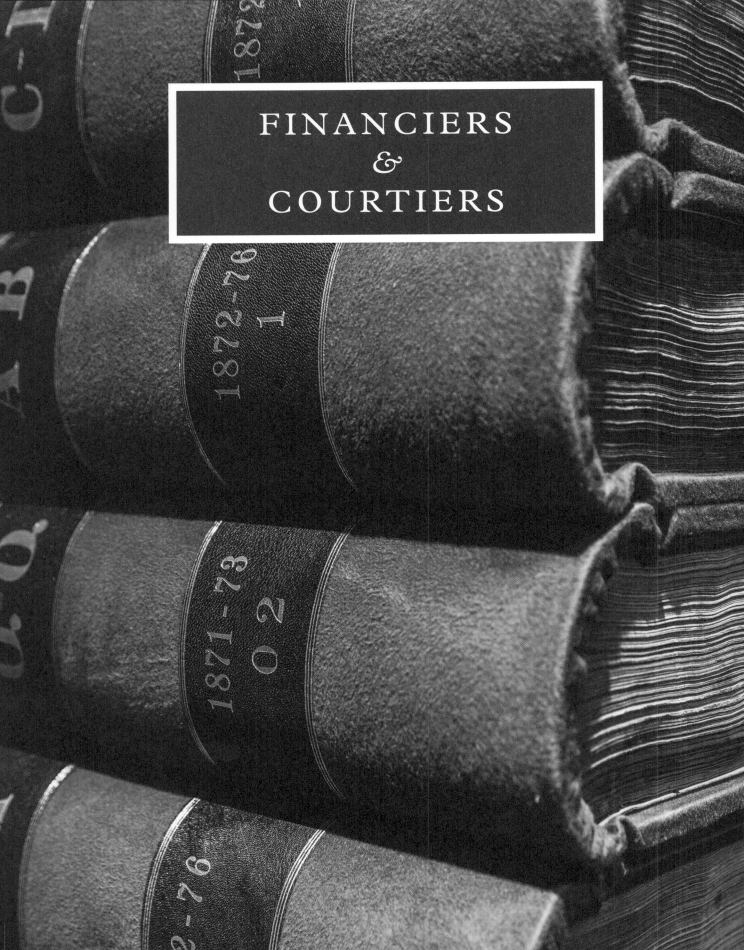

FINANCIERS
&
COURTIERS

BARONESS BURDETT-COUTTS

PATRONAGE 1873

SIGNATURE GARMENT A black silk velvet court dress for nephew
Mr Fraser Money

TOTAL SPEND £81 (£5,070 today)

CONNECTIONS Henry Poole & Co has held an account with Coutts & Co
since 1819 when Henry's father James Poole was guv'nor of the firm.

Baroness Burdett-Coutts (1814–1906) was the granddaughter of Henry Poole's banker, Thomas Coutts. In 1837 Angela Burdett inherited Thomas's fortune from his second wife, Harriot, Duchess of St Albans, having accepted the request to add Coutts to her existing name. She became the wealthiest woman in England after Queen Victoria, with a fortune of £1.8 million (£109 million today). Miss Burdett-Coutts was a prim, level-headed young lady guided by her charismatic governess, Hannah Brown.

Baroness Burdett-Coutts's biographer Edna Healey wrote of her: 'Angela, at twelve, was intelligent and shrewd, Hannah was the perfect companion and teacher.' As soon as she inherited, Miss Burdett-Coutts became a figure of fascination and a target for fortune hunters. *Punch* magazine wrote that 'the world set to work, matchmaking, determined to unite the splendid heiress to somebody'. Miss Burdett-Coutts did not fall, choosing instead to set up home with Hannah Brown at No. 1 Stratton Street, Piccadilly.

In 1839, Miss Burdett-Coutts befriended the Duke of Wellington, hero of Waterloo, who was a near neighbour living at Apsley House. Aged thirty-three, she proposed to the seventy-eight year old Duke, who replied: 'My first duty towards you is that of friend, guardian and protector. You are young, my dearest. You have before you the prospect of at least twenty-years of enjoyment and happiness in life.' They remained friends until the Duke's death in 1852.

Eighteen thirty-nine was also the year Miss Burdett-Coutts met Charles Dickens, who wrote to her: 'I have never begun a book, begun anything of interest to me or done anything of importance to me since I first dined with you.' His courtly love was shared and it was Dickens who helped inspire her lifelong passion for philanthropy. One of their first joint crusades was to establish a home for fallen women, which they called Urania Cottage. Dickens dedicated *Martin Chuzzlewit* to Miss Burdett-Coutts, and she was said to be the inspiration for Agnes Wickford in *David Copperfield*.

Miss Burdett-Coutts's interests were varied. Like Queen Victoria, she supported Florence Nightingale's mission to the Crimean War in 1855 and sent 'the lady with the lamp' a linen dryer that she had designed for a hospital laundry. Previously she had backed Charles Babbage's 'calculating engine'. The woman Victorian Society christened 'Queen of the Poor' would turn her attention to the RSPCA, the NSPCC and London's Royal Marsden Hospital. She held honorary posts with the Temperance Society, the Beekeepers Association and the Spitalfields Sewing School.

Miss Burdett-Coutts had cultivated the great and the good since her childhood Grand Tour and an encounter with King Louis Philippe of France. She was an intimate of the statesmen Benjamin Disraeli and William Ewart Gladstone. In 1871 she was made a peer by her admirer Queen Victoria in recognition of her many charitable works. Forthwith, she was known as Baroness Burdett-Coutts of Highgate and Brookfield. The Baroness chose Highgate because in 1837 she had inherited the district's Holly Lodge Estate from her step-grandmother, the actress Harriot Mellon, second wife of Coutts bank founder Thomas Coutts.

In 1881 Baroness Burdett-Coutts startled London society by marrying her secretary, an American, William Ashmead-Bartlett, whose education as a child she had

paid for. The bride was sixty-seven and the groom twenty-nine, making her a 'cougar' in modern parlance. Queen Victoria was compelled to write that 'it would grieve me very much if Lady Burdett-Coutts were to sacrifice her high reputation and her happiness by an unsuitable marriage'. Lady Burdett-Coutts was unrepentant, saying she 'could not face the future without him'.

By marrying a foreigner, Lady Burdett-Coutts lost her inheritance to her sister, Clara Money-Coutts. She was granted £16,000 (£1,060,000) a year, but it was insufficient to support her philanthropic schemes. When she died in 1906, she was buried near the West Door of the nave of Westminster Abbey. King Edward VII voiced the opinion that, after his mother, Queen Victoria, Lady Burdett-Coutts was 'the most remarkable woman in the kingdom'.

SIR FRANCIS KNOLLYS

PATRONAGE 1872–1889

SIGNATURE GARMENT A black superfine dress coat with silk sleeve linings and breast facings

TOTAL SPEND £5,025 (£332,580 today)

CONNECTIONS Sir Dighton Probyn, fellow courtier to the Prince of Wales (later King Edward VII), was also a Poole's customer. A captain in the Bengal Army during the Indian Mutiny and recipient of the Victoria Cross, Probyn became Comptroller of the Household and Keeper of the Privy Purse to King Edward VII and continued his duties to Queen Alexandra after the King's death in 1910.

Sir Francis Knollys, 1st Viscount Knollys (1837–1924), was Private Secretary to – and keeper of secrets for – Edward VII both before and after he became king. Educated at the Royal Military Academy at Sandhurst, Knollys became Secretary to the Treasurer of the Prince of Wales in 1862. His father, General William Knollys, had been appointed by Queen Victoria as Comptroller and Treasurer of the Prince of Wales's household, with a private mandate to report on his indiscretions to the sovereign.

By 1867, Knollys Senior acknowledged that he could not control the Prince of Wales. In 1870 the Prince appointed Francis as Private Secretary while keeping the services of the General for form's sake and to placate Queen Victoria. Edward VII's biographer Jane Ridley describes Francis Knollys thus: 'a dapper little man with shiny black hair and a beard cut into a strip down his chin. He resembled an Italian waiter. The Queen thought he was not fit for the post demanding instead a clever, able man capable of being of use and giving advice. Her conclusion was that, though useful, Francis Knollys was not considered clever by anyone.'

As Private Secretary, Francis Knollys vetted all official and personal correspondence to and from the Prince of Wales at his London residence, Marlborough House. From 1872, his sister Charlotte was Lady of the Bedchamber to Princess Alexandra, and thus the family were some of the closest confidants of the Prince and Princess of Wales in the land. Knollys knew about the Prince's vices and his failings and made it his life's work to protect the heir to the throne and shield him from scandal. He referred to the Prince's mistresses as his 'actress friends' and was the agent for organizing safe houses for the Prince and his brother Alfred to entertain their paramours.

In 1890 the Prince of Wales became embroiled in the Tranby Croft gambling scandal, an unfortunate case in which his friend Sir William Gordon-Cumming was accused of cheating at baccarat during a house party in the company of the Prince. In the face of persistent rumours and gossip, Gordon-Cumming insisted on his innocence and eventually brought a case of slander against his accusers. Knollys advised the Prince that attempting to keep the case out of court would do more damage to his reputation than appearing as a witness in the highly publicized case. Nonetheless, Gordon-Cumming gained the public's sympathy as the judge was widely considered to be biased in favour of the royal witness. When Gordon-Cumming lost the case in 1891, his former friend the Prince of Wales was roundly booed at Royal Ascot.

Knollys was ruthless in protecting his master from sex scandals, including those involving Lady Mordaunt, Lady Brooke and Lady Susan Vane Tempest, the daughter of the Duke of Newcastle. One major affair squashed by Knollys involved former mistress Lillie Langtry. Mrs Langtry's estranged husband, Ned, had compromising letters written by the Prince of Wales. When Ned Langtry died of drink in Chester Asylum in 1897, his letters were appropriated by his landlord, who attempted blackmail. The letters were retrieved and the blackmailer left unpaid.

The Prince of Wales was a profligate spender – another vice Knollys had to cover up. When it was reported that the prince was £600,000 in debt, Knollys had the *Times* print a retraction. When the Prince of Wales's eldest son, Prince Eddy, Duke of Clarence and Avondale, developed a reputation for living as loosely as his father in the fleshpots of London, it was Knollys who pressed for Prince Eddy to be sent on a tour of India to remove him from temptation.

When Queen Victoria died in 1901, politician Lord Carrington wrote, 'Francis Knollys is the most powerful man in England at this moment'. He had served the Prince of Wales for more than forty years and was rewarded by being made Private Secretary to him when he became king. He continued to write every letter for the King by hand in distinctive black ink.

The year 1909 saw a constitutional crisis that could have resulted in the abdication of King Edward VII. The Liberal government sought to flood the House of Lords with newly appointed peers in order to pass a budget that the Lords were blocking. Prime Minister Asquith snubbed the King's invitation to dine and sleep at Windsor Castle, resulting in his estrangement from the monarch. But fate overtook politics and, in 1910, King Edward VII died

After the King's death in 1910, Knollys was assiduous in his task of burning personal correspondence from 1863 to 1910. Courtiers appointed by the new king, George V, reported that Knollys was losing his reason and that his judgment in destroying so many of the late king's papers was impaired. George V asked for Knollys's resignation in 1913, though he continued to serve as Lord-in-Waiting to Queen Mary until his death in 1924, aged eighty-seven.

J. P. MORGAN

PATRONAGE 1876–1916

SIGNATURE GARMENT A blue cheviot double-breasted short lounging coat

TOTAL SPEND £9,690 (£761,340 today)

CONNECTIONS J. P. Morgan's father, Junius, was a Henry Poole customer,
as was his son, J. P. Morgan Jr.

Of his generation, John Pierpoint Morgan (1817–1913) was the most powerful banker, industrialist and art collector in America. Born in Connecticut, he was the third generation of a banking dynasty that he would go on to dwarf with his financial acumen and bullish instinct. His father, Junius Spencer Morgan, was a partner in a London-based merchant bank and a Henry Poole customer. Another ancestor, James Pierpoint, founded Yale University. Morgan's education was rich and varied. After high school in Boston, he went to Swiss school Bellerive, then on to the University of Göttingen, and could speak fluent Spanish, French and German.

Morgan's first banking job was in London, but in 1858 he returned to New York and joined Duncan, Sherman & Company. In 1871 he formed a partnership with Anthony Drexel (another Henry Poole man); two years after Drexel's death in 1893 the firm was renamed J. P. Morgan & Co.

At the height of his powers in the 1890s, Morgan was said to control one sixth of America's railway lines. In 1895 he and a consortium of bankers rescued America's Gold Standard, loaning the federal government more than $60 million. In addition to the bank that bore his name, Morgan invested in and subsequently bought the Carnegie Steel Company, Edison General Electric and the United States Steel Corporation. He also acquired the *New York Times* newspaper and founded the Metropolitan Club in New York when the Union Club blackballed his friend John King. Deeply offended, he instructed the architects to 'build me a club fit for gentlemen. Forget the expense.'

J. P. Morgan's power was considered by some to be too great and was wielded with ruthless efficiency. Physically, Morgan was an intimidating man and his presence was described 'as if a gale had blown through the house'. He suffered from the chronic skin disease rosacea, which gave him a bulbous purple nose and a disinclination to be photographed. A man with an almost superhuman constitution, Morgan smoked dozens of Havanas, earning his favourite cigars the nickname 'Hercules' Clubs'.

Morgan's first wife, Amelia Sturges, whom he married in 1861, died four months after the wedding. In 1865 he married Frances Louisa Tracey, who bore him four children. They held court in a mansion on Madison Avenue that was the first private residence in New York to be lit by electricity. Morgan also owned a vast summer house called East Island in Glen Cove. His houses were showcases for his enormous collection of antique books, paintings, clocks, gemstones and minerals.

The financier's other interests included a world-famous collection of photographs of Native American Indians and a fleet of yachts. As a fatalistic aside, Morgan had a ticket to sail on RMS *Titanic*'s maiden voyage in 1912, but decided instead to remain on the French Riviera at Aix-les-Bains. J. P. Morgan died in 1913 at the Grand Hotel in Rome. His son, Jack, inherited his estate. On the day of Morgan's funeral, the flags on Wall Street were flown at half mast and the Stock Market closed for two hours in honour of one of America's great financiers.

BARON FERDINAND DE ROTHSCHILD

PATRONAGE 1874–1880

SIGNATURE GARMENT A blue Denmark beaver evening pea cape
with silk collars and cuffs

TOTAL SPEND £205 (£30,370 today)

CONNECTIONS Baron Ferdinand's father, Anselm von Rothschild,
and his father-in-law, Lionel de Rothschild, held accounts with Henry Poole,
as did his uncles and cousins the barons Charles, James, William, Nathaniel,
Solomon, Gustave, Leopold and Alfred de Rothschild.

Baron Ferdinand de Rothschild (1839–1898) was a scion of the Viennese branch of the formidable Jewish European banking dynasty. His father, Baron Anselm von Rothschild, was the head of the Vienna Rothschild bank and was by all accounts dismissive of his second son's prospects. As Baron Ferdinand wrote, 'my mother [Charlotte] was my guardian angel, the one being around whom my existence revolved'. 'Ferdy', as he was known, moved to London in his late teens and gravitated towards the Piccadilly mansion of his uncle Baron Lionel de Rothschild, who headed the London branch of the family bank.

Ferdy fell in love with Lionel de Rothschild's bright and beautiful daughter Evelina and married her in 1865. He said of his bride, 'she has grown into my heart that my only wishes, cares, joys, affections, whatever sentiments in fact a man possesses were directly or indirectly wound with her existence'. Within a year, 'Evy' tragically gave birth to a stillborn son and lost her life in the process. Ferdinand established the Evelina Children's Hospital on Southwark Bridge Road in her memory and never married again.

In 1874 Ferdy began construction of what was to be his great legacy: Waddesdon Manor in Buckinghamshire. Designed by the architect Gabriel-Hippolyte Destailleur, Waddesdon was designed in the style of the great Loire Valley Renaissance châteaux. Ferdy's life's work was the decoration and expansion of Waddesdon, the establishment of the formal gardens that surround it and the collection of paintings and objets d'art that furnish it, with a particular emphasis on Sèvres porcelain, French royal furniture from the reigns of Louis XV and Louis XVI, Savonnerie carpets and 18th-century British paintings.

Though his brother-in-law Nathaniel Meyer de Rothschild thought Ferdy effete and pretentious, this might be the prejudice of a banker against a relative who had no interest in the family business. Ferdy was one of the most well-connected gentleman collectors in late Victorian Britain. The Prince and Princess of Wales were regular guests at Waddesdon, as was his cousin Hannah de Rothschild, who married the 5th Earl of Rosebery, Lord Hartington (the future 9th Duke of Devonshire) and prime ministers Benjamin Disraeli,

William Ewart Gladstone and Arthur Balfour.

Ferdy's landscaping of Waddesdon led the Prince of Wales to seek his advice when improving the formal gardens surrounding his Norfolk retreat, Sandringham House. The Prince wrote: 'I have sufficient confidence in your good taste to be quite easy in my mind that it will be a success.' The Prince's sister the Empress Frederick of Prussia, whom Ferdy visited in 1894, reported to her mother Queen Victoria that 'he is an excellent gardener and good botanist and had a good deal of artistic knowledge and taste'. The future Queen Mary was less kind, writing to say that a fountain in the shape of a pelican given by the Baron to her father-in-law, King Edward VII, made her 'shriek with laughter'.

Though Ferdy served as a Liberal politician from 1885 until his death in 1898, his polit-

ical influence was not best realized at the Palace of Westminster. His power was much more subtly exercised at weekend parties at Waddesdon co-hosted by his sister Alice, who was chatelaine of the estate. The Prince of Wales's friendship with Ferdy broke the taboo against Jewish people taking a place in London Society. In 1890 Queen Victoria honoured the Baron with one of her extremely rare visits to a subject's estate. On his death, Baron Ferdinand de Rothschild left Waddesdon to Alice and gave the choice of his collection of Renaissance objets d'art to the British Museum, of which he was a trustee.

WILLIAM COLLINS WHITNEY

PATRONAGE 1875–1899

SIGNATURE GARMENT Olive Elysian beaver greatcoat

TOTAL SPEND £4,113 (£272,220 today)

CONNECTIONS The 1890s saw America's millionaire tycoons with business
connections in London begining to patronize Henry Poole, including railway
magnate William Henry Vanderbilt, financier John Jacob Astor III and Louis
Lorillard of the tobacco dynasty.

William Collins Whitney (1841–1904) was a financier and founding father of the Whitney family's immense fortune. His aptitude for accumulating wealth was matched by a talent to charm his way into Manhattan society, controlled in the late 19th century by the arbiter of taste Mrs Astor. William Whitney could trace his family's descent back to William Bradford, who had sailed to America on the *Mayflower* in 1620 and settled in Massachusetts. But Whitney's ambition was to take his place in Gilded Age New York society, to which Mrs Astor was gatekeeper.

Whitney graduated from Yale in 1863, where he had befriended wealthy and influential young men such as John D. Rockefeller and Oliver Payne, the latter of whom would become his brother-in-law. He entered Harvard Law School, where a contemporary described Whitney as 'magnanimous, unselfish and generous', concluding that 'we all agreed when we graduated that his success would depend on whether anything would stimulate him to a full development of his powers'. Whitney left Harvard before graduating to pursue his legal career in New York and was admitted to the bar in 1865. His stimulus proved to be not law but money.

Popular, good-looking and charming, Whitney made an advantageous match with Flora Payne, Oliver Payne's 'expressive and vivacious' sister in 1869, with whom he would go on to have five children. According to the Governor of New York, Samuel Tilden, Whitney was 'the ablest political associate I ever had'. It was said of him that 'mediocrity in Whitney is unthinkable'. He served on the Corporation Council of New York between 1875 and 1882, and the powerful Vanderbilt family called on the 'intellectual giant' for financial advice.

Whitney made his first fortune as a streetcar magnate. He and business partner Thomas Ryan used underhand tactics, including bribery and corruption, to secure control of New York's Metropolitan Transit Company, buying shares belonging to rival Jacob Sharp, after the unfortunate man was jailed, for a fraction of their value. According to Greg King's *A Season of Splendor* (2009), 'the Metropolitan Transit Company offered new and frequently dubious opportunities for self-enrichment'.

In 1885 President Cleveland appointed Whitney Secretary of the Navy, an office he held until 1889. While in office he and Flora held court in Washington and made influential political and social alliances. Flora died in 1894, and Whitney rekindled a relationship with the widowed Mrs Edith Randolph, who, it was rumoured, was also the former mistress of J. P. Morgan. The reappearance of Mrs Randolph caused a rift with the deceased Flora's brother, Oliver Payne.

Whitney and Edith married in 1896 and set about remodelling a vast mansion on the southwest corner of 57th Street and Fifth Avneue opposite the Vanderbilt palaces. Architect Stanford White constructed a Venetian palazzo façade for the 'Palace of Art', which contained green onyx walls, 16th-century French tapestries, the largest ballroom in New York, bronze gates taken from the Palazzo Doria in Rome and artworks by Raphael, Tintoretto, Van Dyck and Reynolds. The Whitneys had not yet moved into the mansion when Edith was rendered comatose in a riding accident on their estate in South Carolina in 1898. She barely recovered and lived in great pain for several months before dying in 1899.

As a widower Whitney moved into the Fifth Avenue palazzo in 1900 and gave a debutante ball for 700 guests for his niece Helen Barney. But the mansion was said to resemble a sepulchre without a lady of the house. The American newspapers were dismissive of Whitney's tastes: 'We could wish that Mr Croesus was putting up an American house instead of reproducing a Venetian palace; or that some decorative artists had made a mantel so beautiful and so perfect that it was not necessary for the latest millionaire to ransack an old French chateau to discover something to his liking,' wrote *Munsey's Magazine* in 1901. William Whitney died in 1904 from peritonitis after an emergency appendectomy.

CORNELIUS VANDERBILT II

PATRONAGE   1883–1893

SIGNATURE GARMENT   Check cheviot elastic shooting jacket

TOTAL SPEND   £2,132 (£141,100)

CONNECTIONS   Cornelius Vanderbilt was recommended by his father, William Henry Vanderbilt. He ordered garments for his sons William Henry and Cornelius Vanderbilt III. His nephew William Vanderbilt Jr and niece Consuelo Vanderbilt – wife of the 9th Duke of Marlborough – held accounts with Poole's at the turn of the 20th century.

A favourite grandson of shipping and railroad tycoon 'Commodore' Cornelius Vanderbilt, who founded the family fortune, Cornelius Vanderbilt II (1843–1899) was president of the Vanderbilt family enterprises and investments between 1886 and 1899 and was noted for his philanthropic activities. He commissioned two of the outstanding architectural achievements of America's Gilded Age: the palatial Vanderbilt mansion at 57th Street and Fifth Avenue in New York, and Italian Renaissance 'cottage' The Breakers in Newport, Rhode Island.

The eldest of eight siblings, Cornelius II was born to William 'Billy' Vanderbilt and Maria Louisa Kissam. The Commodore looked kindly on his namesake, who took a clerkship with New York's Shoe & Leather Bank aged sixteen and forged his early career independent of the Vanderbilt family fortune. Aged twenty-four, Cornelious entered his grandfather's firm as assistant treasurer to the New York and Harlem Railroad.

A strict Episcopalian, Cornelius met and married Alice Claypole Gwynne when both were teaching Sunday school classes. It is a curious paradox that this seemingly pious couple would prove to be the most extravagant members of America's wealthiest family and chose to live in splendour to rival a European royal household. The Commodore died in 1877, leaving 95 per cent of his £100 million estate to his eldest son, Billy. He bequeathed $7 million to Cornelius II, who bought a city block on New York's Fifth Avenue, where his Vanderbilt uncles and cousins had chosen to build on Millionaire's Row.

Billy Vanderbilt would survive his father by only three years and on his death in 1880 Cornelius II inherited $70 million. He rose from Vice President to President and Chairman of the New York Central, Michigan Central and Canadian Southern Railroads. In 1883 Cornelius II commissioned architects George B. Post and Richard Morris Hunt to construct a New York mansion that would dwarf the Fifth Avenue palaces recently completed for his sister-in-law Alva Vanderbilt, who was the socially ambitious mother of Consuelo, the future Duchess of Marlborough.

The Vanderbilt mansion was the largest private residence ever built on the island of Manhattan. The façade of the 130-room red-brick and limestone mansion was modelled to scale on the Château de Blois in the Loire Valley and was embellished with towers, turrets, Gothic spires and crenellations as imposing as they were unnecessary. Cornelius said he wanted the Vanderbilt Mansion to dominate the plaza, and constructed a grand porte-cochère entrance on the east side, facing Central Park behind 3-metre (10-foot) high gilded wrought-iron gates.

This folly was razed to the ground in the 1920s to make way for the department store Bergdorf Goodman. The gates were re-erected in Central Park and the fireplace from the Great Hall awcquired by the Metropolitan Museum of Art. Little else survives of this humourless monument to hubris. Alice Vanderbilt's rivalry with her sister-in-law Alva was said to be behind the construction of The Breakers between 1893 and 1895. The Cottage, as the Vanderbilts called the Italian Renaissance palace built on a 5-hectare (13-acre) Newport coastal estate, cost $7 million to build and is now a museum, though the family still retains apartments on the third floor.

In his 1989 book *Fortune's Children: The Fall of the House of Vanderbilt* Arthur Vanderbilt II writes that 'a lifelong acquaintance of Cornelius Vanderbilt II's remarked that he never once recalled seeing him smile'. Cornelius III remembered his father as a joyless man who lived only for work. A second stroke killed the patriarch in 1899. It was reported in the *Times* that Cornelius II had woken in the Vanderbilt mansion at 6.00 a.m., roused Alice and said 'I think I am dying' before promptly doing so. He was fifty-five.

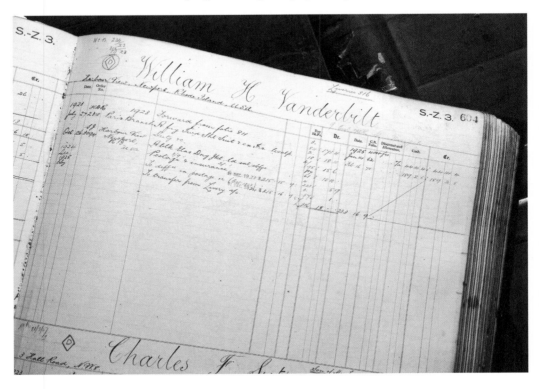

HRH PRINCE VICTOR DULEEP SINGH

PATRONAGE 1892–1904

SIGNATURE GARMENT Chalk-stripe flannel double-breasted short lounging
coat with double-breasted waistcoat and flat-front trousers

TOTAL SPEND £973 (£76,060 today)

CONNECTIONS Prince Victor's best friend in British society, the 5th Earl of
Carnarvon, was a Henry Poole man, whom the ledgers prove introduced him to the
tailor and underwrote the Prince's bills.

Prince Victor Albert Duleep Singh (1866–1918) was an orphan of the British Empire. His grandfather the Maharaja Ranjit Singh of Lahore, the Lion of the Punjab, was the fearless founder of the Sikh Empire. His father, the last maharaja of the Sikh Empire, was deposed after the Second Anglo-Sikh War in 1849 and exiled to London. Maharaja Duleep Singh is credited as being the first Sikh settler in Britain.

The twelve-year-old Maharaja Duleep Singh, forced to perform obeisance before Queen Victoria, presented the sovereign with the Koh-i-Noor diamond and the Timur ruby, treasures of the Punjabi royal dynasty. Queen Victoria made a pet of the exotic young prince, inviting him to Osborne House and commanding court artist Franz Winterhalter to paint his portrait. In her diary Victoria cooed, 'those eyes and those teeth are too beautiful'. In adulthood, the Maharaja would refer to the Queen as 'Mrs Fagin' for stealing the Koh-i-Noor from his people.

The displaced Maharaja met and married his German/Ethiopian first wife, Bamba Müller, in Egypt, and their first child, Prince Victor Albert Duleep Singh, was born in 1866. The boy was named after Queen Victoria's eldest grandson, Prince Albert Victor, and Her Majesty stood as godmother. He was christened in the private chapel at Windsor Castle and a miniature portrait of Prince Victor held in the Royal Collection bears witness to the affection with which the British royal family held the exiled Punjab prince.

Prince Victor Duleep Singh was the first Indian prince educated like a son of the British aristocracy. He learned to shoot on his father's Suffolk estate, Elveden Hall, where the pleasure-loving Prince of Wales (the future King Edward VII) was often a guest. At Eton and at Trinity College, Cambridge, he was a contemporary of his namesake Prince Albert Victor and the heirs to the Earl of Coventry, the Duke of Manchester and the Earl of Carnarvon. His friendship with Lord Porchester, who as 5th Earl of Carnarvon found fame as an Egyptologist, was the cause of much controversy, as was his subsequent marriage to the 9th Earl of Coventry's daughter Lady Anne.

At Cambridge Prince Victor Duleep Singh and Lord Porchester were inseparable. Both young bucks tore through allowances granted by the Indian Office and the Earl

of Carnarvon respectively. They developed a taste for gambling on the French Riviera and allegedly sowing wild oats in the brothels of Cairo. If rumour is to be believed, Lord Porchester contracted a sexually transmitted disease in Egypt that would have repercussions when he married.

Prince Victor required a special dispensation from Queen Victoria to join the Royal Military Academy at Sandhurst in 1887, but his record there was undistinguished. In 1888 the Prince was issued with his first bankruptcy petition. It was settled privately and Prince Victor was commissioned as a lieutenant in the 1st Royal Dragoons. In 1889 he was posted to Halifax, Nova Scotia, as Honorary Aide-de-Camp to General Sir John Ross, but frittered his time and money away in fashionable Newport society and returned to London leaving his debts for the army to settle.

Though the Prince of Wales was asked to keep Prince Victor in check, a despairing Indian Viceroy Viscount Cross wrote: 'I cannot pay his debts again but I mean to keep him in the army if I can. He is, however, a thorough oriental extravagance.' Prince Victor Duleep Singh's records in the Henry Poole & Co archives bear out his extravagance and his reliance on the patronage of his friend the 5th Earl of Carnarvon. Carnarvon recommends Prince Victor to Henry Poole in 1895, the year Carnarvon married heiress Almina Wombwell, who was the illegitimate daughter of Alfred de Rothschild. Prince Victor gives Highclere Castle, Carnarvon's family seat, as the delivery address.

Prince Victor stood as best man to the 5th Earl and accompanied his friend and the Countess of Carnarvon on their honeymoon to Cairo. He appeared to serve as the third person in the marriage, leading to rumours that it was the Indian prince who fathered Carnarvon's heir in 1898. Society was scandalized when Prince Victor courted and won the hand of Lady Anne Coventry, whom he had first met in 1898 when at Cambridge with her brother. The Prince of Wales overruled Lady Anne's family's objections to the mixed-race marriage and Queen Victoria gave her blessing, though she allegedly told the bride at a private audience: 'You must never have any children with the Prince.'

Queen Victoria's words were heeded and Prince and Princess Victor Duleep Singh remained childless. By 1900 Prince Victor owed the colossal sum of £17,000. Bad investments and gambling debts overwhelmed him. With characteristic recklessness, he travelled to Monte Carlo in the vain hope of restoring his fortune at the gaming tables. His losses resulted in a further declaration of bankruptcy in 1902 that necessitated his quitting London to live in Paris. The Prince suffered a fatal heart attack in Monte Carlo in 1918 and was buried in the Anglican cemetery.

SIR ERNEST CASSEL

PATRONAGE   1882–1906

SIGNATURE GARMENT   A stripe flannel short lawn tennis jacket

TOTAL SPEND   £783 (£64,240)

CONNECTIONS   Sir Ernest Cassel followed Baron Maurice de Hirsch –
a Henry Poole account holder – as financial adviser to the Prince of Wales
(King Edward VII) suggesting that patronage of Henry Poole was a rite of passage
for key members of the Prince of Wales's Marlborough House set.

Sir Ernest Cassel (1852–1921) was a German-born banker raised in the Ashkenazi Jewish faith who arrived penniless in Liverpool aged sixteen in 1869 and rose to become King Edward VII's financial adviser and trusted friend. Cassel was one of the most astute financial minds of his generation and showed early promise clerking for an Anglo-Egyptian bank in Paris, where he was mentored by revered European banker Baron Maurice de Hirsch. Hirsch secured Cassel in the London merchant banker Bischoffsheim & Goldsmidt when the Franco-Prussian War necessitated a swift exit from Paris.

Cassel's investments were risky, bold and successful, earning him a salary increase from £200 to £5,000 within a year at Bischoffsheim & Goldsmidt. Before his thirtieth birthday, he was said to have accrued a personal fortune of £150,000 investing in Siberian gold mines, American railways and ore mining in Sweden. In 1878 Cassel married Annette Maxwell, for whom he converted to Roman Catholicism and became a natural British citizen. They had a daughter, Maud, but Annette died three years later of tuberculosis and Cassel never remarried.

The Prime Minister's wife, Margot Asquith, described Cassel as 'a man of natural authority, dignified, autocratic and wise with the power of loving those he cared for'. Asquith thought him kind but cold with no small talk or gossip. Cassel's modus operandi was to avoid investment in the UK in favour of overseas propositions with higher risk and higher returns, such as Mexican railways, mining and transport infrastructure in China, and gold and diamond mining in South Africa.

Social climbing was a necessary occupation to gain access to the highest spheres of influence in world finance. Cassel's wealth opened the door to British aristocratic society and he cultivated friends in high places on the hunting field, at shooting parties, on the racecourse and at the card table. Baron Hirsch, who was the Prince of Wales's financial adviser, introduced Cassel to the future King Edward VII in the 1890s.

When Hirsch died in 1896, Cassel took over the Prince's private investment portfolio, an arrangement sweetened by Hirsch's final instructions for £300,000-worth of loans to the Prince to be written off on his death and Cassel's guarantee that any losses accrued by

Bertie would be underwritten by the banker. The Prince of Wales and Cassel were similar in personal appearance, hence the society jest of referring to them as 'Windsor Cassel'.

Edward VII's biographer Christopher Hibbert wrote in 1976, 'Cassel was careful to join the right clubs and was indefatigable in his pursuit of British as well as foreign decorations … It was felt that, except when he was on the hunting field or inspecting his horses, Cassel's attention never wandered far from the world of finance, international loans, of percentages and profits. Yet unlike most men of comparable riches, he derived as much pleasure from spending money as in amassing it.'

As Hibbert suggests, Cassel was rewarded for supplementing the Prince of Wales's private income with honours that rained down on him when the Prince became King Edward VII in 1901. Cassel was awarded the monarch's Royal Victorian Order in 1901 and was made a Privy Councillor in 1902. The King's patronage ensured his membership of the Jockey Club, and his international investments earned him orders from Germany, Sweden, France and Japan.

King Edward VII was a witness at the wedding of Cassel's daughter Maud to MP Wilfred Ashley in 1901 and stood as godfather to his granddaughter Edwina, who would become the last Indian Vicereine and Countess Mountbatten of Burma. As Hibbert writes, 'the sum of money that Bertie owed to Ernest Cassel has never been fully calibrated but Cassel's role is underpinning the Edwardian monarchy was incalculable'. Cassel was one of the last people called to Edward VII's deathbed on 6 May 1910.

WILLIAM RANDOLPH HEARST

PATRONAGE 1888–1931

SIGNATURE GARMENT Blue Denmark beaver pea coat

TOTAL SPEND £3,958 (£309,400 today)

CONNECTIONS Hearst's British counterpart as a pioneering newspaper
tycoon, the 1st Viscount Rothermere, held an account with Henry Poole & Co.

A merica's 'Sun King', William Randolph Hearst (1863–1951), built the world's largest newspaper and magazine empire, the Hearst Corporation, making him the most influential press baron in the first half of the 20th century. Born in San Francisco, Hearst was educated at Harvard, from which he was famously expelled for giving his professors monogrammed silver chamber pots. His father, George Hearst, was a gold-mining million-aire and US Senator from San Francisco who also had interests in the city's newspapers. By sheer force of personality, two years after Hearst left Harvard, he pressured his father into ceding control of his premier newspaper holding in 1887, having written a strident letter urging, 'give me the *San Francisco Examiner*'.

Investing in advanced print technology, employing high-profile writers such as Mark Twain and introducing campaigns, thundering editorials, cartoons and sensational photography, Hearst was a pioneer of tabloid journalism as we know it today, or 'yellow journalism' as it was known in the US. Like a circus ringmaster, Hearst was a master of ballyhoo. He sponsored the first round-the-world airship voyage in 1929, making his correspondent Grace Drummond-Hay the first woman to circumnavigate the globe, on board the *Graf Zeppelin*. He visited Germany to personally interview Adolf Hitler, telling the Führer bluntly that Americans believed in democracy and were averse to dictatorship.

Hearst married chorus girl Millicent Wilson in 1903. She bore him five sons, but by 1919 Hearst had met the love of his life, actress Marion Davies, whom he remained faithful to until the day he died. He never divorced Millicent, who became something of a society grande dame and tolerated her estrangement from Hearst, telling mutual friend Charlie Chaplin that 'if it weren't Marion it would be someone else'.

Chaplin gives an intriguing portrait of Hearst in his 1964 autobiography: 'If I were asked what personality in my life has made the deepest impression on me, I would say the late William Randolph Hearst … It was the enigma of his personality that fascinated me, his boyishness, his shrewdness, his kindness, his ruthlessness, his immense power and wealth, and above all his genuine naturalness.'

Hearst was most proud of the mansion he called 'The Ranch', more commonly known as Hearst Castle. Hearst Castle was a 'château' built from various castles shipped over in

crates from Europe. The dining room was a smaller-scale replica of Westminster Abbey's nave and could comfortably seat eighty. As Chaplin wrote, 'I never knew a person throw wealth around in such a dégagé manner as did Hearst', who also hosted lavish weekend parties aboard his yacht *Oneida*.

In 1924, Hearst and Davies were rocked by scandal when pioneering Hollywood producer Thomas H. Ince was shot on board the *Oneida* while on a pleasure cruise with guests including Chaplin, celebrated British author Elinor Glyn and Hearst reporter Louella Parsons. Rumour had it that Hearst shot Ince thinking he was Chaplin who he believed was having an affair with Marion. It was whispered that the fatal shooting on board *Oneida* was in Orson Welles's original script for *Citizen Kane*, the 1941 film loosely based on Hearst and Davies.

As with most megalomaniacs, Hearst's end was not a happy one. It was an open secret that Marion drank. Marion also had affairs, falling for one of her young co-stars, William Powell, among others. As the author Anita Loos wrote of him, 'he considered he rated with Napoleon and Gladstone and all the great political figures'. Loos's verdict was that Marion believed the bravado despite having to hock jewels worth $1 million to bail out Hearst's rapidly crumbling empire in the 1930s. Hearst died of a heart attack in 1951 with Marion by his side.

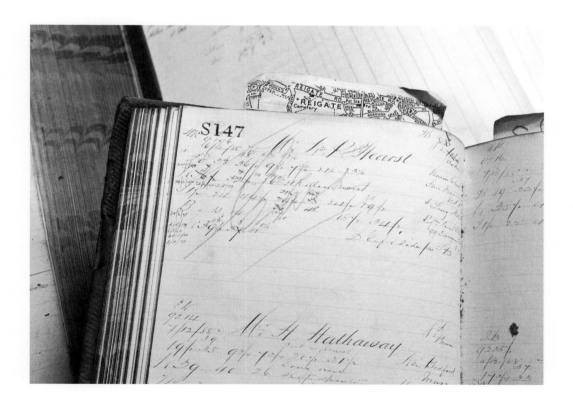

CALOUSTE GULBENKIAN

PATRONAGE   1892–1906

SIGNATURE GARMENT   A black stripe cheviot lounge coat

TOTAL SPEND   £520 (£40,650 today)

CONNECTIONS   Of all Henry Poole's philanthropic customers, Calouste
Gulbenkien left the largest art collection – 6,400 pieces, to be exhibited in his public
gallery in Lisbon. J. P. Morgan left his 1,000-piece gem collection to the Museum of
American History and Baron Ferdinand de Rothschild left his exceptional 300-piece
collection of Renaissance art and *objets de vertu* to the British Museum.

Born in Constantinople (now Istanbul), the son of an American banker and oil trader, Calouste Gulbenkian (1869–1955) would become the wealthiest and most successful oil broker in the Western world and the guardian of a historic art collection of paintings, antiquities and sculptures. Gulbenkian was known as 'Mr Five Per Cent' because that was the seemingly modest percentage he insisted on retaining as payment for brokering deals with the British, French, German and Turkish governments for foreign rights to drill for oil in uncharted territories such as Iraq.

Gulbenkian was educated at Kings College, London, where he studied petroleum engineering. He visited Russia to study the oil business at Baku before fleeing the Ottoman Empire in 1896 in the aftermath of the Hamidian Massacres, when an estimated 300,000 Armenians were murdered in an indiscriminate anti-Christian pogrom. Gulbenkian relocated to Cairo, where he went into business with Armenian oil magnate Alexander Mantashev and formed an alliance with banking heir Sir Evelyn Baring.

In 1902 Gulbenkian moved to London and took British citizenship. In 1907 he was the broker who helped arrange a merger between Royal Dutch Petroleum and Shell Oil. This was the first of his 'Five Per Cent' deals. In 1912, Gulbenkian was the fixer who negotiated the foundation of the Turkish Petroleum Company and developed successful oil exploration in Iraq. It was Gulbenkian who put together the oil alliance between the British, Dutch, German and Ottoman empires that held together through the two world wars.

When World War I ended, the Ottoman Empire was dismantled and Iraq became a British protectorate. Oil reserves were discovered at Baba Gurgur and the Pasha of Iraq gave the control of the entire concession to Gulbenkian, who formed the Iraq Petroleum Company. Gulbenkian retained five per cent, saying, 'better a small piece of a big pie than a big piece of a small one'.

Gulbenkian divided his time between London and Paris, where he filled his palatial houses with museum-quality antiquities, Old Masters, coins, illuminated books and classical sculptures, He displayed his sculpture collection in his four-storey house on the Avenue d'Iéna in Paris. In 1936, Gulbenkian lent thirty of his paintings to London's National Gallery with a view to bequeathing them to his adopted country. He loaned his Egyptian artefacts to the British Museum, intending to make a similar bequest.

Gulbenkian was in Paris when World War II was declared. When the French government fled the Nazi invasion and left Paris for Vichy, he followed them and as a consequence was temporarily declared an enemy alien by the British government. His UK oil assets were sequestered and his citizenship revoked. Though he was compensated after the war, Gulbenkian never forgave the British. In 1942 he relocated to Lisbon, and lived there for the rest of his life.

At the time of his death in 1955, Gulbenkian's fortune was estimated at $840 million; a monumental sum in the mid-20th century. Instead of willing his collection to his children, Gulbenkian left instructions for a foundation to be established in his name. Assets included a collection of masterpieces painted by the greats of the 18th, 19th and 20th centuries, such as Rubens, Van Dyck, Hals, Rembrandt, Gainsborough, Fragonard, Nattier, Manet, Renoir, Degas and Monet.

Gulbenkian called the favourite pieces in his collection his children, a particular favourite being Jean-Antoine Houdon's sculpture of the goddess Diana that had belonged to Catherine the Great and was bought from the Hermitage Museum. Not that Gulbenkian was not as ruthless with his collection as he was in the oil business. He sold pieces that had fallen out of favour at the top of the market to make new acquisitions.

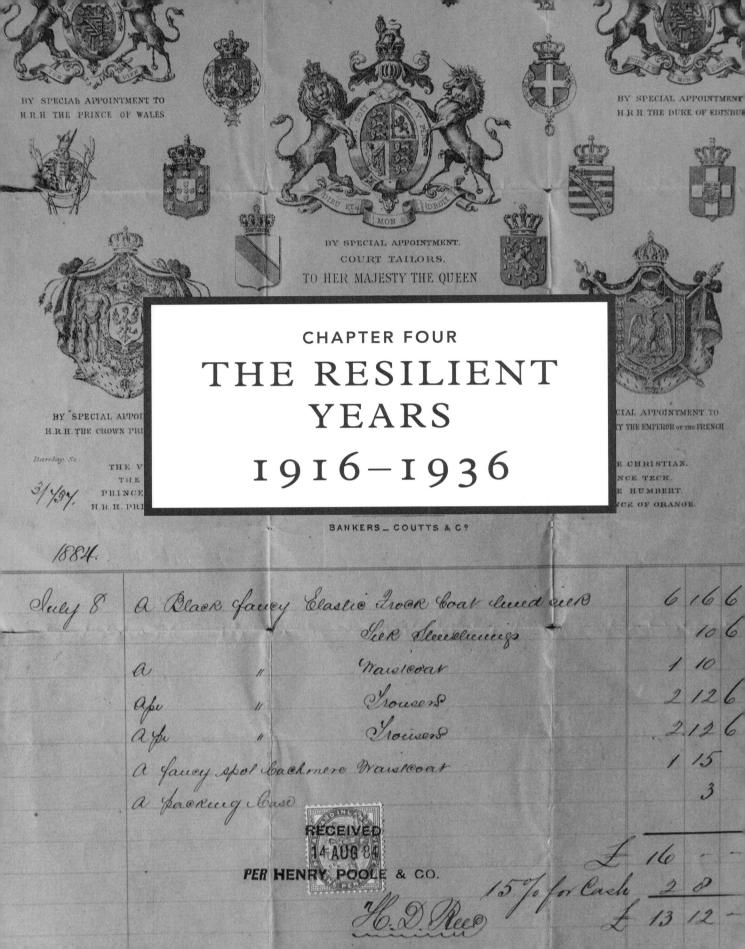

CHAPTER FOUR
THE RESILIENT YEARS
1916–1936

'I have been myself actively employed since the Autumn of 1875 and have consequently had long experience of how the business has been and should be conducted. It has always borne a very high reputation for punctuality and attention to detail, which it has been the constant aim of my predecessors and myself to maintain.'

HOWARD CUNDEY (1916)

The two world wars in the 20th century were catastrophic for London's bespoke tailors. Post-World War I, the ceremonial and livery trade that had reached its apex in the reign of King Edward VII was dealt a staggering blow from which it never fully recovered. Taking one customer ledger, L–R 1909–1925, we see how Henry Poole's customers prepared for battle.

In late 1913, the extravagant Count Larisch, one of Poole's highest-rolling customers, instructed the firm to send a stock of Floris perfume and Briggs hats to the Palais Larisch in Austrian Silesia, knowing the supply could soon be cut off. 'Sunny', 9th Duke of Marlborough, ordered a khaki whipcord service jacket lined with fleece and a khaki camel great coat lined with 'own fur' to be delivered to Blenheim Palace in 1914.

The 5th Earl of Onslow, recruited to the Intelligence Corps in 1915, commissioned Poole's to provide him not only with a khaki service jacket and whipcord trousers but also a Sam Brown belt, cap, haversack, water bottle, revolver, puttees and a folding knife–fork–spoon set. The Earl's order demonstrates the not-uncommon practice of long-standing customers trusting Poole's to purchase items over and above clothing. Only a decade previously these items might have been jewelled cigarette cases with diamond-encrusted regal ciphers and now the firm was purchasing firearms.

Civilian orders during the Great War understandably plummeted. Pre-1914, the A–Z customer ledgers would fill eight volumes of more than 1,000 pages each. From 1914 to 1939, the number of ledgers used was halved. Where once each customer filled a page of a ledger, after World War I they were listed two to four a page. Poole's survived on maintenance, as the 1914 order of wealthy press baron Alfred Harmsworth, 1st Viscount Northcliffe, demonstrates. Ironically, the future Nazi sympathizer's sole requirement of Poole's during the Great War was to pay £5 biannually to store his peer's robes.

Opposite: Poole's magnificent letterhead dated 1884 ablaze with the arms of Queen Victoria, the Prince of Wales, the Duke of Edinburgh, the Crown Prince of Prussia and Emperor Napoleon III of the French.

Head cutter Gustave Brinkman's dismissal from Poole's is recorded in Howard Cundey's Staff Book.

Henry Poole & Co was also at war within the walls of the showroom. In the wake of the Thirty Years' War with Bingley and Sir Reginald Hanson, Howard Cundey found himself facing an enemy within. Poole's was facing legal action again in 1916 when the firm's German-born head cutter, Gustave William Brinkman, instructed his solicitors, Grey & Brooks, to sue Poole's for unfair dismissal. The court transcripts of Howard Cundey's evidence from the witness box give an intriguing account of the politics in the showroom and workshops that Howard Cundey had to finesse.

The troubles begin when Mrs Yarrow of Pinner 'expressed great surprise that the uniform ordered by my husband should be entrusted to a man of German birth for execution'. In a stern but polite letter dated 27 November 1914, Howard Cundey replies that Brinkman had worked at Poole's since 1887, had been married to a Frenchwoman for twenty-six years and had several relatives fighting with the Allies.

Howard Cundey's loyalty to his staff in the face of xenophobia is admirable; particularly considering Mr Brinkman was already a divisive character within the firm. As early as 1909, Mr Chalke complained to the guv'nor that 'Cove and Fortin, English indoor workhands working for Mr Brinkman, were receiving next to no work while Muller, an outside workman and a foreigner employing his assistants, was heaped with work'. The implication was that Brinkman was favouring outworkers over in-house staff.

Mr Brinkman had also been agitating to replace the then head cutter, Mr Dent, claiming that 'he was not the man that he had been and that his work was not cut to the style of the present day and how different the shoulders of Mr. Dent's coats were to his shoulders'. Dent retired in December 1909 and Brinkman was offered a ten-year agreement at a salary of £1,000 per annum. Brinkman forced Howard Cundey's hand to offer him £1,200 after five years or he would take a partnership with neighbours Jones, Chalk and Dawson at No. 6 Sackville Street. This in itself is a time-honoured negotiating tactic and it proves that Howard Cundey valued Brinkman's work.

Like many a head cutter today, Mr Brinkman had the self-assurance of a high-ticket Premier League football player in his skill. According to current livery director Keith Levett, his confidence was justified. 'On many occasions I have examined liveries and ceremonial garments from the Brinkman era,' says Mr Levett, 'and I have been humbled by the man's work.' Brinkman was good and he knew it.

Once appointed head cutter, Brinkman set about removing as many of Dent's old work hands as possible, using the excuse that 'they were incapable of turning out the work as desired by him, that he had taken great pains to try and explain the peculiar way in which his shoulders should be made up and not one of these old work hands was able to grasp his instructions and not one of them was capable of carrying them out even if he could grasp them'. As Brinkman knew, botching a shoulder line of a bespoke coat is tantamount to a treasonable offence on Savile Row.

Pressure mounted on Howard Cundey when, in 1912, one of the firm's best customers, the Earl of Lonsdale, complained by letter of Mr Brinkman's 'neglect of instruction' – a euphemism for impertinence. In the same year, the Amalgamated Society of Tailors demanded an audience to ask why Poole's allowed Brinkman to not employ 'tried and experienced British indoor hands who had been working for so many years for Mr. Dent'. It came to Mr Cundey's attention that Mr Brinkman had also eavesdropped outside his office door when the deputation from the AST came to call. Staff members Messrs Heale and Morton accused Brinkman of using 'obscene language continually when speaking to workpeople'.

In the first year of the Great War, Howard Cundey began receiving acrimonious anonymous postcards and letters about Brinkman. We learn through Brinkman's reluctant acceptance that his salary should not be increased for the duration of the war that Poole's business had 'very much deteriorated owing to the war' and that Mr Cundey was pessimistic about its future. Howard Cundey writes, 'One does not know how long the war may go on and I think the probability is I may find myself going from bad to worse and I shall be contracting an ever-growing loan with my bankers.'

Complaints from the Paris branch of Poole's, which continued to trade during World War I, accused Brinkman of not fitting the facings of his short jackets carefully enough and that 'his work generally might be better finished'. Howard Cundey reminded Brinkman that grievances from the now defunct Berlin and Vienna branches had been constant. The nail in Brinkman's coffin was struck on 20 August 1915, when Poole's American representative, Mr Vassar, told Howard Cundey: 'I left England with a heavy heart because I am so reluctant to make myself responsible for orders executed by Mr Brinkman who could not be relied upon to carry them out either according to instructions given or to have them finished in a proper manner.'

Mr Cundey made his judgment. 'My business has been falling off continuously for several years and I had rather come to the conclusion that it was owing to dissension amongst the head cutter and other members of the staff and that I must either get rid of Mr. Brinkman or run the risk of losing other members of my staff whose services I valued. In fact, I came to the conclusion that it was no longer possible for me to run my business with Brinkman on the premises because he was upsetting everybody.' Brinkman did not go quietly, saying to Cundey, 'Are you going to turn against me?' The answer was a 'yes, Mr Brinkman'.

As the Poole ledgers demonstrate, World War I decimated the firm's turnover. Page upon page of orders from young customers are crossed out with the word 'dead' written in pencil. The enemy debt book for the Great War has not survived but the fall of the Austro-Hungarian, Russian and German emperors erased the European court and military trade. As was customary at Poole's, the firm looked to foreign shores.

In 1913, Howard Cundey had surmised that measures provided by the Japanese ambassador for uniform and mufti were 'presumably for HM the Emperor of Japan'. The emperor in question was Yoshihito, who died in 1926, but it was his son, Crown Prince Hirohito, who established Poole's reputation in the Land of the Rising Sun.

Crown Prince Hirohito was the first prince from the imperial household given permission to travel outside Japan in more than 2,500 years of the dynasty. In 1921, on the recommendation of the Japanese Ambassador to the Court of St James's, Howard Cundey instructed a tailor to meet the Crown Prince's battleship at Gibraltar, measure him up and cable the figures to Poole's telegraph address 'Picky' (as in Piccadilly) so the firm could make a Western formal wardrobe for him.

The Crown Prince arrived aboard the imperial battleship *Katori* in May 1921 and was later met at Victoria Station by King George V and the Duke of Connaught: the wardrobe tailored by Henry Poole & Co was waiting for him. Crown Prince Hirohito was photographed in white tie and orders standing next to the Prince of Wales in St James's Palace.

In 1922 Howard Cundey's eldest son, Sam, who was seventeen, joined the firm on the instruction of his father. As Sam rather lugubriously recalled in 1974, 'and that was that! I was not consulted. Tailoring was not exactly my choice of work.' Sam was shipped to the Paris branch in 1923 with little more French than '*Bonjour*' and spent two years 'acting the doorman' because the Paris staff were wary of instructing the guv'nor's son.

Not that Howard Cundey wanted his son to be a practical tailor, writing to Sam that 'it would be a waste of time for you to become skilled in clothing. Much better that you should engage good staff and make sure they are doing their jobs properly.' The reluctant heir had not long returned to work in the Savile Row showroom before his father's health began to fail.

The August 1927 edition of the *Sartorial Gazette* announced that 'the whole of the members of the tailoring and allied trades of the British Isles will mourn the death of

Impeccably tailored by Poole's, Crown Prince Hirohito of Japan visits the National Gallery in London in 1921.

Howard Cundey which occurred on Sunday, July 10th at the age of seventy'. The *Sartorial Gazette* went on to call him 'diplomatic, tactful and courteous in the highest degree'. Mention was made of Mr Cundey's presidency of the MTBA and his support for the sainted 'Florence Nightingale of the tailoring trade, Angelica Patience Fraser'.

Ill-health had necessitated Howard Cundey's retirement from the trade in 1925. The *Tailor & Cutter* obituary (21 July 1927) reported: 'He leaves a widow, two sons and two daughters. Mr Samuel Cundey has been in the Savile Row business for three years and the younger son, Hugh, will join him as soon as he has passed his examination as a chartered accountant.'

Like his father, Samuel, Howard had left a one-paragraph will that left his entire estate to his widow, Mabel. Presumably the decision was made to avoid the nightmares that ensued following the publication of Uncle Henry's will. Had Mabel Cundey not died aged fifty-nine in 1931, Sam and Hugh Cundey might have been able to accommodate not insurmountable death duties. With both parents' deaths coming so close together, the firm was crippled financially by double death duties. As a solution, Sam and Hugh Cundey agreed to mortgage their inherited properties to the Chartered Bank of India, Australia and China in 1935. This roll of the dice would eventually necessitate the firm doing the unthinkable and being forced to quit Savile Row.

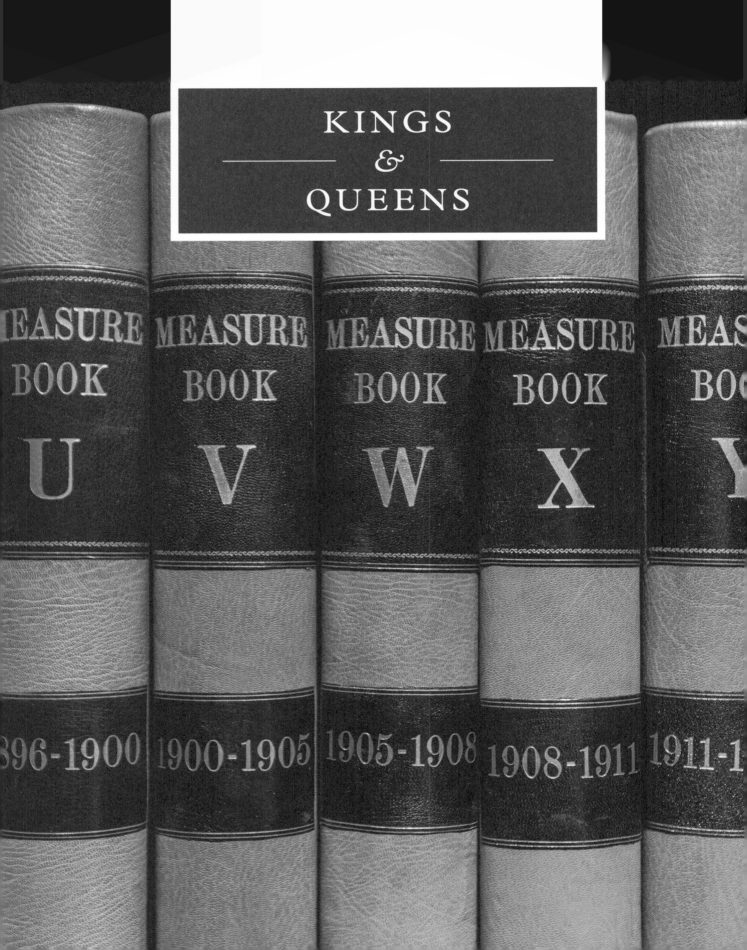

HM KING CHRISTIAN IX OF DENMARK

PATRONAGE   1867–1903

ROYAL WARRANT   HRH Prince Christian of Schleswig-Holstein (1870)

SIGNATURE GARMENT   A black diagonal cloth lounging coat lined with silk

TOTAL SPEND   £668 (£44,210 today)

CONNECTIONS   King Christian was introduced to Henry Poole & Co by his son-in-law the Prince of Wales (the future King Edward VII). His sons the future King Frederick VIII of Denmark, King George I of Greece and Prince Valdemar also held accounts with Henry Poole & Co. Between 1879 and 1883 all of King Christian's orders were placed by his wife, Queen Louise.

King Christian IX of Denmark (1818–1906), who reigned between 1863 and 1906, was not born to rule. A fourth son of the princely house of Schleswig-Holstein-Sonderburg-Glücksburg, born and brought up in Germany, Prince Christian was from a junior branch of the Oldenburg dynasty that had ruled Denmark since 1448. By royal standards his upbringing in Gottorf Castle was parochial and modest. The French ambassador judged him 'of very mediocre mind and very little education'. But Prince Christian was chosen as heir presumptive in 1853, after thrice-married King Frederick VII failed to provide a legitimate heir.

King Frederick was the last absolute monarch of Denmark, who ceded power in favour of a constitutional monarchy. An eccentric man, the King had twice divorced before morganatically marrying a former milliner and ballet dancer. His inability to sire an heir left the Danish throne vacant for whoever the Great Powers of Europe deemed a safe pair of hands. The modest Prince Christian, educated at the Military Academy of Copenhagen, was in many ways not a strong candidate, so was dispatched to Europe to broker an advantageous marriage.

In 1842 Prince Christian married his second cousin, Princess Louise of Hesse-Kassel. Princess Louise and her mother and siblings were very close in the line of succession to the Danish throne: they all renounced their rights in favour of Prince Christian, who was confirmed as hereditary prince of Denmark in 1853.

The marriage proved to be partially a love match, with Louise the stronger, more intelligent partner, who set a moral tone bordering on puritanism in the household. The couple had six children – Frederick, William, Dagmar, Alexandra, Thyra and Waldemar – whose dynastic marriages became an obsession for Princess Louise, earning the King and Queen of Denmark the nicknames 'Father- and Mother-in-Law of Europe'.

In 1862, Prince Christian escorted his daughter Princess Alexandra to England, for her marriage to the Prince of Wales the following year. In November 1863, Frederick VII

died and Prince Christian was proclaimed King of Denmark. Poole's clerks assiduously amended his title in the company ledgers. Within a month of his accession, Denmark was at war with Prussia, which had occupied the Danish territories of Holstein and threatened to annex Schleswig. Despite the new Princess of Wales's considerable diplomatic skills, Britain would not support Danish interests and before King Christian had been on the throne for a year he had lost more than half his kingdom to the hated Prussian Empire.

Christian was unpopular with his people, and his power abroad lay in the match-making skills of Queen Louise, who also had a Henry Poole & Co account. Princess Dagmar married the future Tsar Alexander III of Russia, and Prince Frederick (the future King Frederick III of Denmark) wed Princess Louise of Sweden. Prince William, who would ascend the throne of Greece as King George I of the Hellenes, married Grand Duchess Olga of Russia, and Prince Waldemar wed French Princess Marie of Orléans. Princess Thyra, who had given birth to an illegitimate child in 1870, married the Duke of Cumberland.

Danish politics under King Christian were controlled by long-serving prime minister Jacob Estrup, who kept an iron grip on power between 1875 and 1894. Following a failed assassination attempt in 1885, Estrup imposed draconian laws restricting press freedom and the right to bear arms while giving the Danish police greater licence to crush dissenting political factions. Both King Christian and Queen Louise were conservatives and supported Estrup in the suppression of liberalism. That said, Queen Louise's charitable work and piety were influential in prompting laws passed to introduce old-age pensions, unemployment assistance and tax relief for families.

In an age when monarchies such as Russia were still absolute powers, the King seemed weak at home even though his influence on the international stage remained strong. In 1906 Christian died peacefully of old age at the Amalienborg Palace in Copenhagen after a forty-two-year reign.

HM KING LEOPOLD II OF THE BELGIANS

PATRONAGE 1862–1874

ROYAL WARRANT HM The King of the Belgians (1869)

SIGNATURE GARMENT Fine blue Windsor uniform dress coat with scarlet
collar and cuffs ordered for an 1866 visit to Queen Victoria at Windsor Castle

TOTAL SPEND £641 (£40,130 today)

CONNECTIONS Confirming Poole's reputation as quartermaster for European
royal gifts, King Leopold's last order with Henry Poole & Co was a silk velvet dog
coat, a basket lined with silk and a soft leather collar for his pug Ruby. King
Leopold's wife, Queen Marie-Henriette, held a livery account with Poole's.

Leopold II (1835–1909), King of the Belgians, known nationally as 'the Builder King' for his aggrandisement of his capital city, Brussels, and as 'the Belgian Bull' for his prowess as a lover, casts a long shadow over colonial history as the 'Butcher of the Congo'. Atrocities committed during his personal rule of the Congo Free State between 1885 and 1909 have gone down in history as some of the worst outrages of 19th-century imperialism.

Prince Leopold's father, King Leopold I, was Belgium's first monarch, and his mother, Louise-Marie, was a scion of the French Orléans dynasty. He was an unhappy, unpopular child whose father called him 'the little tyrant' and whose mother thought his hooked nose rendered him deformed. Leopold was also said to be shy and awkward and walked with a limp.

In 1853, he made a dynastic alliance with Austrian princess Marie-Henriette, daughter of Archduke Joseph; benevolent, beautiful and popular, she was known as 'the Rose of Brabant'. In the same year Leopold was appointed to the Belgian Senate and made his imperial ambitions for Belgium known. Between 1853 and 1865, he travelled extensively to India, China, Africa and Europe. It is during this period that he first appears in the Henry Poole & Co ledgers, under the title Duke of Brabant.

The Poole's clerks record the Duke's accession as King Leopold II of the Belgians on a ledger page dated 1865. No sooner was Leopold declared king than he began lobbying Queen Isabella II of Spain to cede the Philippines territories to Belgium. This endeavour failed. Tragedy struck his first year as ruler when the Belgian legation to Mexico – where the King's sister, Carlota, was puppet empress – was massacred. Leopold's brother-in-law, the Emperor Maximilian, was executed by firing squad and his sister driven mad with grief. Dispatching Queen Marie-Henriette to bring Carlota back to Belgium, King Leopold would draw on his sister's not inconsiderable riches to further his colonial ambitions in Africa.

King Leopold's domestic record was largely benign. Under his reign, universal male suffrage was put on the statutes, trade unions were legalized and laws against child labour were passed whereby no child under twelve was allowed to work in a factory, none younger than sixteen allowed to work at night and no woman younger than twenty forced to work underground.

In 1876, King Leopold turned his colonial ambitions to Africa. He set up the deceptively benign-sounding International African Society, led by English explorer Henry Morton Stanley, to colonize the territories that became known as the Congo Free State. The Congo proved to be anything but free. King Leopold was declared sovereign of the Congo Free State – a territory more than seventy-six times the size of Belgium – and commanded a personal army sent to enforce his regime.

Leopold began by exploiting the trade in ivory, and when this dried up turned his attentions to harvesting the sap of rubber plants. The populace was enslaved and labour enforced. The penalty for not meeting the rubber quota was the severing of a hand. King Leopold's personal wealth was estimated at between $100 million and $500 million, making him the richest man in the world and furnishing him with the funds to rebuild Brussels, Antwerp and Ostend on a magnificent scale. The cost in human life of King Leopold's colonial ambitions has been estimated at anything between two and fifteen million Congolese people killed under Belgian rule. The consensus today is ten million deaths.

In 1890 the Brussels International Conference condemned slavery in the Congo, and opposition to the brutality of the regime gathered momentum in the following decade. The King survived an assassination attempt in Brussels in 1902; the same year his estranged queen, Marie-Henriette, died. Mark Twain's satire *King Leopold's Soliloquy* and Arthur Conan Doyle's *The Crime of the Congo* voiced international outrage about the enslavement and massacre of the Congolese people, and the Belgian Senate finally forced Leopold to cede the Congo to the nation in 1908. He died a year later.

HM KING GEORGE I OF THE HELLENES

PATRONAGE 1865–1877

ROYAL WARRANT HM The King of the Hellenes (1877)

SIGNATURE GARMENT Black drill lounging coat lined with silk

TOTAL SPEND £308 (£19,300)

CONNECTIONS King George ordered clothing for his eldest son, the future
King Constantine I, on his Poole's account.

Born a Danish prince in Copenhagen's Yellow Palace, King George I of the Hellenes (1845–1913) was seventeen when he was elected to establish a new dynasty of kings by the Greek National Assembly, which had deposed Bavarian-born King Otto and the unpopular Queen Amalia in 1862. King George had the distinction of ascending to the Greek throne before his father became King Christian IX of Denmark. His nomination was supported by the Great Powers of Russia, France and Great Britain. The Greek government held a plebiscite and although Prince Alfred, Duke of Edinburgh, won 95 per cent of the vote, his mother, Queen Victoria, was adamant that the Prince would not leave England, so Prince George took the prize.

When King George I sailed into Athens in 1863, he said, 'my strength is in the love of my people'. In his accession speech, the King declared that 'in these modern days, princes must strive to be superior in intellect, knowledge and goodness to those around them'. A born democrat, George supported the constitutional monarchy and swiftly mastered the Greek language, as well as national sports such as wrestling and running. He established the modern Olympic Games in Athens and opened the summer games in 1896. His endeavours to endear himself to his people earned him the moniker 'Father of the Nation'. King George would reign for almost fifty years.

In 1867, George married Grand Duchess Olga Constantinovna of Russia. Of their seven surviving children, three married into the doomed Russian Romanov dynasty. The heir, Prince Constantine, married Princess Sophie of Prussia, who was the sister of Emperor (Kaiser) Wilhelm II. A younger son, Prince Andrew, married Princess Alice of Battenberg. Prince Andrew's son Philip, born in the palace of Mon Repos on the island of Corfu, would become the Duke of Edinburgh, consort to Queen Elizabeth II.

Under King George, Greece prospered, enjoying a unique position in Europe thanks largely to the spider's web of royal relations. In 1888, the King celebrated his silver jubilee with a thanksgiving service at the Metropolitan Cathedral of Athens and attended a lunch for 500 on the Acropolis attended by the Prince and Princess of Wales, the Crown

Prince of Denmark, the Duke and Duchess of Edinburgh and the grand dukes Sergei and Paul of Russia.

For the duration of King George's reign, Greece was formally or informally at war with Turkey over sovereignty of the island of Crete. When Greece did declare war, the Great Powers sided with the Turks and George considered abdication. It was only after a foiled assassination attempt in 1898 that he regained the affection of his people. The King had always made a point of walking freely among his people without a bodyguard. After the assassination attempt, he continued to do so, earning the respect of the Greek nation.

In 1913, the King decided to abdicate in favour of his son Constantine after celebrating his golden jubilee. Tragically, on a visit to Greece's second city, Thessaloniki, in March 1913 he was shot through the heart at point-blank range by a socialist anarchist called Alexandros Schinas. The killer was tortured and fell to his death from a police station window before being convicted of regicide.

After the King's death, Queen Olga returned to St Petersburg at the onset of World War I and set up a military hospital in her brother's Pavlovsk Palace. When the Russian Revolution erupted in 1917, Olga was placed under house arrest, but the intervention of the Danish Embassy facilitated her escape to Switzerland. She returned to Athens in 1920 on the death of her grandson King Alexander, and briefly served as regent until her son King Constantine was restored to the throne.

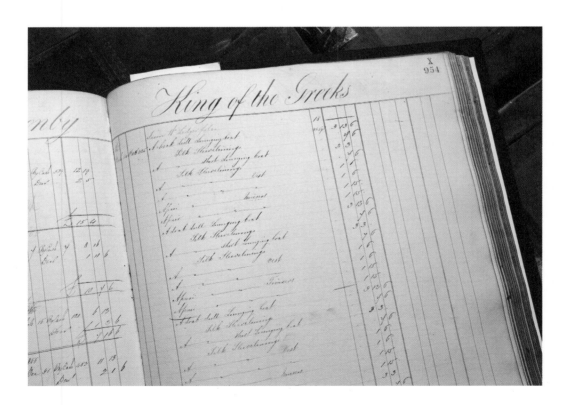

HM QUEEN MARIA SOPHIA OF THE TWO SICILIES

PATRONAGE   1862–1871

SIGNATURE GARMENT   A fine light-blue yachting coat lined with silk with
flat braid, a silk velvet collar and anchor gilt buttons

TOTAL SPEND   £34 (£2,010 today)

CONNECTIONS   Queen Maria Sophia's sister Empress Elisabeth 'Sisi'
of Austria is recorded in company lore as a Poole's customer for riding habits.
Her records do not survive.

Maria Sophia of Bavaria, Queen of Naples (1841–1925), was a heroic woman who had the misfortune to marry into a fragile dynasty. She was one of ten children born to Joseph, Duke of Bavaria, and his wife, Princess Ludovika. Like her elder sister Elisabeth (who would become Empress of Austria), Maria Sophia was considered a bright, beautiful young woman, famed in European courts for her proficiency as an equestrian. Aged sixteen, she was betrothed to Francis, Crown Prince of Naples, who acceded to the throne of the Two Sicilies in 1860. King Francis II was said to suffer from phimosis and the marriage was not consummated.

In 1861, when the Queen Consort of the Kingdom of the Two Sicilies was only twenty-one years old, the independent nations of Naples and Sicily were attacked by the forces of Giuseppe Garibaldi, who was seeking to unify Italy under the rule of King Victor Emmanuel II. The King and Queen abandoned the royal palace in Palermo and made a stand within the walled coastal fortress of Gaeta, near Naples.

It was during the siege that Queen Maria Sophia earned her spurs as the 'warrior queen', the 'heroine of Gaeta' and the 'modern Joan of Arc', rallying the troops, nursing the injured, feeding her forces at her own table and taunting Garibaldi's army from the battlements with the words: 'Go ahead and shoot me! I will be where my men are!' It was said of her that the Queen would 'wipe your brow if you were wounded or hold you in her arms while you died'.

Despite the Queen's heroism, Naples and Sicily fell and were absorbed into the unified Kingdom of Italy. King Francis and Queen Maria Sophia fled to Rome, where they established a court-in-exile centred around the Farnese Palace. In his essay 'The Last Stand of the Italian Bourbons', published in the *Atlantic Monthly* in November 1884, William Chauncey Langdon wrote: 'Pope Pius IX welcomed the late royal family with somewhat ostentatious hospitality. The young Queen ever won upon the kindly interest and sympathy of everyone who looked upon her almost girlish figure, her fair face and placid brow. Francis sat silent, gloomy, saturnine.' Chauncey Langdon concludes: 'These last Bourbon royalties of Italy remained in Rome for some years vainly hoping and attempting to create a favourable occasion for stirring-up reaction, or at least a conspiracy of one kind or another, in the late kingdom of the Two Sicilies.'

A lady who signed her 1872 book *Royal Exiles and Imperial Parvenus* only 'An Englishwoman' wrote: 'The Palazzo Farnese in Rome was, when I knew it in 1863, the refuge of that modern Joan of Arc, the ex-queen of Naples … She seemed to me the most lovely vision I had ever seen. Her dark hair reached halfway down her back and she seemed ready to burst the wide-meshed net that cinched it. Her eyes and colour added to the sprightly, bewitching beauty of her face and her carriage was absolutely the most willowy and graceful I ever saw.' There the adulation ends. 'But there the dream of Joan of Arc must end. The high moral resolve, the far seeing grasp of mind, were utterly wanting. So fair a shrine but so feeble a lamp within.' Yet the ex-queen still had the power to charm in the late 1860s, when English sculptor Harriet Homer declared herself 'still faithful in my violet-eyed heroine of Gaeta' (despite the presence in Rome of the rival Prince and Princess of Piedmont).

Maria Sophia fell in love with an officer of the Papal Guard, Armand de Lawayss, and bore him a daughter, who was given up to the father's family. The loss of this, her first child, was said to have contributed to her bouts of depression in later life.

In 1870 the King and Queen were forced to flee Rome and live a nomadic existence, moving first to Munich and then to Paris. Maria Sophia first appears in the Henry Poole & Co ledgers in 1871, ordering liveries for the household she was establishing in Paris. The ledgers give her the title Queen of Naples though she was if anything ex-Queen Consort Maria Sophia of the Kingdom of the Two Sicilies. In Paris, the ex-Queen was lionized by Marcel Proust as the 'soldier queen on the ramparts of Gaeta' and poet Gabriele d'Annunzio called her 'a stern little Bavarian eagle'.

Ex-King Francis died in 1894 and four years later ex-Queen Maria Sophia's sister Empress Elisabeth of Austria was stabbed to death by an Italian anarchist's stiletto. Ex-Queen Maria Sophia never lost hope that a unified Italy would be defeated and the Two Kingdoms returned to the Bourbon dynasty. Until her death in Munich aged eighty-four in 1925, Maria Sophia still rode astride her favourite horse like a warrior queen going into battle. Sicily's newspaper *Il Mattino* remembered her as 'one of those European princesses who with her great gifts would have had another destiny but for the dramatic events of her time'.

HM KING UMBERTO I OF ITALY

PATRONAGE   1870–1879

ROYAL WARRANT   HM King Umberto I of Italy (1879)

SIGNATURE GARMENT   A black superfine dress coat

TOTAL SPEND   £175 (£10,960 today)

CONNECTIONS   King Umberto's son, Prince Emanuel of Savoy, and nephew,
Prince Emanuele Filiberto, Duke of Aosta, awarded Henry Poole & Co their Royal
Warrants in 1892.

The second monarch of unified Italy, King Umberto I (1844–1900) was born into a dynasty at war. During the Prince's adolescence, his father, King Victor Emmanuel II of Savoy, and Giuseppe Garibaldi were fighting the patchwork of independent ducal states and kingdoms that made up Italy and working towards the union of 1861 known as the Risorgimento. The Savoy dynasty had ruled territories in and around Italy since the year 1003 but their claim to the unified kingdom was not universally popular.

Prince Humbert of Piedmont, as he was first listed in the Henry Poole & Co ledgers, served during the Second War of Independence and witnessed the carnage during the Battle of Solferino in 1859. The battle was the largest fought on European soil since Leipzig at the end of the Napoleonic Wars and an average of 26,000 men were killed every day. The young Prince of Piedmont would fight at his father's side until all the kingdoms of Italy were annexed under King Victor Emmanuel's rule.

As heir to the Risorgimento throne, Prince Humbert was not considered a solid gold match, although a tentative alliance with Archduchess Mathilde of Austria was dashed when the unfortunate girl set her gauze gown on fire smoking an illicit cigarette and burned to death. Instead, in 1868 the Prince married his first cousin Princess Margherita of Savoy, daughter of the Duke of Genoa. The marriage proved to be a political masterstroke.

Though not a beauty, Princess Margherita had charisma and poise. Her effect on patriotic crowds was describe as *margheritismo*. When Prince Humbert became King Umberto I of Italy in 1878, his new queen endeared herself to the crowds waiting in the rain outside the Quirinale Palace in Rome by removing the canopy from the royal carriage.

One of King Umberto's first acts on becoming monarch was to tour Italy showing off Queen Margherita and their heir, Victor Emmanuel, Prince of Naples, who was born in 1869. Like many a European throne, King Umberto's was not secure. In Naples he duelled with a would-be assassin, disarming the man with his sword. The King earned his title 'Umberto the Good' by keeping a close watch on his subjects and appearing at their side in times of crisis and natural disaster, such as the floods that overwhelmed Venice and Verona and an earthquake on Ischia.

The royal family was in residence at the Villa Reale, Monza, in 1900 when the anarchist party finally hit its target. In 1898 the city of Milan had been placed under martial law after riots had broken out protesting against the colonial wars in Africa. Cannons had been turned on demonstrators and the death toll was said to have reached 1,000. Umberto had sent a telegram congratulating commander General Bava-Beccaris for crushing the insurrection and the incident had become known as the Bava-Beccaris massacre.

King Umberto was returning to the Villa Reale when Italo-American anarchist Gaetano Bresci shot him in the heart at point-blank range. On being apprehended, Bresci said: 'I have not shot Umberto. I have killed the King. I have killed a principle.' He claimed the assassination was revenge for Bava-Beccaris. Bresci was found dead in his cell less than a year into a life sentence. Only two more Savoy kings would rule Italy. The dynasty was voted out in a referendum in 1946.

HM QUEEN RASOHERINA OF MADAGASCAR

PATRONAGE 1862

SIGNATURE GARMENT A rich crimson Genova velvet mantle lined
with silk and embroidered with gold

TOTAL SPEND £100 (£5,910 today)

CONNECTIONS The date of Queen Rasoherina's order for a coronation robe,
1862, anticipates the 1863 coup that saw her husband, King Radama II,
assassinated, leading to the supposition that the coup and the Queen's accession
was long in the planning.

When Queen Rasoherina of Madagascar (1814–1868) was born, her despotic aunt, Queen Ranavalona I, ruled the island nation off the southeast coast of Africa as an absolute – and, some surmised, mentally unbalanced – monarch. Under Ranavalona I, Christianity was banned in Madagascar and more than 3,000 of her subjects were put to death under the system of trial by the ordeal of tangena, whereby the accused's guilt or innocence would be proved by whether they survived ingesting the poisoned nut (tangena).

As the fourth largest island in the world, Madagascar was of colonial interest to the British and French, who were held at bay by Queen Ranavalona until her death aged eighty-three in 1861. The Queen's son and heir, the future King Ramada II, despised his mother's tyranny and had already signed a secret treaty with the French called the Lambert Charter in 1855, six years before her death. The animosity between mother and son might have stemmed from the rumour that Ramada was the bastard child of Ranavalona and a handsome general in her army.

King Ramada II chose his first cousin Rasoherina (born Princess Rabodo) as first consort. Princess Rabodo had previously been married to a much-decorated diplomat who had served as Secretary to the Embassy to Great Britain. They divorced in 1847 and in the same year Rabodo married the heir to the throne.

In his book *Madagascar: Its Mission and its Martyrs* (1863), historian Ebenezer Proud said of King Ramada: 'That the son of such a mother, trained up under a despotism so dark, restrictive and cruel, should have adopted such principles of religious freedom and political economy as equal civil liberty and universal free trade was little short of a miracle.' Christian missionaries were welcomed back to Madagascar, schools were opened, trial by tangena was abolished, political prisoners were freed and confiscated property returned to enemies of the dead Queen Ranavalona I.

Ramada II's reign was to be short-lived. He rejected his mother's isolationism, ended the persecution of Christians and reopened his kingdom to the influence of the French and the British, enraging his prime minister, the improbably named Rainivoninahitriniony,

who would prove to be Queen Rasoherina's nemesis as well as leader of the coup in which her husband was ostensibly assassinated.

In the 1863 coup that deposed King Ramada, Queen Rasoherina pleaded for his life but was forcibly removed from the palace. Soldiers strangled the King with a silk sash, avoiding the curse of shedding royal blood. Though it was later suggested that King Ramada survived the assassination attempt and lived out the rest of his natural life in obscurity on a remote coast of Madagascar, the rumours have never been proven. The Prime Minister announced that King Ramada had committed suicide and that Queen Rasoherina would accede to the throne, with the proviso that 'for the future, the word of the sovereign alone was not to be the law' and on the condition that the Queen's command alone could not put a Madagascan citizen to death.

With the Prime Minister as de facto ruler, Queen Rasoherina was crowned. The sole entry in the Henry Poole & Co ledger books for 'The Queen of Madagascar' is dated 1862 and is for a crimson velvet robe embroidered in gold and lined in silk, which Queen Rasoherina is pictured wearing in her coronation portrait.

Drunk with power and not a little alcohol, the Prime Minister was said to have abused the Queen, even threatening her at knifepoint when she would not bow to his will. In retaliation and with public support, the Queen cast down the Prime Minister and replaced him with his younger brother, Rainilaiarivony.

Queen Rasoherina attempted to continue her late husband's policies and sent ambassadors to London and Paris. In 1865 she signed a treaty with the United Kingdom giving its subjects the right to rent lands and buy property on Madagascar as well as retain an ambassador at her court … probably a posting most British diplomats considered a punishment more than a promotion. She treated with the US in 1867 to limit import of weapons and export of cattle and was in talks with the French government, but her health began to falter and the question of her successor became paramount.

In 1868 a coup was staged and a howling mob armed with guns and swords invaded the royal palace in the capital city of Antananarivo, but neither Queen Rasoherina nor the Prime Minister was in residence. With Rainilaiarivony's encouragement, the Queen addressed her people and invited them to lead her back to her palace in Antananarivo to demonstrate popular support. The gambit paid off, but four days later Queen Rasoherina, who had hidden her profound ill-health from her people, breathed her last. The Queen was received into the Roman Catholic Church on her deathbed and was succeeded by her cousin Queen Ranavalona II, who declared Madagascar a Christian nation in 1869.

HM KING PETER I OF SERBIA

PATRONAGE 1905

SIGNATURE GARMENT A state uniform and pantaloons delivered to the
Royal Palace, Belgrade

TOTAL SPEND £153 (£12,020 today)

CONNECTIONS Fellow Balkan monarch King Ferdinand I of Romania held
an account with Henry Poole, as did his wife, Queen Marie of Romania, when she
was titled Princess Marie of Edinburgh.

In the cauldron of Balkan politics, King Peter I of Serbia (1844–1921) was considered a
national hero for ending the deadlock between two warring families, the Karadordević
and the Obrenović dynasties, who fought for the Serbian throne. When Prince Peter was
born, his father, the Karadordević Prince Alexander, ruled. Alexander was deposed by
Obrenović Prince Milan in 1858.

Prince Peter was fourteen when the ex-royal family fled first to Wallachia, then on to
Geneva and eventually to France, where he studied at the prestigious Saint-Cyr military
academy in Paris. As a deposed prince from a dynasty that had little likelihood of being
reinstated, Peter's prospects were low. He resolved to fight and, between 1870 and 1871,
served as a mercenary in the Franco-Prussian War. He joined the French Foreign Legion,
taking the nom de guerre 'Kara'.

In 1883 the nomadic Prince Peter married Princess Zorka, the eldest daughter of King
Nicholas I of Montenegro, and the couple lived at the Montenegrin court for a decade
before drifting to Paris and Switzerland. Unlike her sister Elena, who would become
Queen of Italy as consort to King Victor Emanuel III, Princess Zorka did not live to see
her husband crowned king. She bore the prince five children but died in childbirth in 1890.

By the end of the 19th century, thunder rolled around the throne of Serbia. King
Alexander I (Prince Milan's son) had marred a commoner, Draga Mašin, twelve years his
senior. Her father had died in a lunatic asylum and her mother was a dipsomaniac. The
concern of the political class and the military was that the childless Queen Draga would
persuade King Alexander to proclaim one of her two brothers heir to the Serbian throne.

In 1903, the royal palace of Belgrade was invaded by troops headed by Captain Dragutin
Dimitrijević, a leading member of the Black Hand, the Serbian terrorist society that
would assassinate Archduke Franz Ferdinand in 1914, thus lighting the touchpaper for
World War I. The King and Queen were dragged from their hiding place in a wardrobe,
brutally stabbed, shot, partially dismembered and then thrown out of a window on to a
compost heap in the garden below.

In the wake of this brutal regicide, Prince Peter was proclaimed King of Serbia and the throne was restored to the Karađorđević dynasty after forty-five years. Peter was fifty-eight years old when he returned in triumph to Belgrade and was crowned in 1904. Thus began a reign remembered as the golden age of Serbia. The King supported a benign, constitutional monarchy ruled by a democratic parliament. He was also a vocal supporter of the unified Yugoslavia.

His eldest son and heir, Crown Prince George, who was demonstrably unsuited to rule, was the thorn in King Peter's side. A wild, reckless man, the Crown Prince attacked one of his servants in 1909, kicking him repeatedly in the stomach until he haemorrhaged and subsequently died. After this episode and following pressure from the military and the political class, Prince George was forced to renounce his claim in favour of his younger brother, Alexander.

As the Ottoman Empire entered its death throes, King Peter led Serbia into the Balkan Wars of 1912–1913 and by doing so doubled the size of his country, gaining territories previously occupied by Turkey. But ill-health forced the King to retire from public duties and cede his role to Crown Prince Alexander. During World War I, the King visited Serbian troops in the trenches, where it was reported on one occasion that the old soldier picked up a rifle and began shooting at enemy troops.

In 1915, Serbia was invaded by the combined forces of Germany, Austria-Hungary and Bulgaria. King Peter led the withdrawal of the Serbian Army, together with tens of thousands of civilian refugees, over the Albanian mountains to the Adriatic Sea, where Allied ships transported them to the Greek island of Corfu. Serbia's government in exile chose Corfu as its seat of high command and the King remained on the island for the duration of the war. In December 1918, King Peter was proclaimed King of the Serbs, Croats and Slovenes. He returned to the royal palace in Belgrade, where he died in 1921 aged seventy-seven.

HM KING ALFONSO XIII OF SPAIN

PATRONAGE 1886–1898

SIGNATURE GARMENT King Alfonso's orders were almost exclusively for his aide-de-camp His Excellency Joseph Palomino and his brother Raphael.

TOTAL SPEND £901 (£73,930 today)

CONNECTIONS In the year of his coronation, 1874, the seventeen-year-old King Alfonso XII (the subject's father) placed his only order with Henry Poole & Co.

King Alfonso XIII of Spain (1886–1941) was born a reigning monarch. The death of his father, Alfonso XII, aged twenty-seven left the throne vacant and his wife, Queen Maria Cristina of Austria, expecting their child. King Alfonso XIII's minority necessitated Queen Maria Cristina's acting as regent until the boy reached his sixteenth birthday in 1905. As Julie Gelard writes in her 2014 biography *Born To Rule: Granddaughters of Queen Victoria, Queens of Europe*, 'the young boy king grew into a lively and spirited individual. Maria Cristina noted that he is good but so eager, so turbulent, so desperate for liberty'.

King Alfonso's reign would prove to be a turbulent period in Spanish history. Under the regency, Spain lost its colonial territories of Cuba, Puerto Rico, Guam and the Philippines during the Spanish-American Wars of 1898, which saw Cuba gain independence with the support of the US Navy. Seeking a diplomatic alliance with England, the young king embarked on a state visit to the court of Queen Victoria in 1905, where he met the Queen's granddaughter Princess Victoria Eugenie of Battenberg at a Buckingham Palace ball. The King began a correspondence with Victoria Eugenie and resolved to make her his queen.

The wedding was blighted by a Catalan anarchist, Mateu Morral, who threw a bomb at the royal carriage, killing several bystanders. The future King George V and Queen Mary attended the wedding and wrote to Queen Victoria describing the sight of Victoria Eugenie returning to the royal palace in Madrid with her white wedding dress spattered with the blood of her subjects. In 1907 an heir, Alfonso, Prince of the Asturias, was born. When the infant was circumcised, he did not cease to bleed for hours, confirming that the heir was haemophiliac, a condition he inherited from his mother.

King Alfonso was said to hold Victoria Eugenie responsible for tainting the Spanish royal bloodline – another son, Gonzalo, born in 1914, also had the disease – and the couple became estranged. The King subsequently fathered five illegitimate children. Alfonso was, however, a benign and diligent ruler who kept Spain's neutrality during World War I. In his 1938 memoir *Great Contemporaries*, Winston Churchill praised Alfonso's 'vigilant care for the interest of his country and his earnest desire for the material welfare and progress of its people', noting that the King refused to retreat behind palace walls despite a further five attempts on his life.

Between 1920 and 1926 Spain fought the Rif War to preserve colonial rule over northern Morocco. King Alfonso supported the military coup of 1923, when General Miguel Primo de Rivera seized power, ruling as dictator with the King's support until 1930; but the alliance foundered as the Spanish economy faltered. In 1931 the Republican and Socialist parties won landslide victories in the municipal elections, and the Second Spanish Republic was proclaimed. Though King Alfonso refused to abdicate, he fled the country and would remain in exile for the rest of his life.

The wandering king lived at Le Meurice hotel in Paris and Brown's hotel in London before establishing permanent residence in Rome. Queen Victoria Eugenie returned to England but eventually settled in Lausanne, Switzerland. The royal children proved to be a disappointment. The King's heir, Alfonso, renounced his claim to the throne and married a commoner in 1933. His second son, Jaime, a deaf mute following a botched operation in childhood, also renounced all rights to the Spanish throne in the same year. The youngest son, Gonzalo, died in a car crash in 1934, meaning that the only surviving son, Juan, Count of Barcelona, was now sole heir.

When General Franco came to power in 1936, he declared that King Alfonso XIII would not be reinstated. Four years later Alfonso abdicated in favour of the Count of Barcelona and died in Rome, where he was interred in the Spanish national church. Five years after Alfonso's grandson, King Juan Carlos I, restored the Spanish monarchy in 1975, his body was repatriated and buried at the royal residence of El Escorial.

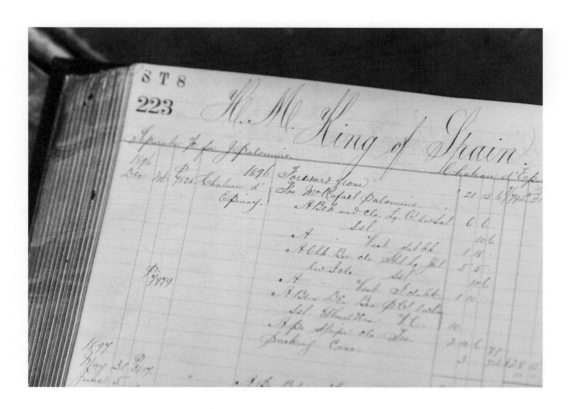

HM QUEEN MARIE OF ROMANIA

PATRONAGE 1887

SIGNATURE GARMENT Black riding habit lined with silk

TOTAL SPEND £15 (£990)

CONNECTIONS The Henry Poole 1887 measure books record measurements
for Princess Marie of Edinburgh and her sisters Princess Victoria (the future Grand
Duchess Maria Alexandrovna of Russia) and Princess Alexandra (the future
Princess Alexandra of Hohenlohe-Langenburg).

Princess Marie of Edinburgh (1875–1938) was the eldest daughter of Prince Alfred, Duke of Edinburgh, Queen Victoria's second son, and the Grand Duchess Maria Alexandrovna of Russia, who was Emperor Alexander II's beloved daughter. She was destined to become the last Queen of Romania and 'mother-in-law of the Balkans'. Her cousin the future King George V was besotted by Princess Marie but the Duchess of Edinburgh objected because the Russian Orthodox Church would not countenance marriage between first cousins. Instead, she chose Crown Prince Ferdinand of Romania as a suitable dynastic match and the couple wed in 1891.

'Nando', nephew of the reigning King Carol I of Romania, was bookish, introspective and inclined towards international pursuits. Marie was a flirtatious, mischievous sixteen-year-old who danced with abandon and rode like a daredevil Hussar. The old Duke of Cambridge's verdict was blunt: 'It does seem too cruel a shame to cart that nice pretty girl off to semi-barbaric Romania and a man to the knowledge of all Europe desperately in love with another woman.' The lover in question was a lady-in-waiting to Prince Ferdinand's aunt, Queen Elisabeth, who encouraged the liaison.

The new Crown Princess's early years in the royal palace of Bucharest were lonely. King Carol was an autocrat and the Queen (who wrote literary works under the name of Carmen Sylva) dabbled in the occult. Carol considered his daughter-in-law 'too English, too free and easy, too frivolous, too fond of dress, of riding, of outdoor life, too outspoken, with not enough respect for conversations or etiquette'. When Marie gave birth to a son, Prince Carol, in 1893 he was taken away from her, the King and Queen believing that it was inappropriate for the youthful parents to raise their own children.

The infidelities of Crown Princess Marie's husband led her into the arms of Lieutenant Zizi Cantacuzène, the first of many amours, with which the Empress Frederick of Prussia sympathized: 'I think Missy of Romania is more to be pitied. The King is a great tyrant and has crushed the independence in Ferdinand so that no one cares about him. His beautiful and gifted little wife, I fear, gets into scrapes and like a butterfly, instead of hovering over flowers burns her pretty wings by going rather near the fire.'

In 1900, the Duchess of Edinburgh spirited Princess Marie away to Coburg, where she bore a third daughter who may or may not have been Cantacuzène's. Ferdinand accepted the child; Princess Marie later wrote: 'It is such a shame that we had to waste so many years of our youth just to learn how to live together.' In 1902 Marie formed an attachment with Waldorf Astor while attending the coronation of King Edward VII, though his wife, Lady Astor, privately called her 'the lunatic Princess'.

Back in Bucharest, Princess Marie fell under the spell of Prince Barbu Stirbey, who schooled her in Balkan politics and advised King Carol that 'it is essential not to break her will. If we can persuade her to take herself and her duties more seriously, her natural intelligence will do the rest.' Princess Marie proved her mettle during the Second Balkan War (1913), when she served as a field nurse, ministering to an army plagued by a cholera epidemic. After this experience, she declared: 'I am a changed person.'

Facing the horrors of the battlefield prepared Marie for the German invasion. King Carol died in 1914 and the new queen's response was heroic: 'I knew that I had won, that the stranger, the girl who had come from over the seas, was a stranger no more. I was theirs with every drop of my blood.' Queen Marie persuaded King Ferdinand to fight on the Allied side in World War I, earning her the accolade 'truly the only man in Romania'.

When Germany bombed Bucharest, Queen Marie was forced to flee, and she resumed her duties as a nurse on the front line. The American ambassador believed, 'there is no doubt in my mind that if she could have led the soldiers, the Romanian army would have been unconquerable'. On Armistice Day in 1918, Queen Marie was awarded the Croix de Guerre by the French ambassador. She sallied forth to attend the Paris Peace Conference and signed the treaty that united Romania and Transylvania.

In 1918 the Queen's eldest son, Crown Prince Carol, eloped with a commoner called Zizi Lambrino, though their marriage was quietly annulled. In 1921 he bowed to his parents' wishes and wed Prince Helen of Greece and Denmark. They had a son, Michael, but the marriage foundered when Prince Carol took up with the divorcee Magda Lupescu, telling his mother he would renounce his throne and she could inform the press he had drowned in Lake Maggiore.

King Ferdinand died in 1927, shortly after Queen Marie had returned from a triumphant tour of America. Her grandson Michael was proclaimed king under a regency council, but the reign of a boy king in the volatile Balkans was doomed. His father made a triumphal re-entry into Bucharest in 1930, revoked the act of succession and proclaimed himself King Carol II of Romania. Dowager Queen Marie was starved of finances, forced to live in a reduced household and surrounded by her son's spies. On her death in 1938, Marie was accorded a state funeral and wrote a valedictory letter to her people, telling them: 'I became yours through joy and sorrow and now I bid you a fond farewell forever.'

KING BORIS III OF BULGARIA

PATRONAGE 1936

ROYAL WARRANT HM The King of the Bulgarians (1936)

SIGNATURE GARMENT Black superfine tailcoat lined with satin

TOTAL SPEND £166 (£8,050 today)

CONNECTIONS King Boris of Bulgaria's custom at Henry Poole is the shortest on record. An evening dress tailcoat was measured, cut, stitched and pressed for him within twelve hours when the monarch arrived at Poole's needing the garment for a reception at Buckingham Palace that evening. The firm's rapid response earned Poole's its thirty-seventh Royal Warrant.

King Boris of Bulgaria (1894–1943) began his reign prematurely when his father, King Ferdinand I, abdicated following a humiliating defeat during World War I that lost his nation territories and saddled Bulgaria with crippling reparations payments to neighbouring countries. He had been nineteen years old when Bulgaria was crushed in the aftermath of the Second Balkan War in 1913 following defeat against the united forces of Serbia, Greece and Romania.

Prince Boris was educated in the Palace Secondary School established by King Ferdinand to educate his royal sons. He enrolled in Sofia's Military School and served in the Second Balkan War, proving himself a model soldier. In the aftermath of Bulgaria's defeat in the Great War, German general Erich Lundendorff proclaimed Boris wise beyond his years and preferred to agree terms with him rather than King Ferdinand. Boris III was proclaimed king in 1918.

Republicanism was rife in Bulgaria in the first years of Boris's reign. His prime minister, Alexander Stamboliyski, was a member of the Bulgarian People's Agrarian Union and, though popular with the proletariat, was despised by the Bulgarian military and royalists. Stamboliyski was deposed in 1923 and imprisoned in his village of birth, Slavovitsa, where he was tortured and murdered. The former prime minister's hand was cut off and his head sent to Sofia in a box of biscuits.

In 1925 anarchists attacked the cavalcade King Boris was travelling in but he escaped unharmed. Two days later, a bomb was detonated in Sofia that killed 150 members of Bulgaria's military and political class. In 1930 King Boris married Princess Giovanna, daughter of King Victor Emmanuel III of Italy, in a Catholic ceremony in Assisi attended by Benito Mussolini. Queen Giovanna gave birth to a daughter, Maria Louisa, in 1932, and an heir, Simeon, in 1937.

Boris was reduced to the role of puppet king in 1934 when a military dictatorship overthrew the government and abolished political parties. The King staged a counter-coup and regained his power as absolute monarch. Under the 'King's government', Bulgaria prospered, enjoying a 'golden age' that lasted five years. On the outbreak of World War II, Adolf Hitler attempted to win Boris's loyalty by demanding Romania give certain territories back to Bulgaria. Although the King allied Bulgaria with the Axis powers, he resisted declaring war on Russia. He appeared on the cover of *Time* magazine in 1941 wearing full military uniform, vowing not to send Bulgarian troops to fight with the Germans against Russia.

Bulgaria's prime minister, Bogdan Filov, was a Nazi sympathizer and passed laws in accordance with Hitler's Nuremberg Laws that were hostile to the nation's Jews. In 1943, Hitler's emissary Theodor Dannecker was sent to negotiate with King Boris, demanding that the monarch deport 20,000 Jews from Bulgarian territories Thrace and Macedonia. Just over 11,000 Jews were deported but this did not meet the Nazi quota so Dannecker demanded that Bulgarian Jews were deported to make up the number. Boris intervened personally to stop this monstrous proceeding.

Despite only having declared 'symbolic' war, Bulgaria was bombed by US and UK forces in 1943. In the same year, King Boris III died of heart failure while visiting Hitler, athough doctors suspected he had been poisoned. In 1946, the Soviet Army oversaw a referendum, in which 97 per cent of Bulgarians voted to abolish the monarchy. After years in exile, however, the ex-king Simeon returned to Bulgaria, by now a republic, and served as prime minister from 2001 to 2005. King Boris III's body was disinterred and has since disappeared. His heart was found buried in the courtyard of the Vrana Palace in Sofia.

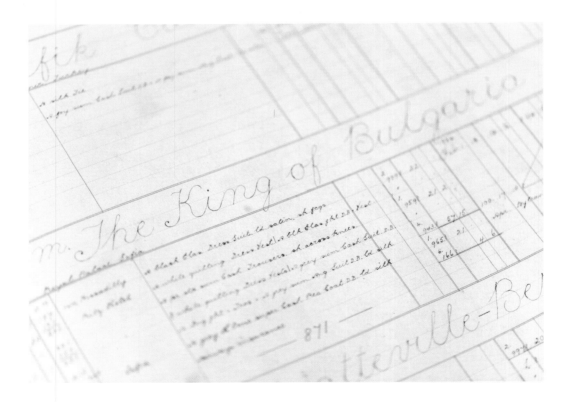

MINISTRY, HARROGATE
6094

Extn.................

munications on the
f this letter should
sed to:—

NDER SECRETARY
TE, AIR MINISTRY,

following number

35.

29/39/E.13.

AIR MINISTRY,
DEPT. ZA,
HARROGATE,
YORKS.

23rd April, 1940.

24 APR 1940

Royal Air Force Officers' Uniform.

entlemen,

I   ated 19th

nstant and   n shirt

approved for wear by Royal Air Force officers has double c

I am,
Gentlemen,
Your obedient Servant,

for Director of Equipmen

Messrs. Henry Poole & Co.,
37-39, Savile Row,
London, W.1.

CHAPTER FIVE
POOLE'S AT WAR
1936–1976

'The premises of Henry Poole may be taken as the exemplar:
traditional in design, solid in construction and
utterly English in atmosphere, they provide the ideal
ambiance for the master craftsman.'

*MAKERS OF DISTINCTION: SUPPLIERS TO THE TOWN
AND COUNTRY GENTLEMAN* BY THOMAS GIRTIN (1959)

The Cundey brothers, Sam and Hugh, inherited Henry Poole & Co two years before the Wall Street Crash and the Great Depression. Then, as now, American trade accounted for 40 per cent of the firm's turnover, and the Depression was the beginning of a turbulent tenure for the new generation as reluctant guv'nors of Poole & Co.

Savile Row, and Henry Poole & Co in particular, has always had a genius for finding a new generation of elegant, affluent men to replace those to whom fortune has not been favourable. Before 1914, Poole's order books were ablaze with Romanovs: after the Russian Revolution in 1917, Poole's had to write off all orders made by now-impoverished White Russian customers as enemy debt.

Fortunately for Sam and Hugh Cundey, between the two world wars it had become fashionable among India's maharajas to spend their summers attending the London season, send their sons to Eton and order Western dress for the royal families from Savile Row tailors. Between 1918 and 1939 the maharajas of Jodhpur, Jaipur, Kolhapur, Kapurthala, Bikaner, Darbhanga and Patiala chose Henry Poole.

In 1938 Sam and Hugh Cundey were moved to write a letter to the editor of the *Times* in response to rumours about the firm's future printed in the newspaper. 'Sir – The fear expressed in your recent issue relative to the fate of Poole's in Savile Row may perhaps be allayed if it be known that our kinsman of a century ago, in building his business, builded [sic] not for himself alone, but for the succeeding generations upon whom he counted for the continuance of his art, and so ensured that their tenure should be such as could resist the vagaries of time.'

Sam Cundey's letter was not written only with the weight of James Poole's, Henry Poole's and his father Howard Cundey's legacies on his shoulders but also in the knowledge that he had a responsibility to pass on the world's most famous tailor to his son Angus Cundey, the company's present chairman, who was born in 1937.

Opposite: The Air Ministry writes to Poole's in 1940 approving dress regulations for Royal Air Force officers' uniform.

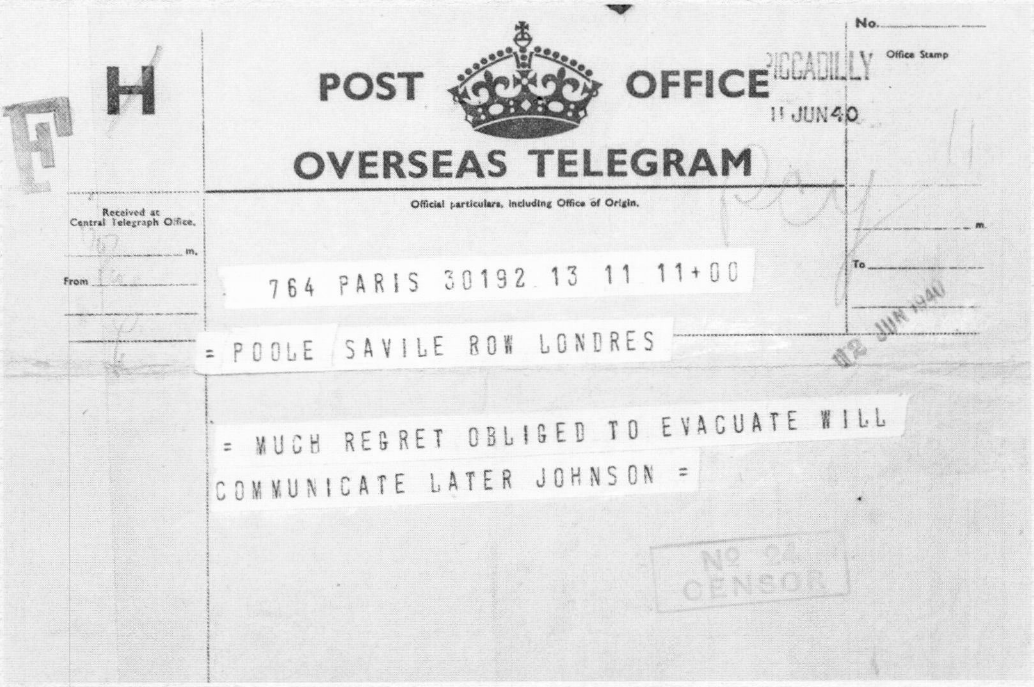

POST OFFICE OVERSEAS TELEGRAM

PICCADILLY
11 JUN 40

764 PARIS 30192 13 11 11+00

= POOLE SAVILE ROW LONDRES

= MUCH REGRET OBLIGED TO EVACUATE WILL
COMMUNICATE LATER JOHNSON =

June 1940 telegram from Paris branch head Mr Johnson announcing the evacuation
(and final closure) of the Rue Tronchet shop.

'My grandfather Howard Cundey did not give my father a choice whether he wanted to go into the family business or not,' says the chairman. 'In fairness, Father took over at a very difficult time for Savile Row and was crippled for money, having inherited double death duties. It devastated him to have to sell our premises in 1946.'

To Sam Cundey's credit he showed grace under pressure and did everything in his power to keep Henry Poole & Co trading under the most hostile of circumstances through the worst run of luck. He had steered Poole's through the Great Depression that had forced many of London's bespoke tailors to close. One such was the hundred-year-old Hill Brothers, which Sam and Hugh Cundey agreed to buy out in 1939 and eventually amalgamate with Henry Poole.

No sooner had Poole's taken this step to expand the business than on 3 December 1939 Prime Minister Neville Chamberlain declared that Britain was at war with Germany. In 1939, Sam Cundey showed a journalist from *Tailor & Cutter* around the premises to demonstrate Poole's preparations for war. In addition to a fully equipped air-raid shelter to hold seventy-five workers, 'on the roof rests a big cistern, well sandbagged. Fire appliances are set at various parts of the building with stirrup pumps and pails. Wire netting protects four sky-lights. Poole's possess thousands of customers' paper patterns, which have been laid flat on (the) ground (and) compressed ... Blankets saturated with soap and water are put over doors to form an airlock. A fire shelter of glazed brickwork has the virtue of not absorbing gas, and is supported by strong girders.'

As the half-empty ledgers for the first half of the 1940s demonstrate, civilian tailoring dropped off a cliff. Worse was to come when the Nazis occupied France. On 11 June 1940 Poole's Paris branch was obliged to evacuate: the last of Henry Poole's European branches closed and would never open its doors again.

In 1940 King George VI decreed that court dress was to be abolished. In June 1941 clothing rationing was introduced and would remain in place until 1949. German bombs landed ever closer to Poole's, destroying rival tailors in the West End such as Gieves Ltd, Meyer & Mortimer, Jones, Chalk & Dawson and Dege. In 1941 two incendiary bombs hit Poole's. The flames were swiftly extinguished by the fire brigade but the water cannon flooded the basement and caused serious damage to the company's customer ledgers. In November 1945, *Leader* magazine reported that 'because of the terrible ravages of the Blitz, nearly a dozen of the Row tailors now find temporary refuge in the premises of the first and most famous of them all, Henry Poole'.

The British aristocracy had formed the backbone of Poole's business before World War I not only for personal orders but also for household liveries. Death duties and exorbitant income tax imposed by Labour governments in the first half of the 20th century saw estates sold off and palatial London houses razed to the ground. The World War II ledgers show only a smattering of aristocratic customers, such as the 12th Duke of Bedford, the 14th Duke of Hamilton and the 2nd Viscount Astor.

Reminiscing in 1976 of the postwar years, Sam Cundey told *Men's Wear*: 'until [the war], a peer of the realm would have, say, three establishments: a town house; a country house; and a shooting lodge. He would want clothes to wear at each and there was a much more regular buying pattern. People would come in during early spring and order their summer suits, and early autumn for their winter suits. And if, after the initial order, they came in for a fitting, you could very often tempt them to buy another.'

Henry Poole & Co and its venerable premises were metaphorically towed like Turner's *Fighting Temeraire* into the 1950s. The livery department was reinvigorated with the accession of Queen Elizabeth II in 1952 and the Coronation the following year. But Poole's showroom appeared frozen in aspic. In 1955 the *Wall Street Journal* described a visit to Henry Poole thus: 'Inside you'll see a musty showroom that hasn't changed since Dickens' days. Scattered around a well-worn carpet there's a stand-up reading stand bearing the *London Times*, an ancient weighing chair, several roll top wooden desks topped with windup clocks and calendars where clerks still keep the company's books by hand.'

That said, the weight of Henry Poole's history was a guarantee of quality and correctness for the American businessmen and wealthy travellers who kept London's purveyors of luxuries solvent. 'So many Americans stayed in Britain after the war,' says the chairman. 'They became very valuable customers. From 1946 onwards, the firm became totally dependent on America.'

Angus Cundey remembers visiting Poole's in the war years but knew nothing of the firm's reputation until he was called before the headmaster at his boarding school, Framlingham College, Suffolk, in 1954. 'The headmaster summoned me and said, "Now

Cundey, what are you going to do when you leave here at the end of Christmas term?" I said I was going into the Royal Air Force and that I was going to learn to fly an aeroplane. "Cundey!" he replied. "Don't you know your family has the most famous tailoring company in the world?"'

'I had never heard my father speak like that,' says the chairman. It was on a train to Liverpool Street that Angus wrestled with the RAF or Savile Row. On meeting his father at the station, he said, 'Dad, would there be a place for me at Henry Poole?' 'A big smile crossed my father's face,' says Angus, 'and he said of course. After two weeks' holiday, he sent me to Paris to apprentice in Lanvin's bespoke department for a year.'

The optimism of the new queen's reign in the 1950s offered only temporary relief to Sam and Hugh Cundey. Having sold the freehold of Nos 36–39 Savile Row, the lease on the premises expired in 1960, with the owners denying the firm a chance to renew. After 114 years of dominating the British bespoke trade from the grandest façade on Savile Row, Henry Poole & Co was exiled to Cork Street in 1961. It would be almost inconceivable today that a Thomas Cubitt-designed structure would be flattened to make way for a municipal car park, but that was the fate of Henry Poole & Co's home.

In 1961 *Tailor & Cutter* wrote: 'Henry Poole & Sons, Ltd [sic] have gone from Savile Row. On Saturday March 11, the doors and shutters were closed on the famous premises for the last time. Inside, the showrooms that are steeped in tradition are now quiet and empty, gone is the bustle that has reigned over them since 1846 and now they stand ready for the heavy booted demolition gangs to do their worst.'

Sam Cundey's comment was short and profoundly sad: 'I feel that life will never be the same after we leave here.' The fact that the Savile Row address was lost on his watch seems to show on Sam's face in all the photographs of him taken after 1961.

Sam Cundey instructed his son Angus to sell the three tonnes-worth of paper for a sum just shy of £19 (£400 today). With it went priceless documentation of the fluctuating physiques, assets and imperfections of historical giants such as Bismarck, Napoleon III and Churchill that historians, and master tailors, cannot decipher from the opaque system of numerals recorded in the Henry Poole measure books. But even without the pick of the most famous paper patterns, the Henry Poole archive of documents relating to bespoke tailoring is the oldest and most complete on Savile Row, if not in the world.

While Sam Cundey was mourning the past on his way to the Lyons Corner House, brother Hugh was looking to the future and brokering an overseas deal with Japanese department store Matsuzakaya to export Poole's expertise to Tokyo. Matsuzakaya's managing director, Suzusaburo Ito, had ordered his first British bespoke suit from Poole's in 1936 when he was an undergraduate at Cambridge. In 1959 he returned to order a further four suits and declared to Sam Cundey: 'I would like to have a little bit of Henry Poole in my shop on the Ginza in Tokyo.' 'My father was horrified and said "certainly not",' says Angus, but with Hugh Cundey's agreement, the deal was made in 1964.

Back in London as the Sixties began to swing and the peacock revolution in men's fashion ruffled establishment feathers, Savile Row was besieged by taste-makers such as

The Cork Street Poole's showroom interior: home to the firm from 1961 to 1982.

society photographer Cecil Beaton, who drawled, 'It is ridiculous that they go on turning out clothes that make men look like characters from P. G. Wodehouse in 1965'.

In London Poole's could not afford to be as radical as fashion boutiques such as Mr Fish at No. 19 Clifford Street or Rupert Lycett Green's Blades in Burlington Gardens. But neither was Angus Cundey dismissive when Tommy Nutter and Edward Sexton opened Nutters of Savile Row on Valentine's Day 1969 on the site of Poole's demolished showroom.

Angus Cundey was the first to acknowledge that a redesign of Cork Street in 1969 – with windows that made the shop visible from the street – was directly influenced by Tommy Nutter. As the *Times* wrote of Henry Poole's new groove, 'today's gilded youths, lost to Savile Row for too long, are returning. They have brought with them their ladies and a less tolerant attitude to traditions of dress and décor. Wisely Poole's realize it, and this week reopened clad in a splendid mantle of green and gold.'

In the 15 January 1976 edition of *Men's Wear*, Sam Cundey bowed out of Henry Poole & Co with a reflective interview. Of his time as a seventeen-year-old apprentice in 1923 he said: 'We had a very large staff in those days, about 250 including the counting house and showroom personnel. We have about fifty-five staff now. In those days, too, there was more rivalry and much less friendship between tailors.' His critique of new tailoring might apply to 2019: 'The whole pattern of tailoring, too, has altered: thinner materials, new techniques, clothes more carefully fitted.' But Sam Cundey ended on an elegant, polite note: 'However difficult things get, there will always be room for the best.'

WILKIE COLLINS

PATRONAGE 1860–1861

SIGNATURE GARMENT A double-breasted fancy stripe buckskin lounging vest

TOTAL SPEND £40 (£2,370 today)

CONNECTIONS Wilkie Collins's friend and colleague Charles Dickens was previously mistaken as a Poole's customer when a cheque to the firm signed by the author came up at auction. The cheque, drawn in 1861, was to settle an unpaid order placed by Dickens's son Charles Jr.

William Wilkie Collins (1824–1889) was a novelist, playwright and short story writer and the father of the modern English detective novel. Dorothy L. Sayers declared his masterpiece, *The Moonstone*, to be 'probably the very finest detective story ever written'. Though he wrote thirty novels and more than sixty short stories, *The Moonstone* and *The Woman in White* have emerged as giants in the 'sensation' genre characterized by sinister Italian counts, haunted mansions, abductions, insanity and mistaken identity.

Collins was born in London and named after his father, the landscape artist William Collins, and his godfather, Sir David Wilkie. He attributed his genius for storytelling to a boy at Reverend Cole's boarding school who would not let him sleep until he had invented an original yarn to send the chap to sleep. He later said: 'It was this brute who first awakened in me, his poor little victim, a power of which but for him I might never have been aware.' He also credits family trips to Italy with educating his imagination, writing that in Italy he learned more 'which has been of use to me among the scenery, the pictures, and the people, than I ever learned at school'.

Collins was called to the bar in 1851, but never practised law. In the same year he met Charles Dickens, already a famed novelist, and proprietor of the literary journal *Household Words*. Apart from a memoir of his late father and a smattering of journalism, Collins, then twenty-seven, was unpublished. His first contribution to *Household Words*, in 1852, was the short story 'A Terribly Strange Bed', a tale of terror and the supernatural.

Collins was inducted into Dickens's amateur theatrical company and performed in Edward Bulwer-Lytton's *Not So Bad As We Seem* with Dickens at Devonshire House in front of Queen Victoria and the Prince Consort in 1851. They performed on tours of Italy, Switzerland and France, holidayed together and were a familiar sight in the West End dining at Verrey's on Regent Street, haunting the music halls and café-concerts and holding court at the Garrick Club. Collins grew in stature, writing first short stories then novels serialized in *Household Words*.

Like Dickens, Collins was a bohemian at heart with an unconventional private life. He was a gourmand, drank deep, wore flamboyant costume and formed two long-term relationships with women that he did not marry. He lived with a widow, Caroline Graves, and her daughter, while simultaneously maintaining a household with Martha Rudd, with whom he had three children born out of wedlock.

The Woman in White was published in 1859 and Collins's other major novels, *Armadale*, *No Name* and *The Moonstone*, were all completed within the following decade. Not coincidentally, Collins began to take laudanum (a mixture of alcohol and opium) in 1860 to treat chronic arthritis, and became addicted. Laudanum-induced hallucinations were a major plotting device in *The Moonstone* and Collins admitted to writing the novel under the influence of the drug. Collins has Miss Gwilt in *Armadale* asking, 'Who was the man who invented laudanum? I thank him from the bottom of my heart.'

Following Dickens's death in 1870, Collins's dependence on laudanum overwhelmed him and his novels of the following two decades were undistinguished. He was lauded by literary lions such as George Eliot and Anthony Trollope, though he would never again receive the acclaim that greeted *The Woman in White*. Collins became increasingly desperate about his declining health and would say that he took more laudanum per day 'than would have sufficed to kill a ship's crew or a company of soldiers'.

Collins died in 1889 at his Wimpole Street town house of a paralytic stroke. He was buried in Kensal Green Cemetery and would be joined in death by Caroline Graves. His four great novels are classics of Victorian 'sensation fiction', with *The Moonstone* and *The Woman in White* being adapted many times for film and television.

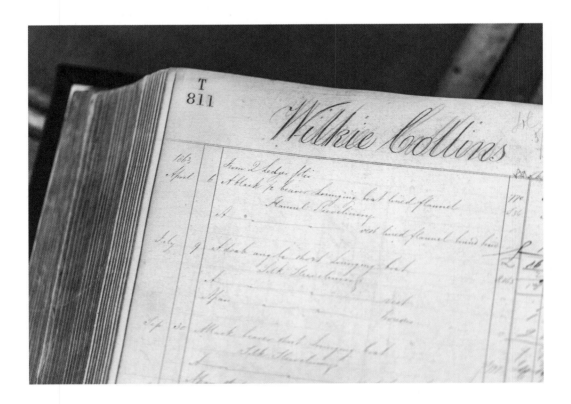

RICHARD D'OYLY CARTE

PATRONAGE 1881–1894

SIGNATURE GARMENT Check Angola lounge coat

TOTAL SPEND £240 (£19,690 today)

CONNECTIONS Arthur Sullivan, composer of the comic operettas with librettist W. S. Gilbert that were produced by Richard D'Oyly Carte between 1775 and 1789, was a customer of Henry Poole & Co.

In the last three decades of Queen Victoria's reign Richard D'Oyly Carte (1844–1901) was a colossus on the landscape of London's theatres and grand hotels. Carte's father was a flautist and also sold musical instruments at Rudall, Rose & Co on Charing Cross Road; though he became a partner in the firm, it was tacitly understood that his wife, Eliza, had married beneath her. Richard Carte Jr's education at University College London was cut short when he was co-opted to assist his father in the family firm.

D'Oyly Carte's theatrical ambitions began with him writing and publishing his own music, but the young man conceded that his talents lay elsewhere. In 1874 he established a talent agency representing 200 artists and composers including Adelina Patti, Matthew Arnold, James McNeill Whistler, Oscar Wilde and Jacques Offenbach. In the same year Carte leased the Opera Comique, a theatre off the Strand, and declared 'my desire to establish in London a permanent abode for light opera'.

Carte instinctively knew that there was a distinctly English alternative to racy French operetta: light, lyrical entertainment that the *Times* later classified as 'a combination of good taste and good fun'. As the *Observer* said of him, 'Carte took what other people thought were risks but he felt were certainties. He knew everyone worth knowing and his practical judgement was as sure as his sense of artistry.'

In 1875 D'Oyly Carte was managing the Royalty Theatre and brought together dramatist W. S. Gilbert and composer Arthur Sullivan, suggesting the latter write the music for Gilbert's libretto *Trial by Jury*. Recognizing a winning team, Carte found investors to bankroll his new 'Comedy Opera Company', which produced Gilbert and Sullivan's forthcoming collaborations, including *The Sorcerer* (1877) and *HMS Pinafore* (1878).

Such was the success of the partnership that Gilbert, Sullivan and Carte each put up £1,000 to form 'Richard D'Oyly Carte's Opera Company' and oust the original investors. The split was acrimonious as the two warring sides fought for the rights to *HMS Pinafore* but the D'Oyly Carte Opera Company eventually broke away, and the impresario built his 'permanent abode for light opera' in 1881, christening it the Savoy Theatre.

Gilbert and Sullivan wrote a string of operatic pearls for the Savoy stage, including *Princess Ida* (1884), *The Mikado* (1885), *Ruddigore* (1887), *The Yeoman of the Guard* (1888)

and *The Gondoliers* (1889). With his wealth, Carte built the magnificent Savoy Hotel next to the theatre in 1889. Under the guidance of manager Cézar Ritz and chef Auguste Escoffier, the Savoy became the most fashionable hotel in London, if not the world.

The relationship between Carte, Gilbert and Sullivan soured in 1890 when Gilbert took exception to Savoy Theatre renovations being charged to the partnership rather than to Carte's account. Gilbert and Sullivan's last light opera, *The Grand Duke*, was staged in 1896 but flopped spectacularly.

Undeterred, Carte constructed the Royal English Opera House (now known as the Palace Theatre) in 1891 on Cambridge Circus. In the same year, a 'Spy' cartoon of Carte appeared in *Vanity Fair* depicting him dressed like a swell with top hat, cane, spats and an overcoat not only lined with sable but also trimmed with an extravagant fur collar and cuffs. Like Gilbert, Carte had been tailored by Henry Poole & Co since the mid-1880s. Being a Poole's man complemented Carte's sybaritic lifestyle. He lived in a palatial apartment in the Adelphi Building behind the Savoy with a games room painted entirely in baize green by his friend the artist Whistler. He also owned an island in the Thames called Folly Eyot, which name he changed to D'Oyly Carte Island.

Carte's hotel empire grew throughout the 1890s. He bought Claridge's in 1893 and the Grand Hotel in Rome in 1896, along with the Berkeley in 1900 just so he could poach its general manager, George Reeves-Smith, to replace Cézar Ritz at the Savoy. Richard D'Oyly Carte died from heart disease in 1901 aged fifty-six.

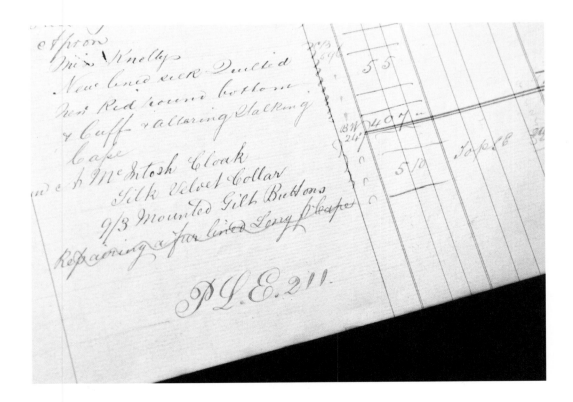

BRAM STOKER

PATRONAGE   1893–1901

SIGNATURE GARMENT   A black thin cashmere elastic lounge coat

TOTAL SPEND   £201 (£16,490 today)

CONNECTIONS   Only the most successful authors found their way to Henry Poole & Co. In addition to Wilkie Collins, Edward Bulwer-Lytton and Benjamin Disraeli, Poole's also dressed Henry James, author of *The Portrait of a Lady* (1880), *The Turn of the Screw* (1898) and *The Wings of the Dove* (1902). During World War II, travel writer Patrick Leigh Fermor patronized Henry Poole.

In the words of his grandnephew Daniel Farson, Abraham 'Bram' Stoker (1847–1912) is 'one of the least known authors of one of the best known books ever written'. The book in question is late Victorian Gothic horror novel *Dracula*, published in 1897. As befitting the father of the cult of the undead, Stoker's success as a novelist was largely posthumous and his masterpiece of the vampire genre not even mentioned in his *Times* obituary.

Bram Stoker's life before *Dracula* does give clues as to how a civil servant turned theatre manager could create such a powerful, monstrous myth. Stoker was born in a suburb of Dublin and was bedridden for the first seven years of his life. The sickly child's mother would recite stories from Irish folklore, which sparked an early interest in mystical narrative. As Stoker wrote, 'the leisure of long illness gave opportunity for many thoughts which were fruitful according to their kind in later years'.

Stoker read mathematics at Trinity College, Dublin, and was president of the Philosophical Society, where he delivered his first paper, on the subject 'Sensationalism in Fiction and Society'. On graduation, Stoker worked as a civil servant at Dublin Castle for ten years while also writing unpaid theatre reviews for the *Dublin Evening Mail*, a paper co-owned by Gothic novelist Sheridan Le Fanu, whose 1871 vampire tale *Carmilla* brought the blood-drinking undead back into fashion in popular fiction.

In 1876 the celebrated actor-manager Henry Irving appeared at the Theatre Royal, Dublin in *Hamlet* and his performance entranced Stoker. The young reviewer was invited to a supper party at which Irving recited Thomas Hood's poem *The Dream of Eugene Aram*. As the *Leeds Times* reported, 'one of Irving's auditors, a young man with a brilliant reputation at Trinity College, was so affected by the tragedian's delivery that he burst into tears'.

Stoker married his sweetheart, Florence Balcombe, in 1878, and at Irving's invitation the couple moved to London, where Stoker worked as secretary to the Victorian age's greatest actor. He was swiftly promoted to business manager of Irving's Lyceum Theatre: a position he would hold for nearly thirty years until the actor's death in 1905.

The 1890s was a golden age for horror, science fiction and supernatural literature with H. Ryder Haggard, Rudyard Kipling, Robert Louis Stevenson, Arthur Conan Doyle and H. G. Wells exploring the dark side of fiction. But *Dracula*'s epistolary form most closely followed fellow Henry Poole & Co customer Wilkie Collins's 'sensation novels' such as *The Woman in White* and *The Moonstone*. Henry Irving is acknowledged as the model for Count Dracula's appearance, mannerisms and mesmeric character.

Aft *Dracula*'s publication in 1897, the *Spectator* review read: 'Mr Bram Stoker gives us the impression – we might be doing him an injustice – of having deliberately laid himself out in *Dracula* to eclipse all previous efforts in the domain of the horrible – to go one better than Wilkie Collins, Sheridan Le Fanu and all the other professors of the flesh-creeping school.' Arthur Conan Doyle penned a note to say: 'I write to tell you how very much I enjoyed reading *Dracula*. I think it is the very best story of diablerie that I have read for many years.'

Though favourably compared with Edgar Allan Poe, Mary Shelley and even Emily Brontë's *Wuthering Heights*, *Dracula* did not make Bram Stoker's fortune. Soon after Henry Irving died in 1905, Stoker suffered the first of a series of strokes. He wrote *Personal Reminiscences of Henry Irving* in 1906, and continued to write horror fiction titles such as *The Lady of the Shroud* (1909) and *The Lair of the White Worm* (1911) that deserved more attention than they received. A year before his death, Stoker petitioned the Royal Literary Fund for a compassionate grant of funds to relieve poverty. Stoker died in dire financial straits in 1912, with hypotheses for cause of death including syphilis, exhaustion and a fatal stroke. A year later his widow auctioned the *Dracula* papers at Sotheby's.

SIR HENRY IRVING

PATRONAGE 1881–1905

SIGNATURE GARMENT A black superfine frock coat lined with silk

TOTAL SPEND £3,637 (£298,410 today)

CONNECTIONS Actors were a rarity on Henry Poole's books until the 20th century, when Broadway and silent movie star Lionel Barrymore ordered from the firm. In 1960 Poole's tailored Robert Mitchum's on-screen wardrobe for *The Grass is Greener* co-starring Cary Grant, Deborah Kerr and Jean Simmons.

Actor-manager Sir Henry Irving (1838–1905) was considered the greatest Shakespearean actor of his generation and was the first member of the profession to be honoured with a knighthood. Irving was born in Somerset to a strict Methodist family and was christened John Brodribb, hence wag Max Beerbohm's cruel dubbing of him 'the knight from nowhere'. Irving's mother disapproved of his ambitions to be an actor so at the age of thirteen he began working at a local law firm.

In 1856 the disillusioned Brodribb saw Samuel Phelps play the title role in *Hamlet* and this inspired him to turn his back on the law, change his name to Henry Irving and begin acting, touring the United Kingdom in stock companies. In his first ten years in the profession, Irving played more than 600 minor roles and honed his craft. He arrived in London in 1866, but it was another five years before his breakthrough role in *The Bells*.

A three-act tragedy by Leopold David Lewis, *The Bells* opened at the Lyceum Theatre, London, and ran for an unprecedented 160 performances. The opening night audience were, apparently, stunned by the intensity of Irving's performance but rose to give him a standing ovation. Critic Edward Gordon Craig wrote: 'The thing Irving set out to do was to show us the sorrow which slowly and remorselessly beat him down. The sorrow which he suffers must appeal to our hearts.'

Irving had married Florence O'Callaghan in 1869, with whom he had two sons. The marriage broke down on the first night of *The Bells* in 1871. Mr and Mrs Irving were returning home in a carriage when she turned to him and said: 'Are you going to make a fool of yourself like this all your life?' Without saying a word, Irving got out of the carriage at Hyde Park Corner, and never saw or spoke to his wife again. The couple did not divorce and when Irving was knighted, Florence rather presumptuously styled herself Lady Irving.

Henry Irving took over the management of the Lyceum Theatre in 1878. His reputation as an actor-manager was built on the foundations of working only with the best – including his lover, the actress Ellen Terry. He employed Arthur Wing Pinero, Alfred, Lord Tennyson, Victorien Sardou and Arthur Conan Doyle to write new works for his

company and commissioned celebrated artists Lawrence Alma-Tadema and Edward Burne-Jones to design productions. The Lyceum was one of the first London theatres to use gaslight to great effect. As David Garrick had been in the 18th century, Irving was renowned as the greatest Shakespearean actor of his age.

After Irving's death, his long-term leading lady Ellen Terry declared that 'we were terribly in love for a while'. Irving and Terry were a celebrated couple in all but name, and became the toast of the US when they undertook eight major tours between 1883 and 1904. Queen Victoria knighted Sir Henry at Windsor Castle in 1895. Irving gave his last performance at the Lyceum in 1902 as Shylock in *The Merchant of Venice*. In 1905 he was on a final tour when he died in the lobby of the Midland Hotel, Bradford. The chair in which he breathed his last is now at the Garrick Club in London.

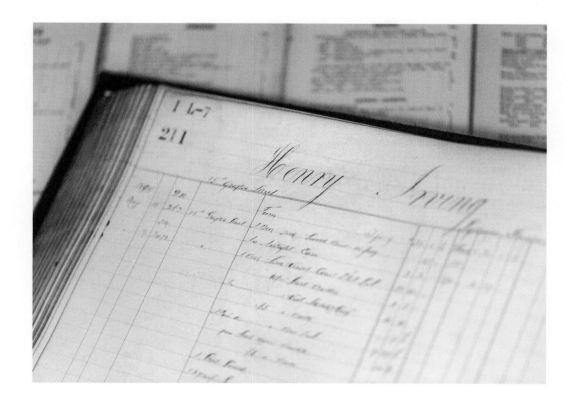

LILLIE LANGTRY

PATRONAGE 1885–1903

SIGNATURE GARMENT A black diagonal cloth riding habit

TOTAL SPEND £1,907 (£156,470 today)

CONNECTIONS Female friends of Bertie, Prince of Wales, would commission
Poole's to tailor waistcoats as birthday and anniversary gifts. Mrs Langtry did so, as
did Louise, Duchess of Manchester and Devonshire and Hannah Rothschild, wife
of the 5th Earl of Rosebery.

Royal mistress and actress Lillie Langtry, dubbed the 'Jersey Lily' by Pre-Raphaelite artist John Everett Millais, was one of the most celebrated beauties and successful social climbers of her age. Born Emilie Charlotte Le Breton, she was the daughter of the Dean of Jersey. A precocious child in a household full of men, she rejected a governess and was educated with her brothers by a series of tutors. This would stand her in good stead. George Bernard Shaw said of her in her prime: 'I resent Mrs Langtry, she has no right to be intelligent, daring and independent as well as lovely.'

Lillie secured her first husband, landowner Edward Langtry, in 1872. She seemed more taken with his yacht the *Red Gauntlet* than with the man himself, and was rather exasperated not to settle in London. After a near-fatal bout of typhoid, she persuaded Langtry that London would be good for her health and they took a town house in Eaton Place in 1874. Under the patronage of Lord Ranelagh and painter George Francis Miles, Mrs Langtry was introduced to London society and bewitched rakes such as Lord Randolph Churchill. Copies of her portraits by Miles, Millais and Edward Burne-Jones were sold as postcards to a public enchanted by her charms.

On 24 May 1877, a private dinner was arranged to introduce the famous Mrs Langtry of the violet eyes and sharp wit to the playboy Prince of Wales (the future Edward VII). Christopher Hibbert's definitive biography of Edward VII (1976) says the Prince was 'immediately captivated by this tall, graceful, glowingly voluptuous woman who had recently established herself as one of the most sought-after beauties in London. Led by the Prince's long-suffering wife Alexandra, Society accepted the presence of Langtry at any occasion attended by the Prince of Wales.'

Ditties were penned for Langtry, including one with the couplet 'London Society has gone quite silly, Fallen at the feet of the Jersey Lillie'. Oscar Wilde said, 'I would rather have discovered Lillie Langtry than America', and Queen Victoria received the royal mistress, who mischievously wore the Prince of Wales's three ostrich feathers in her hair. In 1877 the Prince built a love nest for her outside Bournemouth. A window with their initials and entwined hearts etched by Langtry still exists in the building, now a hotel.

Langtry had numerous affairs; her lovers included the Earl of Shrewsbury, Prince Louis of Battenberg (father of Lord Louis Mountbatten) and Arthur Jones, an illegitimate son of Lord Ranelagh. In 1881 she gave birth to a daughter, born in Paris, whose father was always assumed to be Prince Louis, although recent evidence suggests that Arthur Jones may have been the more likely candidate. Her affair with the Prince of Wales lasted until 1880, when Lillie allegedly put ice down her prince's collar at a private dinner.

Removal of the Prince's patronage could have proved fatal for Langtry. Her husband's alcoholism had resulted in a dwindling of their fortunes. Not to be defeated, she made her stage debut a year later at the prompting of Sarah Bernhardt, in a production of *She Stoops to Conquer*. It was the first time a London society woman had appeared on stage and her appearance caused a sensation. Largely thanks to the Prince of Wales's support – he attended her performance numerous times – Langtry was a success, despite possessing limited talents as an actress. She went on to manage the Imperial Theatre in London, and also conquered America, touring with her own theatre company and finding several wealthy patrons on the road.

Langtry also went on to own a successful racing stable; she married Hugo Gerald de Bathe in 1899 on the day her horse Merman won the Goodwood Cup. On the death of his father in 1907 she became Lady de Bathe. The marriage later foundered and she lived out her final years in Monaco. Lillie Langtry died of pneumonia in Monte Carlo in 1929.

MADAME ADELINA PATTI

PATRONAGE 1877–1879

SIGNATURE GARMENT A blue livery greatcoat lined with Angola with eighteen plated crest buttons

TOTAL SPEND £94 (£6,220 today)

CONNECTIONS Madame Patti and Lillie Langtry were the only female stage performers to hold livery accounts with Poole's in a galaxy of royal and aristocratic women including Queen Alexandra, Empress Eugénie of the French, Queen Marie-Henriette of the Belgians, Queen Olga of the Hellenes and the Duchess of Edinburgh (Grand Duchess Maria of Russia).

Adelina Patti, 'Queen of Song' (1843–1919), was the highest-paid soprano of her generation and a definitive interpreter of bel canto roles whom Giuseppe Verdi considered 'a stupendous artist beyond compare'. At the height of her fame in the 1870s and 1880s Patti was paid £5,000 per performance: more than the president of the United States was paid in a year.

Patti was born in Madrid to Italian parents. The family emigrated to America, and Patti made her operatic debut in 1859 aged sixteen, performing Donizetti's *Lucia di Lammermoor* at the New York Academy of Music. In 1860 she performed in Montreal for the Prince of Wales, who was touring Canada on a state visit that his mother, Queen Victoria, would not undertake herself. The Prince would become one of Madame Patti's most ardent admirers and was a guest at her Welsh home, Craig-y-Nos Castle.

Patti made her London debut in 1861 at Covent Garden in the role of Amina in Bellini's *La Sonnambula*. Verdi, who was in the audience, wrote: 'When I heard her for the first time in London I was astounded not only by the marvellous performance but also by a great number of stage traits that revealed her great acting talent.' She chose England as her home and bought a house in South London.

Madame Patti travelled as tirelessly as a diplomat, establishing her fame in Paris, Vienna, Washington and St Petersburg. Her performance in Paris in 1862 earned her the attention of the lascivious Emperor Napoleon III. She was immortalized by the Empress Eugénie's court painter Franz Xaver Winterhalter, dazzled Russia's Emperor Alexander II (who awarded her the Russian Order of Merit in 1870) and sang one of her favourite songs, 'Home! Sweet Home!', for President Abraham Lincoln at the White House in 1862. It was in Paris in 1868 that she met her first husband, Marquis de Caux, an equerry of Napoleon III, whom Patti divorced in 1885, costing her £64,000 – half of her not inconsiderable fortune.

The Diva, as she was called, burnished her fame with demands that only the greatest prima donna of her age could get away with. Her £5,000 fee was paid in gold before a

performance. Her name was always top of the bill and printed in larger type than that of any other performer. She was not obliged to rehearse, though reserved her right to attend and criticize her fellow artists and the orchestra. According to English opera promoter James Henry Mapleson, Patti travelled with a parrot that she trained to shriek, 'Cash! Cash!' whenever a theatre manager walked into the room.

Reporting on her 1884 *La Traviata* at Covent Garden, *The Theatre* magazine wrote: 'The Queen of Song was enthusiastically greeted by such an audience as she alone, of all the living *prime donne*, can draw to the largest of London theatres. She was looking lovelier than ever, having acquired a becoming embonpoint during her sojourn in the States. Her singing and acting were in every respect as inimitable as they have been for many a past year.' When Patti heard the first of her thirty gramophone recordings, she was alleged to have said: 'Now I understand why I am Patti. Oh yes. What a voice! What an artist!'

Patti invested wisely and bought the Welsh castle Craig-y-Nos in 1878, adding a theatrical auditorium based on Wagner's theatre in Bayreuth. Here she gave private recitals, entertained and made gramophone recordings of her greatest roles. She retired in 1903 after a farewell tour of the US that was a critical, financial and personal failure owing to the deterioration of her once perfect voice. Her last performance was at the Royal Albert Hall in 1914 for a Red Cross concert to benefit World War I widows. She died in 1919.

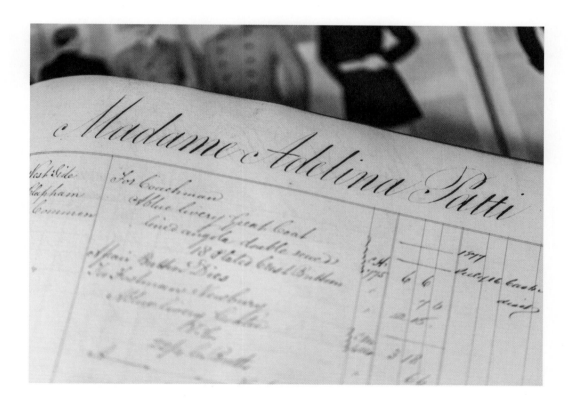

SERGE DIAGHILEV

PATRONAGE 1895–1903

SIGNATURE GARMENT A blue Elysian beaver pea coat

TOTAL SPEND £51 (£3,990 today)

CONNECTIONS Impresario Richard D'Oyly Carte was a contemporary of
Serge Diaghilev's at Poole's, as were Russian grandees Prince Alex Dolgorouky,
Prince Dimitri Soltykoff, Count Serge Stroganoff and Prince Nicolas Troubetskoi.

Serge (Sergei) Diaghilev (1872–1929) was arguably the most influential ballet impresario of the 20th century. His Ballets Russes company, performing between 1909 and 1929, was a magnet for creative giants such as artists Pablo Picasso, André Derain and Henri Matisse, couturier Coco Chanel, composers Igor Stravinsky, Nikolai Rimsky-Korsakov, Claude Debussy and Maurice Ravel, and dancers Vaslav Nijinsky, Anna Pavlova, Serge Lifar, Ninette de Valois, Tamara Karsavina, Léonide Massine, Michel Fokine, Anton Dolin and Alicia Markova.

Russian-born Diaghilev trained as a law student in St Petersburg in 1890 and belonged to a group that established the influential magazine *World of Art*, which introduced him to elite artistic circles including the Imperial Ballet. He became artistic adviser to the Maryinsky Theatre under the patronage of flamboyant homosexual Prince Sergei Volkonsky, who was 'patron' of dancer Vaslav Nijinsky. Diaghilev resigned in 1901 to tour an exhibition of Russian art to Paris. In 1908 he brought a successful production of the opera *Boris Gudonov* to Paris and followed this with a season of opera and ballet at the Paris Opera.

Spurred by his success, Diaghilev formed the Ballets Russes in 1909, building avante-garde new works around his lover Nijinsky, with music composed by Stravinsky (*The Rite of Spring*) and Debussy (*L'apres-midi d'un Faune*). In the latter a scantily clad Nijinsky appeared to simulate orgasm, scandalizing audiences in Paris and London.

The Ballets Russes championed the modernist movement in classical music, commissioning composers such as Debussy, Ravel, Prokofiev and Stravinsky. The great works – *Scheherazade* (1910), *The Firebird* (1910), *Le Spectre de la rose* (1911) and the later *Les noces* (1923) *Les biches* (1924) and *Le Train bleu* (1924) – evolved from the exotic, erotic Orientalism brought to life by designer Léon Bakst into the Art Deco aesthetic such as the sporty Jazz Age beach costumes Coco Chanel designed for *Le Train bleu*.

Diaghilev and the Ballets Russes never returned to Russia after the 1917 Revolution and the company served as a focus for exiled White Russian aristocrats who flooded Paris and the Riviera after the murder of the Tsar and his family in 1918. Diaghilev considered himself a father to the company, though Nijinsky fell foul of the impresario when he got married suddenly in Buenos Aires during a Ballets Russes South American tour. Sadly, schizophrenia stole Nijinsky's mind and he spent much of the rest of his life institutionalized. Léonide Massine, who likened sleeping with Diaghliev to 'going to bed with a nice, fat old lady', was fired when discovered having an affair with ballerina Vera Savina.

Diaghilev was famed for his acid tongue. Dame Ninette de Valois said that he dismissed her stage name as 'half tart, half royal family of France'. His autocratic style was captured in the 1948 Powell and Pressburger ballet film *The Red Shoes*, in which he is depicted as Svengali-like ballet impresario Lermontov. As in the film, Diaghilev demanded absolute loyalty and dedication to the craft from his dancers.

Commercially the Ballets Russes constantly teetered on the brink of bankruptcy but was always rescued by Diaghilev's genius for flattering wealthy patrons, such as Princess Edmond de Polignac, who rescued the company in 1921 and secured for it an annual residency at the Grand Théâtre de Monte Carlo thanks to her royal connections.

Serge Diaghilev died in Venice in 1929, leaving an unpaid hotel bill, and was buried in the island cemetery of San Michele. But as Prokofiev said, 'Diaghilev is a giant, undoubtedly the only one whose dimensions increase the more he recedes into the distance'.

RONALD FIRBANK

PATRONAGE   1911–1925

SIGNATURE GARMENT   A pair of grey flannel trousers

TOTAL SPEND   £215 (£6,250 today)

CONNECTIONS   Louis Comfort Tiffany – the master of Art Nouveau
glass, mosaics, jewellery and interiors – was a contemporary of Ronald
Firbank's at Henry Poole.

An exotic bloom in the mould of Oscar Wilde and Aubrey Beardsley, Ronald Firbank (1886–1926) was an author who achieved little recognition in his short life but has since been reassessed as a leader of the Aesthetic movement. Arthur Annesley Ronald Firbank was born into privilege on Mayfair's Clarges Street. His father was MP Sir Thomas Firbank. He was sent to Uppingham School aged ten, and won a place at Trinity Hall, Cambridge, though he did not complete his degree. During his tenure at Trinity Hall, Firbank converted to Catholicism in 1907. His crises of religious faith may not be unconnected to his chronic alcoholism and homosexuality.

In his online biography *Concerning the Eccentricities of Ronald Firbank*, James J. Conway writes 'a Bright Young Thing before his time, Firbank was born blushing. His associates never fail to mention his social awkwardness, particularly the incessant fluttering of hands (or compulsive washing of same) and the hysterical laughter that would periodically erupt leaving him incapable of completing an anecdote. Attempting to embolden himself with drink merely exacerbated the problem.' Openly gay, Firbank was an inspiration for the character of Cedric Hampton in Nancy Mitford's *Love in a Cold Climate* (1949).

Suffering from delicate health for most of his life, not aided by his addictions to cannabis and alcohol, Firbank was the very model of a wilting Aesthete. His eccentricity manifested itself at Cambridge, where he was acquainted with Oscar Wilde's son Vivyan Holland. Holland recalled seeing Firbank 'incongruously dressed in the costume of sport. Confounded, Holland enquired what he had been doing and, learning that he had apparently been playing football, further enquired whether it was rugby or soccer. "Oh," Firbank replied, "I don't remember".'

Firbank's stories, short novels and plays were mostly published posthumously and never performed. They are baroque, surreal and absurd in the highest degree. His most famous novel, *Concerning the Eccentricities of Cardinal Pirelli* (1926), sees the eponymous prince of the church christening his dog in a cathedral service and dying of a heart attack chasing a choirboy round the altar. *Sorrow in Sunlight* (1924) examines a socially ambitious black family in a fictional Caribbean republic and satirizes pretension and social climbing. Art imitated life. When he met the flamboyant, sinister artists' muse the

Marchesa Luisa Casati, Firbank was said to have laid lilies at her feet and suggested they embark immediately for America.

The author's prose style displays a mastery of comic dialogue tinged with decadence comparable to that of Oscar Wilde. For example, one of his most famous aphorisms was: 'The world is disgracefully managed, one hardly knows to whom to complain.' Of one of his characters he writes: 'Mentally, perhaps she was already three parts glass. So intense was her desire to set up a commemorative window to herself that, when it was erected, she believed she must live behind it, forever, a little ghost.'

Firbank died alone in a hotel room in Rome of lung disease aged forty, and – in a muddle he would have appreciated – was mistakenly buried in a Protestant graveyard by his friend Gerald Berners. One might write off Ronald Firbank as an inferior talent to Wilde – a literary gadfly – but for the devotees who resurrected his work in the 1940s. Evelyn Waugh, Nancy Mitford, E. M. Forster and W. H. Auden all expressed admiration for his slim opus, as did Susan Sontag in her seminal 1964 essay 'Notes on "Camp"'.

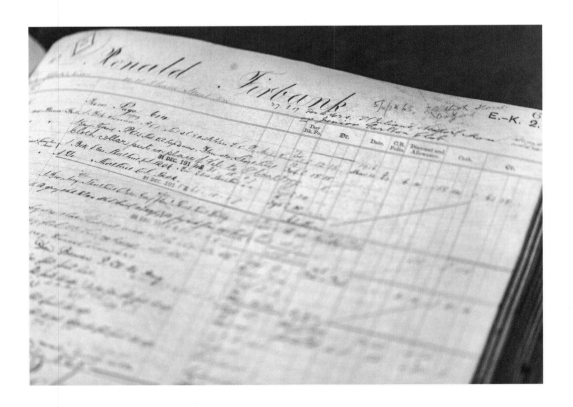

IRVING BERLIN

PATRONAGE 1920

SIGNATURE GARMENT Blue Angola short suit lined with silk

TOTAL SPEND £19 (£550 today)

CONNECTIONS Showbusiness customers were still quietly discouraged at
Poole's in the 1920s. The only contemporary of Irving Berlin's in the business was
film director the Hon. Anthony Asquith, who would go on to direct *Pygmalion*
(1939), *The Winslow Boy* (1948) and *The Importance of Being Ernest* (1952).

Israel Isidore Baline, popularly known as Irving Berlin (1888–1989), was arguably the most celebrated 20th-century 'Great American Songbook' composer. George Gershwin declared, 'I frankly believe that Irving Berlin is the greatest songwriter that has ever lived.' Berlin wrote both the words and the music for eighteen Hollywood films, nineteen Broadway shows and more than 1,500 songs, of which twenty-five topped the US charts. He won one of his seven Academy Award nominations in 1942 for the film *Holiday Inn*. The most popular song from the movie, 'White Christmas', was sung by Bing Crosby and sold more than fifty million records and four million copies of the sheet music.

The violent antisemitic pogroms in Tsarist Russia had forced the Baline family to emigrate to America in 1893 after their village was burned to the ground by Cossacks. They settled in a slum tenement building on New York's Lower East Side. Berlin left school aged eight and delivered newspapers for a pittance in the Bowery, where he sang in the street for coins. He later graduated from busking to a job as a singing waiter at the Pelham Café in Chinatown, where he became known as 'the Yiddishe Yankee Doodle'.

Berlin was fiercely proud to be an American and live in the land of opportunity. He said of his music: 'My ambition is to reach the heart of the average American … the real soul of the country.' In 1911, he wrote his first great American song, 'Alexander's Ragtime Band', which showed off his talent for lyrics penned in the vernacular. It became a worldwide dance sensation. In England, Lady Diana Manners recalled Poole's customer Prince Felix Youssoupoff 'wriggling around the ballroom like a demented worm screaming for more ragtime and more champagne'.

In 1912 Irving Berlin married Dorothy Goetz. She died six months later from typhoid fever, prompting him to pen his first ballad, 'When I Lost You', which sold a million copies of the sheet music. When he wooed his second wife, Ellin Mackay, an heiress from a Catholic family that disapproved of the Jewish composer, Berlin wrote one of his most enduring love songs, 'Always', which Noël Coward made a centrepiece of his 1941 play *Blithe Spirit*.

Berlin was drafted in 1917, leading one New York paper to post the headline 'Army Takes Berlin'. Already a star on Tin Pan Alley, Berlin was a prolific composer for musical

revues. His composition 'A Pretty Girl is like a Melody', written for the Ziegfeld Follies of 1919, was such a hit it remained in all subsequent Follies shows. Berlin also constructed his own theatre, the Music Box on Broadway, in which he produced his own revues.

Journalist Walter Cronkite said that 'Irving Berlin helped write the story of this country, capturing the best of who we are and the dreams that shape our lives'. During the Depression, he wrote some of his most glamorous, escapist melodies, which Fred Astaire and Ginger Rogers performed on film, such as 'Puttin' On the Ritz', 'Cheek to Cheek', 'Top Hat' and 'Let's Face the Music and Dance'. Neither was Berlin shy of 'message songs', such as the anti-slavery ballad 'Supper Time' sung by Ethel Walters.

Berlin was particularly adept at writing celebratory holiday songs, including 'White Christmas' and 'Easter Parade', which would become synonymous with the occasions themselves. 'There's No Business Like Show Business', recorded by Ethel Merman in 1954 for the film of the same name, became a hymn for entertainers worldwide. Written in 1918, 'God Bless America' became a national anthem in all but name during World War II and, after the 9/11 atrocities, was revived and recorded by Celine Dion.

In 1962, after his last stage musical, *Mr President*, closed on Broadway, Berlin announced his retirement. He lived an increasingly reclusive life in his Beekman Place apartment in New York and his weekend home in the Catskill Mountains. Irving Berlin died of natural causes in 1989 at the age of 101.

CHAPTER SIX

POOLE TRIUMPHANT
1976–2019

Henry Poole & Co. (Savile Row) Ltd.
into the place and quality of
Livery Tailors
to Her Majesty
To hold the said place until this Royal Warrant
shall be withdrawn or otherwise revoked.
This Warrant is granted to
Simon Howard Cundey Esquire
trading under the title stated above and empowers the holder to
display the Royal Arms in connection with the Business but does
not carry the right to make use of the Arms as a flag or trade mark.
The Warrant is strictly personal to the Holder and will
become void and must be returned to the Lord Chamberlain in any
of the circumstances specified when it is granted.

'Whenever I am asked whether I'd sell the family business
I will always reply not on my watch. In your lifetime of running
the show, all you ask is to make it better for the next generation.
I have two sons – Henry and Jamie – and if the eldest does come
into the business he will be the eighth generation of the family
to do so: Henry VIII.'

**SIMON CUNDEY, JOINT MANAGING DIRECTOR,
HENRY POOLE & CO (2017)**

Angus Cundey was president of the Federation of Merchant Tailors when the Fifteenth World Congress of Master Tailors was held in London in 1973. A matter of urgency was the 'modern tailor's concern not only with the source of his material but the problems he may meet in handling new textiles'.

In short, the heavy 20 oz (560 g) cloths that were necessary for insulation before the advent of central heating could practically be moulded like sheet metal and hold their shape. The lighter modern cloths necessitated more finesse in the cutting and a more delicate touch when being sewn. Savile Row's tailors would have to adapt or die.

Angus pointed out that, to compound the problem, the reputation of the trade among young people was little short of abominable: they thought tailors still worked in Victorian conditions below stairs for very little money. This perception had to be changed, and a new generation of apprentices was needed to revitalize the trade. Fashion was a more attractive industry, particularly since the glamour of ceremonial work had largely faded by the mid-1970s. As the punk movement that caught fire in 1977 proved, the royal family was not immune to criticism now that the age of reverence seemed to have passed.

In the 1970s there were few opportunities to demonstrate the magnificent ceremonial work that had made Henry Poole & Co's fortune. An order by Prince Aserate Kassa of Eritrea caught the imagination of the British press. The Prince's civil uniform coatee was hand-embroidered with gold shola leaves on the bib and cuffs and cut with a short-fringed shoulder cape embellished with doves. The Emperor Haile Selassie's ciphers on the stand collar and the Lion of Judah buttons were solid gold. Twelve craftsmen laboured for three months to deliver the uniform at a cost of £1,500 (£11,450 today). The bill was still unpaid when the Emperor was overthrown and Prince Aserate executed with sixty other members of Selassie's court.

Opposite: Simon Cundey's Royal Warrant as Livery Tailors to HM Queen Elizabeth II hangs in the showroom next to those of his father, Angus, his grandfather Sam and his great-grandfather Howard.

The monogrammed selvedges from a selection of Henry Poole & Co House Cloths.

In a move to justify the price of a handmade suit, Angus told the press that the average man was willing to spend the equivalent of his weekly wage on a suit and, at £48, 'our prices are within the range of many pockets today'. Poole's trade was robust but the social and economic upheaval in Britain in the 1970s sabotaged many businesses with hyperinflation, power cuts and the imposition of a three-day working week.

But Poole's had powerful customers and a loyal workforce. Throughout the three-day week Poole's tailors voted to work a twelve-hour day from 7.00 a.m. to 7.00 p.m. Coat-maker Mr Goggin told the *Times*: 'If a firm treats you well you do not mind going out of your way to return the favour.' Proving his point, Goggin retired after fifty-two years working for Henry Poole.

A demand by the French customs chief in 1975 for Angus Cundey to divulge his robust Parisian customer list to be audited for alleged import tax evasion was strongly resisted. When the chairman sent letters to his customers telling them fittings were to be delayed, one of them took action. His name was Bernard Destremau and he was the French Secretary of State for Foreign Affairs. Business was immediately resumed as usual.

In 1980 Angus made the decision to bring Rex Harrison's tailor Sullivan & Wooley into Cork Street. Sullivan & Wooley's Alan Alexander would be senior cutter at Poole's until 2018, while Philip Parker served as managing director from 1998 to 2012. Angus's most monumental decision came in 1981, when he announced to his ailing father: 'I have found suitable premises and I am going to take Henry Poole back to Savile Row.' He recalls: 'My father couldn't speak but a huge smile came across his face. Three days later, he died.'

The premises Angus had found were No. 15 Savile Row. The chairman told the *Daily News Record* in 1982: 'As we are credited with starting the whole Savile Row legend by being the first tailor to set up shop there, we are particularly pleased to be going back.' The *Guardian* wrote: 'One of Savile Row's oldest tailors had a comparatively frugal wine party to celebrate their moving back into Savile Row after twenty-one years' exile in Cork Street.'

It was on the chairman's watch that a number of 'house specials' were developed, such as the short-lived Henry Poole & Co cologne and the house check cloth designed in 1989 by Harrisons of Edinburgh managing director Cameron Buchanan and woven by Reid & Taylor that is still in service today. In recent years the weaving of Henry Poole exclusives such as the Fox Brothers & Co Churchill chalk stripe has been directed by the chairman's son and present managing director, Simon Cundey.

Pride in the craft and in the firm had been instilled in Simon from a very young age, when he decided in his early teens that he wanted to join the family business. 'I would travel up to town with Angus and spend weekends with Bill and George in the packing department to earn pocket money,' he says. 'Part of the job was to deliver, so I was introduced to the Connaught, Claridge's, the Reform Club, the Athenaeum, Boodle's and the RAC. In the holidays I was offered a job at Ferragamo on Old Bond Street. When all the glamorous ladies signed their bills I recognized their husbands' names as customers of Henry Poole. I liked that world of Mayfair and London's West End and that's what made me decide I'd like to work at Poole's at such a young age.'

From 1986 Simon studied for three years at the London College of Fashion, before spending a formative four months at cloth mill Taylor & Lodge. 'That was invaluable experience for me,' he says, 'learning about the different jacquards, the looms, the faults, the mending, scouring, warping and wefting. Cloth is a passion for me and knowing the different properties is so important when you are guiding customers through their choices. After Taylor & Lodge I spent a number of months working in Chester Barrie's factories in Crewe. That's when I learned that the nine to five wasn't for me. When you're making a customer a suit, you don't go home at 5.00 p.m. You are invested in quality service and you think about it twenty-four hours a day'.

Nineteen eighty-nine proved to be a baptism of fire for Simon Cundey, who had elected to carve his path at Poole's as a salesman rather than a cutter. He had been due to replace the chairman on the European trips and, having spent four months in Paris, had been sent on a whistle-stop tour of the firm's licensees and factories in Tokyo, Osaka and Nagoya in Japan. On his return to London, the director in charge of Poole's American interests, Patrick Mead, was diagnosed with a fatal illness. 'Poole's had to make a quick decision,' says Simon, 'to send me along with the cutters known to our customers.' The first trip – New York, Chicago, Boston, Washington, Houston and Seattle – was a three-week marathon and the first time Poole's operated a trunk show across the Atlantic.

'Simon is the one who introduced fittings on the American trips,' says Angus, 'and he has never looked back. His knowledge of cloths is enormous and he is a natural salesman. From day one Simon's trips to America have been a great success.' 'At a very early stage I understood that the days of a gentleman choosing his tailor and staying for life for his entire wardrobe had gone,' says Simon. 'Fortunately Poole's has always had a reputation for dressing titans of industry. I'd say we cut a very refined suit and in 2017 business attire for men in London, Tokyo, New York, DC, Singapore and Beijing is still suits. Regardless of nationality, these men get their salaries and bonuses and chop them into what they need. A suit is still a necessity.'

'Dress-down Friday' was a threat to the suit, bespoke or otherwise, in the mid-1990s, though it proved a rod for most men's backs. 'They didn't know how to dress casually,' says Simon Cundey, 'and it proved much easier to wear a navy suit rather than smart casual.'

One of the most high-profile casualties was French prime minister Edouard Balladur, who had been a Poole's customer since 1979 and whose Savile Row suits had caused comment. 'When Balladur ran for the presidency in 1994, his advisers cautioned that he should not wear British bespoke,' says the chairman, 'especially when his slogan was "Believe in France!" So Monsieur Balladur stopped wearing Henry Poole suits, was photographed wearing a trenchcoat and promptly lost the election.'

Henry Poole & Co mounted the landmark exhibition 'Dressing the Part: 190 Years of Savile Row Tailoring by Henry Poole' at Merchant Taylors' Hall in 1995 and then at the Victoria & Albert Museum in 1996–97. The combination of historical and contemporary garments showed the Gap T-shirt and combat shorts brigade that no matter how men's fashion fluctuates, the suit always rises to the top percentage of influential men.

The elephant in the room was the lack of young blood entering the trade so, in 2004, the Savile Row Bespoke association was formed to promote and protect the craft of bespoke tailoring on and around the Row. SRB was established to address the shortfall in apprentices coming up on the Row. The apprenticeship scheme, co-designed by Poole's Philip Parker and Su Thomas, has since trained 200 young people, sixty-four of whom are now employed as bespoke cutters and tailors.

In 2001 Simon Cundey was appointed managing director of Henry Poole & Co, a position he shares with head cutter Alex Cooke. 'We are blessed with our staff,' he says. 'There isn't much turnover at Poole's because I'd like to think we look after our own. As a family business the last thing we want to do is hire and fire. The cutters are still king but if you have a cutter who doesn't have rapport with the customers you are in trouble. Cutters like Alex can travel, sell and sew. We also have another generation coming up, with Tom Prendry taking over the Europe and China trips.'

It is one of the managing director's ambitions to rebuild the European business and also reassess how Henry Poole & Co negotiates the global trade it has had since the days of his great-grandfather Howard Cundey. 'Men looking for the best tailoring in the world will always find their way to Savile Row, but I think we might need to be more flexible in our ability to make short unscheduled trips and go to them when necessary.'

Poole's being a seventh-generation family business does give a reassuring sense of quality and continuity. In 2001 the chairman received a letter from the 13th Duke of Bedford that read: 'After all these years, I think of you every day with gratitude for all

Gary Oldman as Winston Churchill and Ben Mendelsohn as King George VI in a scene from the 1917 film *Darkest Hour*, for which Poole's tailored the costumes shown.

the beautiful fine quality suits you made me. I have not bought a new suit for thirty years and the old ones still look as impeccable as ever.'

Savile Row has always been wary of public relations and Henry Poole & Co's past has harvested a rich seam of film work for which the firm uniquely pays zero for product placement. 'We're seeing renewed interest at Poole's for film costume,' says Keith Levett, 'now that the skills necessary to recreate 19th- and 20th-century tailoring have largely been lost by the costume and prop houses.'

The most recent commission was to recreate 1940s tailoring for Gary Oldman as Winston Churchill and Ben Mendelsohn as King George VI for the 2017 film *Darkest Hour*. Though the firm has always been reticent about naming the high-profile customers they dress, the nature of fame today allows ambassadors such as male model David Gandy to praise his tailor in the press.

'The fact that we manufacture on the Row, rather than just retail, is the magic,' says Simon Cundey. 'That said, I also think we need to go out and find new business. We can be the best in the world but the world has to know it.' Under Simon Cundey, Poole's is expanding its global reach, with the latest new additions to the calendar being Beijing, Shanghai and Hong Kong. With his two sons showing an interest in Henry Poole & Co, Simon Cundey has the succession in place. As he says, 'society will always change but a bespoke suit from Henry Poole remains a constant'.

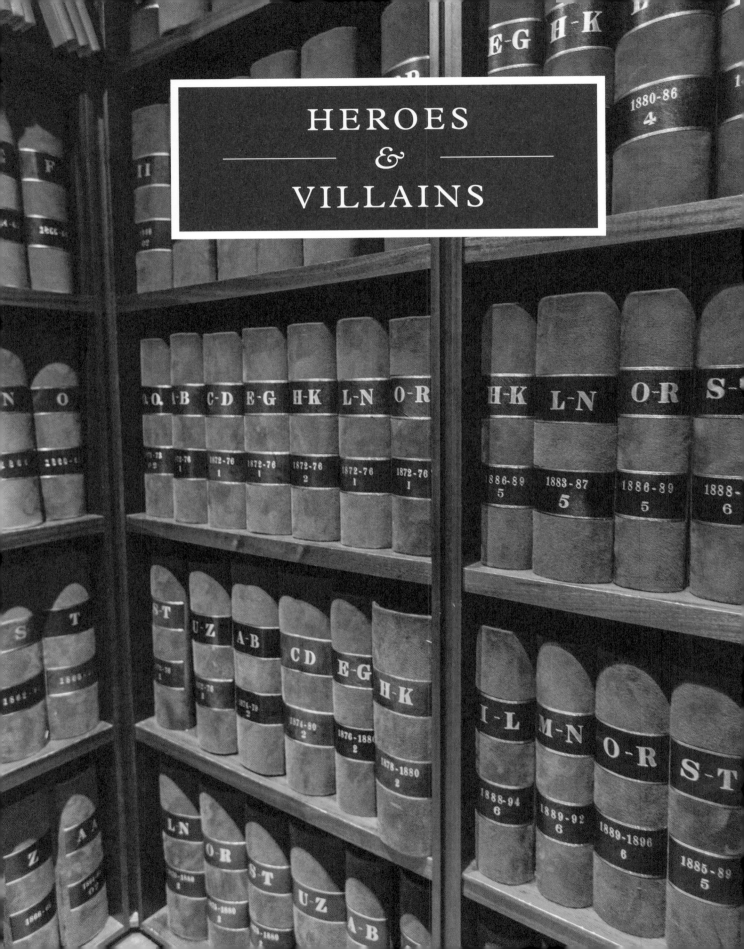

HEROES
&
VILLAINS

PRINCE ALBERT VICTOR, DUKE OF CLARENCE AND AVONDALE

PATRONAGE 1873–1875

SIGNATURE GARMENT A lavender check doeskin round jacket lined with
silk, a lavender check vest and trousers

TOTAL SPEND £529 (£33,120 today)

CONNECTIONS Both Prince Albert Victor and his brother, the future
King George V, were tailored by Poole's throughout their childhood and
adolescence, with orders placed on the accounts of their parents, the Prince
and Princess of Wales.

Queen Victoria's eldest British-born grandson and heir apparent to the throne, Prince Albert Victor (1864–1892), was a fragile infant born two months prematurely to flighty Princess Alix of Denmark and her rumbustious husband, Bertie, the Prince of Wales. In his brief but eventful life, the child who would forever call his fairy princess of a matriarch 'Motherdear' would inspire great love and protectiveness in the closed circle who surrounded him, thus making the facts of his life obscure at best and obtuse at worst.

The Prince of Wales had suffered under a draconian academic and physical regime set down by his parents that he failed to attempt to even scale let alone conquer. So it seems odd that Bertie would push his delicate, indolent eldest son, Eddy, as he was known by the family, into a naval cadetship at Dartmouth next to his more competent younger brother George, Duke of York. It was to Henry Poole & Co that the Prince of Wales took his sons to be fitted for cadet uniforms on his personal account, suggesting that there was a minimum age of sixteen before a Poole's boy could become a Poole's man and have his own account.

Perhaps it was Bertie's neglect and Alix's weakness that allowed a charlatan of a tutor, John Dalton, to be appointed keeper of the royal princes for so many years at the command of their formidable, stubborn grandmother Queen Victoria. It was Dalton who first branded Prince Eddy's an 'abnormally dormant mind', while Sir Henry Ponsonby speculated that he had inherited his charming mother's deafness and her blindness to all that failed to please her.

In 1877 the princes Eddy and George were shipped off on a world tour aboard HMS *Britannia*, again in the company of tutor John Dalton, who sounds not dissimilar to Evelyn Waugh's egregious Mr Samgrass in *Brideshead Revisited*; both men ghostwrote travel diaries for their less-than-enthusiastic charges. For three years the royal princes and their keeper toured the British Empire, the Americas, South Africa, Australia, Fiji, Singapore, Ceylon, Aden, Egypt, the Holy Land and Greece.

Prince Eddy, like his father before him, was ceremonially sent up to Trinity College, Cambridge. And like the Prince of Wales, Prince Eddy did not graduate, though he did meet sinister, charismatic tutor James Stephen, who was both a misogynist and a homosexual. Stephen said of his prince: 'I do not think he can possibly derive much benefit from attending lectures at Cambridge. We hardly would like to make a man of the world of him … not that he would refuse to be initiated.' Prince Eddy did, in fact, contract gonorrhoea at Cambridge, presumably with a fellow man.

Prince Eddy was gazetted as an officer of the 10th Hussars, during which time his uncle Prince George, Duke of Cambridge, called him 'an inveterate and incurable dawdler'. Though Eddy's prowess on the parade ground was lacklustre, the same could not be said about his boots, blacked and polished to shine like vinyl, or the frogged and furred skin-tight No. 1 Mess Dress tunic and breeches he wore to pose for *Vanity Fair*'s 'Spy' cartoon portrait of 1888, or the 'Masher' style of exaggerated shirts that earned him the mocking nickname 'Eddy Collars and Cuffs' from his father.

Rumours began to circulate around Prince Albert Victor in 1889 during what the tabloid press dubbed the Cleveland Street Brothel Scandal. Lord Arthur Somerset, Extra Equerry to the Prince of Wales (and another Henry Poole & Co client), along with several other prominent aristocrats, was accused of visiting a male brothel (illegal at the time) in Cleveland Street, and Prince Albert Victor's name (under the initials PAV) was also dragged into the affair. Somerset escaped prosecution by fleeing abroad, and Albert Victor's involvement was never proven. In October 1889 the Prince embarked on a seven-month tour of India that spirited him away from rumour-laden London society.

Despite his manly good looks and the expectations that attended him, Prince Albert Victor was unlucky in love. His cousin Princess Alix of Hesse and by Rhine refused him, and Princess Hélène of Orléans was deemed unacceptable for her Catholicism. The plain but resourceful minor royal princess Mary of Teck was agreed upon and the union proposed at a Syon House ball in December 1891 to the great pleasure of all concerned. Tragically, a week after his twenty-eighth birthday, Prince Albert Victor, Duke of Clarence and Avondale, succumbed to a severe bout of influenza at Sandringham in January 1892.

Commenting on his son's death, the Prince of Wales said he would have 'gladly given his own life' to save Prince Eddy, and Princess Alexandra never fully recovered from the loss of 'beloved Eddie-dear'. The black and white marble Art Nouveau tomb erected above the Prince's body in St George's Chapel, Windsor, is a masterpiece of high Victorian mourning sculpture and romanticizes the doomed youth. He was all but forgotten until rumours that Prince Eddy was a suspect in the 1888 Jack the Ripper killings in East London began to circulate in 1962. They have since been soundly dismissed on account of geography alone: in other words, the Prince was nowhere near London when the killings occurred. But Prince Eddy's connection to the Cleveland Street scandal has kept him alive in the canon of gay Victorian history and is invariably the headline of his brief life story.

STEPHEN WARD ESQ

PATRONAGE   1947–1948

SIGNATURE GARMENT   A fawn Shetland tweed single-breasted jacket and trousers

TOTAL SPEND   £190 (£6,750 today)

CONNECTIONS   Poole's chairman, Angus Cundey, recalls that all three protagonists in the Profumo affair – the 3rd Viscount Astor, Secretary of State for War John Profumo, and society osteopath Stephen Ward – were all contemporaries at Henry Poole & Co.

Society osteopath Dr Stephen Ward (1912–1963) was indirectly responsible for the most infamous political sex scandal of the 1960s, which brought down a minister and cost Ward his reputation and then his life. He was the link that brought together the 3rd Viscount Astor, Secretary of State for War John Profumo, Soviet military attaché Yevgeny Ivanov and nightclub hostess Christine Keeler. None would emerge from the scandal unscathed.

The son of a Hertfordshire vicar, Ward had a peripatetic but undistinguished early life. In 1934 he began a four-year osteopathy course in Missouri that allowed him the title 'doctor' in the United States but not in the United Kingdom, where osteopathy was still an alternative therapy unrecognized by the medical profession. Neither was Dr Ward accepted by the Royal Army Medical Corps, which turned him down in 1939. As a private in the Royal Armoured Corps, he served as a stretcher-bearer in World War II.

In 1944 Ward was posted to India, where his evident skill as an osteopath resulted in his treating Mohandas Gandhi – 'the most important meeting of my life', according to Ward. Following a nervous breakdown and admission to a psychiatric unit, he was repatriated and discharged from the army in 1945. Dr Stephen Ward worked first from the Osteopathic Association Clinic in Dorset Square, then his own practice in Cavendish Square, his card being passed among those in the highest circles, including Winston Churchill.

Affable and amusing, Ward was welcomed on the periphery of London society, but it was his own parties – where a phalanx of pretty young girls oiled the wheels of the social mix – that made him the man to know. His professional and social success is reflected in the two visits he made to Henry Poole & Co in 1947 and 1948, when his address is listed as Flat 1 Harcourt House, 19A Cavendish Square. The 1948 order – a fawn Shetland tweed single-breasted jacket and trousers lined with alpaca – was settled in cash by Christopher E. North, begging the question of whether it was payment in kind.

According to Ward, 'the truth is that I loved people of all types. And I don't think there are many people the worse for having known me.' As well as practising osteopathy, he studied at the Slade art school and became renowned as a portrait artist. He was commissioned by the *Illustrated London News* to produce a series of portraits of the royal family, including Prince Philip and Princess Margaret, making him even more of a darling on the social scene in London.

Lord Astor, a patient of Ward's, had given his popular friend the Cliveden cottage for a peppercorn rent in 1956, allegedly as a thank you for introducing the peer to London's demi-monde. Ward would usually bring one or two of his London party girls (his 'alley cats') to Cliveden for the weekend. Ward met teenage Christine Keeler in 1959 at Murray's Cabaret Club in Soho, where she was a dancer and hostess. She would live with him platonically at his home in Wimpole Mews, seeming to confirm the 4th Lord Astor's opinion that Ward was 'the ultimate voyeur … a perverted Professor Higgins'.

It was a summer weekend in July 1961 that the 3rd Lord Astor's house party including John Profumo chanced upon a naked Christine Keeler in the pool at Cliveden. The cabinet minister and the nightclub hostess began an affair conducted in Ward's Wimpole Mews flat. Keeler was also sleeping with another of Ward's friends, Yevgeny Ivanov, whom British Intelligence suspected of being a member of the GRU (Soviet miltary intelligence).

Profumo was forced to deny the affair in a statement to the House of Commons, only to resign from cabinet when the police investigation – and Ward – revealed his guilt. In a clear attempt to convict a scapegoat, Ward was arrested and indicted. He took an overdose of barbiturates before the guilty verdict was read in absentia and never woke from a coma. In a suicide note, he wrote: 'The ritual sacrifice is demanded and I cannot face it.'

HAROLD HARMSWORTH,
1ST VISCOUNT ROTHERMERE

PATRONAGE 1911–1940

SIGNATURE GARMENT   A viscount's coronation robe and coronet

TOTAL SPEND   £697 (£29,620 today)

CONNECTIONS   The 1st Viscount Rothermere was far from being the only
pro-appeasement newspaper editor in Britain in the lead-up to World War II.
Poole's customer and owner of the *Observer* Waldorf Astor, 2nd Viscount Astor, and
his wife, MP Nancy Astor, lobbied for an entente with Nazi Germany.

As co-founders of the *Daily Mail* and *Daily Mirror*, press barons Harold Harmsworth, 1st Viscount Rothermere (1868–1940), and his brother Alfred, Lord Northcliffe, were pioneers in popular tabloid newspapers. When Lord Northcliffe died without an heir in 1922, Lord Rothermere became sole proprietor of Associated Newspapers and the third richest man in Britain. The last decade of his life was clouded by his support for Hitler's Germany and his relationship with Austrian 'Nazi Princess' Stephanie von Hohenlohe, also known as 'the vamp of European politics'.

A grammar school boy and clerk for the Board of Trade, Harmsworth took employment at his brother Alfred's newspaper company in 1888. Alfred's instinct for journalism and his brother's for business bore fruit in 1896 when they founded the *Daily Mail*, which was modelled on the American press and sold as 'the busy man's daily news'. Simple, short and readable, the *Daily Mail* pioneered banner headlines on the front page, human interest and sports coverage and the first women's section in a British newspaper. By 1899 its circulation was over a million.

The *Daily Mirror* was launched in 1904 as a 'women's newspaper' with a female editor, Mary Howarth, but little success. As Lord Rothermere ruefully said: 'Some people say that a woman never really knows what she wants. It is certain she knew what she didn't want. She didn't want the *Daily Mirror*.' Hiring editor Hamilton Fyfe, Lord Rothermere turned the *Mirror* into a pictorial and within a month the circulation rose sevenfold.

With the *Daily Mirror* the most popular newspaper on the Western Front during World War I, Lord Rothermere's support was vital for Prime Minister Lloyd George, who appointed him president of the Air Council. He tragically lost two of his three sons within a week in the Great War, which might well have influenced his actions in the years leading up to World War II.

In 1919 Lord Rothermere was created a viscount, his titles rising with the circulation of his newspapers. Between them, Rothermere and the *Daily Express* proprietor, Lord Beaverbrook, could bring down a government. In 1922 Rothermere paid £1.6 million for the controlling interest in Associated Newspapers after his brother's death. By 1926, the *Daily Mail* had two million readers and the *Daily Mirror* more than three.

Lord Rothermere joined the fashionable world spending three months of the year gambling in Monte Carlo, where he met the exotic Princess Stephanie von Hohenlohe in 1927. A political adventuress, it was she who brought Rothermere's attention to the idea of restoring lands to Hungary that had been ceded by the Treaty of Versailles. His thundering editorials in the *Daily Mail* called for a return of the Hungarian monarchy. According to Jim Wilson, author of *Nazi Princess: Hitler, Lord Rothermere and Princess Stephanie von Hohenlohe* (2011), 'a group of monarchists even offered the throne to Rothermere himself. Briefly, he took that offer seriously but he quickly realised it was totally unrealistic.'

In his 1939 book *My Fight to Rearm Britain*, Lord Rothermere wrote that he chose Fascism as a defence against the spectre of Bolshevism. As early as 1933 he wrote that 'the minor misdeeds of individual Nazis will be submerged by the immense benefits that the new regime is already bestowing on Germany'. In 1934 he wrote a piece for the *Daily Mail* headlined 'Hurrah for the Blackshirts', referring to Oswald Mosley's British Union of Fascists. He visited Nazi Germany for the first time in 1934 and hosted a dinner at the Hotel Adlon in Berlin attended by Hitler, Goebbels, Goering and Princess von Hohenlohe.

The Princess was the conduit between Hitler and Lord Rothermere. British, French and American secret services all suspected her of being a German agent, and she was named in the newspapers as 'London's leading Nazi hostess'. The Princess was 'exposed' for having Jewish blood and a disillusioned Lord Rothermere retreated to Bermuda, where he died on 26 November 1940.

COLONEL WILLIAM 'BUFFALO BILL' CODY

PATRONAGE 1892–1903

SIGNATURE GARMENT A black frock coat with silk facings and a double-breasted black vest preserved in the Buffalo Bill Center of the West in Wyoming

TOTAL SPEND £36 (£2,950 today)

CONNECTIONS Poole's most famous hero of the Wild West after Cody was Captain William W. Cooke, adjutant to Colonel George Custer, who fell at the Battle of the Little Bighorn in 1876 and was subsequently double-scalped.

Colonel William 'Buffalo Bill' Cody (1846–1917) was a frontiersman and hero of the American West who perpetuated his own legend as a travelling showman and impresario. Cody was born and raised on the prairies of Iowa; moving to Kansas when his father died in 1857, he worked as a mounted messenger before trying his luck as a prospector in the Peak Pines gold rush of 1858. At the age of fourteen he answered the advertisement of horseback mail service the Pony Express for 'skinny, expert riders willing to risk death daily'.

In 1867 Cody took up the trade that made his name, becoming a buffalo hunter rounding up and dispatching the wild beasts that fed the construction workers building the Kansas Pacific Railroad. By his own account, Buffalo Bill killed 4,280 head of buffalo in seventeen months, and earned his moniker by winning an eight-hour shooting match with rival hunter William Comstock. In 1868 Cody was appointed Chief of Scouts for the Fifth Cavalry and served in sixteen battles, including the Cheyenne defeat at Summit Springs, Colorado in 1869. He was awarded the Congress Medal of Honour in 1872.

Like Daniel Boone, Kit Carson and Davy 'King of the Wild Frontier' Crockett, Buffalo Bill became a national folk hero and subject of sensational dime store novels. The novelist Ned Buntline met Cody in 1869 and published his first adventure, *Buffalo Bill: King of the Border Men*, in the *New York Weekly*. In 1872 Buntline penned a play, *The Scouts of the Plain*, and invited Cody to appear as himself in a Bowery Theatre production in New York.

Though no actor, Cody could spin a good yarn and continued to appear as himself in national theatre tours. In between theatre seasons, Buffalo Bill would escort rich Americans and European nobility, including Russia's Grand Duke Alexei, on expeditions to the Wild West. General Philip Sheridan identified in Cody 'a public relations windfall' for the US Army and recognized that the army needed good PR during the controversial annexing of Native American Indian territories. Cody's expeditions, accompanied by General Sheridan and Major General Custer, were widely publicized.

In 1876 Cody was called back to service as an army scout in the campaign that followed General Custer's defeat at Little Bighorn, during which he famously duelled with

Cheyenne chief Yellow Hair, whom he allegedly shot, stabbed in the heart and scalped in less than five seconds. Never missing an opportunity to capitalize on his own heroics, Cody took a show called 'The Red Right Hand: or Buffalo Bill's First Scalp for Custer' on the road, displaying Yellow Hair's feathers, shield and scalp to audiences who thrilled at his tales of derring-do.

In 1883 Cody produced his first outdoor spectacular, 'Buffalo Bill's Wild West', re-enacting his heroic life as a frontiersman, Pony Express rider, buffalo hunter and scourge of the Indians. When Cody took his show on the road to Europe, he gave a royal command performance for Queen Victoria at Olympia in 1887 to celebrate her golden jubilee. The show was seen by more than two million people. 'Nature's nobleman' was feted throughout the courts of Europe, including a performance in Rome for Pope Leo XIII in 1890.

By 1903 Cody had made a fortune. He invested heavily in stock breeding, coal mining, oil drilling, construction, tourism and publishing in his home state of Wyoming. His newspaper the *Cody Enterprise*, founded in 1899, is still published today. Cody also used his status as one of the world's most famous Americans to lobby for women's suffrage and fair treatment of Native Americans. Yet within a decade he was bankrupt, thanks in no small part to mismanagement of his spectacular shows and increasingly dubious investments. He was finally reduced to performing as an employee in the Sells-Floto Circus: a double-hander of a show featuring performing dogs and ponies as well as circus acts. On his death in 1917, Cody's reputation as 'nature's nobleman' was restored.

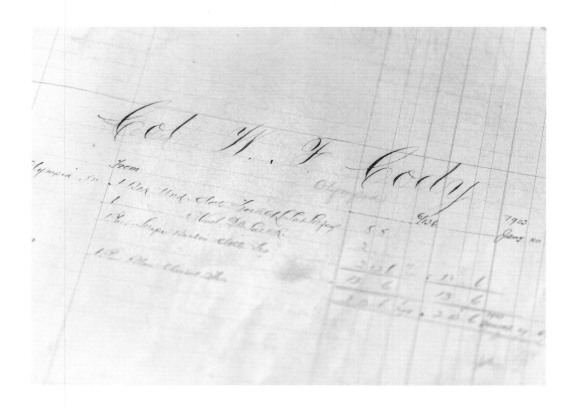

CROWN PRINCE RUDOLF OF AUSTRIA

PATRONAGE 1878

SIGNATURE GARMENT A black broad diagonal cloth frock coat
lined with silk

TOTAL SPEND £74 (£4,900 today)

CONNECTIONS Though her orders are lost, Crown Prince Rudolf's mother,
the famous beauty the Empress Elisabeth 'Sisi' of Austria, patronized Henry Poole
for their famous ladies' riding habits.

The mysterious death of Crown Prince Rudolf of Austria (1858–1889) at his imperial hunting lodge has inspired films, ballets, poems and musicals about the 'Mayerling Incident'. The thirty-year-old prince was discovered sitting up in a chair with a bullet to his head next to the bed on which his mistress Countess Marie Vetsera lay dead, naked but for a rose in her hair. As an only child and heir apparent to the Austro-Hungarian Empire, Crown Prince Rudolf's death started a chain of events that led indirectly to World War I.

Born a crown prince at the Schloss Laxenburg, Rudolf was the eldest son of Austro-Hungarian Emperor Franz Joseph and his beautiful but remote, skittish wife, the Empress Elisabeth. A keen ornithologist and sociologist in his youth, Crown Prince Rudolf accompanied his mother on her hunting expeditions to England where he became a great favourite of Queen Victoria and learned to appreciate her liberal, constitutional monarchy.

Franz Joseph's uncle the Archduke Albrecht judged a teenage Rudolf ill: 'The young, overexcited mind of the Crown Prince, the immaturity of his way of thinking, the extravagance of his undoubtedly high intelligence, makes me worry that he will assimilate ideas and tendencies which would not be compatible with the conservative character of a future monarch.' In 1880 Rudolf did his duty and married Princess Stéphanie, daughter of King Leopold II of the Belgians. The marriage was not a success.

Rudolf's impetuous character was blamed on the influence of his mother, the Empress, who was flirtatious, contrary and in thrall to her melancholy cousin King Ludwig II of Bavaria. In turn, Emperor Franz Joseph was exasperated by his empress's wanderings around Europe and commenced a thirteen-year affair with sixteen-year-old Anna Nahowski and, later, an affair with the actress Katharina Schratt.

In a private memorandum, the Crown Prince was critical of his father and wrote that 'our Emperor has no friends, his whole character and natural tendency do not permit it. He stands lonely on his peak.' Rudolf shared the Empress Elisabeth's temperament, and a courtier perceived that 'like his mother, he had a way of talking that held everybody, and a facility for setting all about him agog to solve the riddle of his personality'.

After two years of marriage, Crown Princess Stéphanie gave birth to a daughter, Elisabeth, but the marriage disintegrated. At the time Rudolf was embroiled with a dancer

called Mizzi Caspar. A year before Rudolf's death, Caspar reported to chief-of-police Baron Kraus that the Prince had confessed he found life too great a burden, that it was lonely to die alone and that he wanted her to join him in a suicide pact.

In 1887, Crown Prince Rudolf bought his hunting lodge, Mayerling, outside Vienna. Near the end of 1888, he transferred his affections to seventeen-year-old Baroness Marie Vetsera, whose mother was one of his previous conquests. According to Joan Haslip's *The Lonely Empress: Elizabeth of Austria* (1965), 'Mary was considered to be fast. She was known as a girl who wore too much jewellery and flirted with married men. From her earliest youth she had been brought up with only one aim in view, to attract and to please men.'

Prince Rudolf and Maria would die together within months. Vienna in the 1880s had the highest suicide rate in Europe and the Empress Elisabeth was haunted by the apparent suicide of her cousin King Ludwig. When Emperor Franz Joseph insisted his son give up Countess Vetsera, he retreated to Mayerling with his paramour. Their bodies were discovered on the morning of 30 January 1889 by the same valet who had served them pheasant and two bottles of Tokay the night before.

It was announced that the thirty-year-old prince had died of an aneurism, but a private investigation proved that Crown Prince Rudolf had shot his mistress before turning the gun on himself. The Countess's body was clothed, smuggled away from Mayerling and buried in an unmarked grave. The Crown Prince was given a Catholic burial in the Imperial Crypt at the behest of his parents, having been declared 'in a state of mental unbalance'.

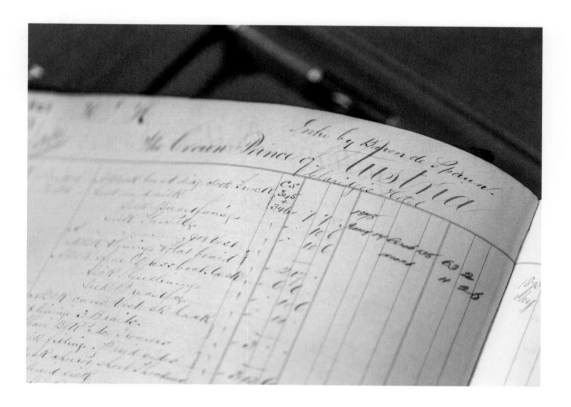

HIM EMPEROR WILHELM II OF GERMANY

PATRONAGE 1902

SIGNATURE GARMENT Black frock coat with black satin facings

TOTAL SPEND £205 (£16,030 today)

CONNECTIONS Kaiser Wilhelm II's grandfather Wilhelm I was a customer of
Henry Poole & Co, as was his father, Emperor Frederick III of Germany, and his
mother, the former Princess Victoria, Princess Royal of Great Britain.

Emperor (Kaiser) Wilhelm II of Germany (1859–1941) was the quixotic, vain tyrant whose love–hate relationship with his English royal relatives was largely responsible for Germany's entry into World War I and the fall of the Emperor's dynasty. The eldest son of Prince Frederick of Prussia and Princess Victoria of Great Britain, 'Willy', as he was known, was born with a withered arm. He later declared, 'An English doctor killed my father and an English doctor crippled my arm – which is the fault of my mother.'

In 1863 Prince Wilhelm accompanied his parents to England to attend the wedding of the Prince of Wales (Uncle Bertie) to Princess Alexandra. Though the little boy in full Highland dress pleased his grandmother Queen Victoria ('such a dear, good boy'), he bit the kilted Prince Alfred, his uncle, on the leg during the service, beginning a lifetime as the thorn in the side of his Uncle Bertie.

Prince Wilhelm idolized his grandfather the absolute monarch Emperor Wilhelm I, and, in retaliation against his liberal anglophile parents, fell under the thrall of the 'Iron Chancellor', Otto von Bismarck. As Crown Princess Victoria's biographer Hannah Pakula writes in *An Uncommon Woman* (1996), 'although there is no indication that Willy had yet begin to suffer from the grandiosity or breakdowns that punctuated his years on the throne, it is clear that he already had emotional problems. Sometimes these manifested themselves sexually.'

In 1877, on his eighteenth birthday, Prince Wilhelm's grandmother Queen Victoria awarded him the Order of the Garter. He had developed an obsession for military uniform and would henceforth flatter the Queen and wheedle for further orders and decorations: what Queen Victoria called 'fishing for uniforms'. Enrolling with the First Regiment of Foot Guards, Prince Wilhelm said he had 'really found my family, my friends, my interests – everything of which I had up to that time had to do without'.

With Bismarck's encouragement, Emperor Wilhelm I sent his grandson on diplomatic visits to the emperors Alexander III of Russia and Franz Joseph of Austria. He also attended Queen Victoria's golden jubilee in 1887. Prince Wilhelm had fallen in unrequited love with Princess Elisabeth of Hesse-Darmstadt, who would marry a Russian grand duke and be murdered during the Revolution. Instead he married Princess Augusta 'Donna' of Schleswig-Holstein, who idolized her husband and bore him six sons and a daughter.

Emperor Wilhelm I died in 1888 and Prince Wilhelm's father was crowned Emperor Frederick III. The new emperor was already suffering from terminal throat cancer, and died ninety-nine days after his accession. The bereft Dowager Empress Victoria was brushed aside, as was Bismarck, who was forced to fall on his sword in 1890. Bismarck had astutely said of his protégé that 'he wishes every day was his birthday'. Rejecting Bismarck's peaceful foreign policy, Emperor Wilhelm II set about furthering Germany's colonial ambitions and building a fleet to rival his British grandmother Queen Victoria's.

Queen Victoria died with her grandson at her bedside in 1901 and was succeeded by Uncle Bertie, who acceded as King Edward VII. Emperor Wilhelm had long loathed 'the old peacock' and any vestige of respect for Great Britain was subsumed by his hatred for and isolation from the new regime. Yet the Emperor continued to visit England and did so in 1902 for Uncle Bertie's coronation. It was on this occasion that he visited Henry Poole & Co. In an attempt to fit in, the Emperor forsook his military uniforms and wore classically tailored Savile Row suits. His account was paid for by his old friend the Earl of Lonsdale.

Increasingly the Emperor's pronouncements on world politics became erratic and aggressive. He believed the Jews were waging a war against his reign, cautioned the world about the threat of the 'Yellow Peril' in China and told the *Daily Telegraph* in 1908 that 'the English are mad, mad, mad as March hares'. He would later call the Jews 'a nuisance that humanity must get rid of some way or other. I believe the best thing would be gas': a presentiment of the rise of Nazism.

Ironically, the Emperor's influence was diminished during the Great War, largely thanks to the military powers he had personally promoted. Germany was ruled by a military dictatorship which in the dying days of the war forced the Emperor to abdicate and go into exile in the Netherlands. The 1919 Treaty of Versailles made provision for prosecuting him as a war criminal and his cousin King George V called him 'the greatest criminal in history'. But the Netherlands would not extradite him and the deposed emperor escaped the hanging that Lloyd George called for in the House of Commons. Wilhelm died of a pulmonary embolism in 1941 and was buried with full military honours, his coffin flanked by swastikas.

GEORGE EDWARD STANHOPE MOLYNEUX HERBERT, 5TH EARL OF CARNARVON

PATRONAGE 1892–1923

SIGNATURE GARMENT A fur-lined travelling tool bag

TOTAL SPEND £2,576 (£151,960 today)

CONNECTIONS The period leading up to World War I was the last time
Poole's ledgers were ablaze with British titled aristocrats. Contemporaries of the
Earl of Carnarvon include the earls of Dalhousie, Cawdor, Ancaster, Carysfort,
Crawford and Balcarres, Crewe, Camperdowne, Cavan, Essex, Feversham, Howth,
Kilmorey, Grey, Lovelace, Onslow, Mayo, Listowel, Lindsey, Jersey and Verulam.

Born at Highclere Castle, Hampshire, and educated at Eton and Trinity College, Cambridge, George Herbert, 5th Earl of Carnarvon (1866–1923), was the noted Egyptologist and financial backer of archaeologist Howard Carter, who discovered the tomb of Tutankhamun in the Valley of the Kings in 1922. The treasures discovered in the boy king's burial chambers dazzled the world and continue to do so. Tutankhamun's burial chamber was the first pharaoh's tomb in centuries to be discovered intact, though its outer chambers had been pillaged by grave robbers.

The Earl's early interest in archaeology manifested itself in amateur digs on the Highclere estate when he was a boy. In 1890, he acceded to the earldom aged twenty-four, and he married heiress Almina Wombwell five years later. There were rumours that the Countess was the illegitimate daughter of Lord Alfred de Rothschild (a Henry Poole man), who named Almina his heiress, bringing Highclere a dowry equal to £25 million today. The Earl lost little time in pursuing his interest in thoroughbred racehorses and automobiles that he took great delight in driving at high speed, and collecting photographs of semi-naked ladies either commissioned or photographed clandestinely by himself.

The charismatic Prince Victor Duleep Singh, son of the last Maharaja of Lahore and godson of Queen Victoria, was the Earl's partner-in-crime from their Eton days. Prince Victor was a friend of the Prince of Wales and, by all accounts, rather a corrupting influence on the 5th Earl of Carnarvon. It was he who allegedly organized a lady of the night to take the Earl's virginity. It was later alleged by author William Cross that Prince Victor fathered Lady Almina's eldest son, Lord Porchester, but this has been disputed by the present Earl and Countess of Carnarvon.

The 5th Earl first travelled to Egypt in 1903 to recover from a near-fatal car crash in Germany in 1901. While convalescing, the Earl began sponsoring archaeological digs. Lady Almina would accompany him on expeditions dressed as though for a Marlborough House garden party and dripping in jewels. The Earl met Howard Carter in 1907 and

financed his excavations in the Valley of the Queens in Luxor and the Valley of the Nobles. The duo had some success excavating the lost temples of Ramses IV and Queen Hatshepsut, but work was suspended for the duration of World War I and the Earl's funds began to dwindle.

In 1922, the Earl called Carter to Highclere to tell him that the funds had dried up for further excavations. But he agreed to a final dig in the Valley of the Kings because Carter put his case so passionately. On 4 November, Carter discovered a staircase beneath the sand and, on excavating further, the stele of 'boy king' Pharaoh Tutankhamun on the sealed doorway to the tomb. Carter telegraphed the Earl, who travelled to Egypt immediately, accompanied by his daughter, Lady Evelyn. In their presence, Carter broke the seal to the mummy's tomb. When the Earl asked, 'Can you see anything?' Carter replied, 'Yes, wonderful things!'

The Earl of Carnarvon did not live to see Tutankhamun's most precious treasures removed from the burial chamber, such as the gold and lapis death mask that is perhaps the most famous of the Pharaoh's treasures. He died in the Continental Savoy Hotel, Cairo, in April 1923 from an infected mosquito bite that led to a fatal bout of pneumonia. The Countess and his son and heir, Lord Porchester, were at his deathbed. Tutankhamun's treasures are now permanently displayed in the Cairo Museum and the Earl's personal bounty was sold to the Metropolitan Museum in New York by the Countess for $145,000 against death duties.

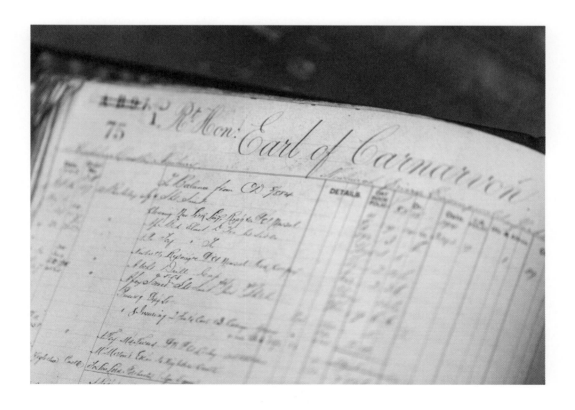

MISS CATHERINE 'SKITTLES' WALTERS

PATRONAGE 1863–1906

SIGNATURE GARMENT A superfine light-blue riding habit lined with silk and trimmed with braid; light-blue riding trousers lined with silk and trimmed with braid

TOTAL SPEND £10,495 (£694,600 today)

CONNECTIONS The last of the Victorian courtesans, Catherine Walters, had affairs with at least three of Henry Poole's more notable customers: the Prince of Wales, Prince Bonaparte and the 8th Duke of Devonshire.

Catherine 'Skittles' Walters (1839–1920) was the last of the great Victorian courtesans. Her benefactors included emperors, prime ministers, dukes and several members of the British royal family, including the future King Edward VII and Prince Alfred, Duke of Edinburgh – Henry Poole & Co men both. Skittles – so named because she briefly worked in a bowling alley near Chesterfield Street in Mayfair – possessed a classical beauty that was matched only by her proficiency as one of her era's most elegant horsewomen, leading to many *bons mots* about Skittles astride.

Skittles was one of London society's tourist attractions and rose to fame as a 'horse-breaker', exercising thoroughbreds on Hyde Park's Rotten Row. She drew huge crowds of sightseers who swooned with lust or envy at her skin-tight riding habits tailored by Henry Poole & Co and worn without underwear. She counted among her lovers the Marquess of Hartington, Emperor Napoleon III and the poet Wilfred Blunt. Unlike her Regency predecessor Harriete Wilson (to whom the Duke of Wellington wrote 'publish and be damned!'), Skittles was discreet and loyal to her many lovers, earning her a lifetime of annual stipends and the gratitude of her many admirers in public office.

Catherine Walters was born in Liverpool in 1839. In *Skittles: The Last Courtesan* by Rupert Hart-Davis (1970), he says of her early years 'beauty does not flower readily amidst squalid surroundings, and a young girl does not long retain a good figure, a clear eye, a fresh complexion and pearly teeth … where malnutrition, inadequate ventilation, lack of even the most elementary medical attention, dirt, disease [and] ignorance combine together to drag her down'. Her father, a Liverpool customs officer turned innkeeper in Cheshire, was a drunk. Her mother died in childbirth.

Skittles escaped her poor upbringing by taking up with George, Lord Fitzwilliam when she was sixteen years old. Lord Fitzwilliam set her up in London and settled £2,000 pounds on her and a £300 annual pension when they parted. Of her endlessly fascinating charms, diarist Henry Labouchère mentioned her grey-blue eyes, chestnut hair, 18-inch (46 cm) waist and the fact that Skittles had 'the most capricious heart I know and must be the only whore in history to retain her heart intact'.

Skittles became famed in London's demi-monde in 1861 when celebrated in poems, ballads and a painting exhibited at the Royal Academy called *The Pretty Horse Breaker* (or *The Shrew Tamed*) by Edwin Landseer. When the Hartington affair ended, Skittles tried her luck in Paris during the decadent Second Empire regime of Emperor Napoleon III. She was famed for driving her own carriage pulled by two thoroughbreds through the Bois de Boulogne flanked by two grooms astride.

In addition to the 8th Duke of Devonshire's 'pension', Skittles picked up further lifetime annuities from King Edward VII, who was eternally grateful for the return of 300 of his love letters. Skittles escaped the fate of many of the ladies in her profession who were left destitute and had to flee to the Continent to escape their debtors. She moved to her final address, 15 South Street in Mayfair, in 1872, where she lived as 'Mrs Baillie', though she never married a man of that name. In addition to South Street, she also owned two hotels: one in England and one in France. In 1879 the forty-year-old courtesan took up with a final grand passion, the nineteen-year-old Gerald de Saumerez, who would inherit her estate on her death in 1920.

The blue plaque identifying Catherine Walters's town house at No. 15 South Street in Mayfair.

LUCIUS BEEBE

PATRONAGE 1958–1960

SIGNATURE GARMENT A brown shantung silk single-breasted dressing
jacket and a pair of lightweight black barathea dining trousers

TOTAL SPEND £238 (£5,680 today)

CONNECTIONS Post-World War II, Poole's business was supported by
high-rolling American visitors such as Lucius Beebe. His American contemporaries
include George Whitney, J. P. Morgan Jr and His Excellency C. Douglas Dillon.

Café society columnist and bon viveur Lucius Beebe (1902–1966) cut a swathe through 'crazy luxe' Jazz Age New York with all the swagger of a seasoned flâneur. Describing his magpie mind, Beebe said, 'the Renaissance Man did a number of things, many of them well, a few beautifully. He was no damned specialist.' Like Oscar Wilde, he had a genius for aphorism and was entirely unacquainted with self-denial. He believed 'there is no food or time of the day and night when the service and consumption of champagne is not both appropriate and agreeable', and said of parsimony: 'Nowhere is moderation so debilitating and destructive of character as in the expenditure of money.'

Born into Boston wealth, Beebe had the distinction of being expelled from both Harvard and Yale for his elaborate practical jokes. When the bearded Dean of Yale endorsed Prohibition, Beebe donned fake whiskers, heckled from a box at the theatre and lobbed an empty liquor bottle on to the stage. At Harvard he would sport full evening dress, a monocle and a gold-tipped cane to morning class and kept a roulette wheel and fully-stocked bar in his rooms. He was credited with introducing white linen plus fours to Yale.

After publishing several volumes of florid poetry, Beebe found his metier in journalism as a social columnist. His dispatches from booths at New York's fashionable nightspots Sardi's, Quo Vadis, the Colony, 21 and Chasen's would become legendary. He judged the performance of Manhattan café society like a theatre critic, taking great delight in the new social order, in which stripper Gypsy Rose Lee was feted more than 'poor little rich girl' Barbara Hutton. In 1929 he was hired by the *New York Herald Tribune*. His column 'This New York' ran until 1944 and was read by one and a half million New Yorkers every morning.

Lucius Beebe was one of the few columnists who became as famous as the social circle he examined. At noon he could be found in the Oak Room at the Plaza ordering his first gin martini of the day and would close the Stork Club or El Morocco before retreating to a Broadway dive with Noël Coward to devour chopped chilli beef with beer. Like Coward, Beebe was a fixture on Cunard's transatlantic liners, travelling with a wardrobe that would shame a maharaja.

Beebe rightly said that 'no woman can stand seeing a man as well or painstakingly dressed as herself', while blithely doing just that. His wardrobe consisted of forty bespoke suits, two mink-lined overcoats with sable collars, numerous silk top hats and doeskin gloves and a collection of evening canes and gold cigarette cases. He favoured Henry Poole suits, shoes made by John Lobb and Charvet ties. In a lengthy paean to Poole in *The Holiday Magazine*, Beebe wrote: '[Henry Poole] is to tailoring what Rolls-Royce and Cartier are to automobiles and diamonds respectively.'

In 1944 Beebe attended a dinner held by Evalyn Walsh McLean, a lady famed for owning the Hope diamond. Also in the party was a square-jawed, handsome photographer called Charles Clegg. Clegg and Beebe became lovers – or partners as Beebe preferred to say – and would remain so for the rest of Beebe's life. They shared a passion for railway trains that would result in numerous co-authored books on the subject and the purchase of two private railway cars.

Together Beebe and Clegg bought the *Territorial Enterprise* newspaper in Virginia City and built its circulation up to being the bestselling weekly in the West. The *Territorial Enterprise*'s editorial policy was wryly described as 'pro-prostitution, pro-alcohol, pro-private railroad cars for the few and fearlessly anti-poor folks, anti-progress, anti-religion, anti-union, anti-diet, anti-vivisection and anti-preparing breakfast food'. Beebe actively campaigned when a city brothel was threatened with closure because of its proximity to a school. His headline? 'Don't move the girls: move the school!' But any antipathy between him and his neighbours was deflected when Beebe bought Virginia City a fire engine.

Beebe and Clegg were inseparable and travelled extensively in Europe and across America in their private railway cars the *Gold Coast* and the *Virginia City*, accompanied by their 11.7-kilo (18.5-stone) St Bernard, T-Bone Towser. The *Virginia City* was decorated by Hollywood set designer Robert Hinley in a style Beebe christened 'Venetian Renaissance Baroque'. The antique furniture that would not have shamed Versailles cost half a million dollars. There were a 7-metre (23-foot) observation drawing room, a dining room for eight, a fifty-bottle wine cellar, three state rooms, staff quarters and a small Turkish bath on board. When film director Cecil B. DeMille clapped eyes on the *Virginia City* he said: 'Tell the Madam I'll have a drink, but I'm too old to go up the stairs.'

In 1960 a new column, 'This Wild West', was offered to Beebe by the *San Francisco Chronicle*. By now he had written more than thirty-five books and was a familiar presence in the *New Yorker*, *Town & Country* and *Playboy*, as well as being honoured with a top-hat-and-tails front cover of *Time* magazine. He and Clegg sold the *Territorial Enterprise* in 1961 and bought a house in San Francisco. Beebe described ageing as 'high blood pressure, cheeriness at breakfast, a mellowing political philosophy and an inability to drink more than half a bottle of proof spirits at cocktail time without falling over the fire irons, all suggesting dark wings hovering overhead and the impending midnight croak of the raven'. He died of a heart attack aged sixty-three.

LIFE

LUCIUS BEEBE SETS A STYLE

JANUARY 16, 1939 **10** CENTS

REG. U S PAT OFF

SAVILE ROW TODAY

ALEX COOKE, HEAD CUTTER AND JOINT MD

In recent years we have witnessed the largest change in men's silhouettes since the 1980s – the very short, slim jackets and ankle-length trousers – and I feel this has influenced much of present-day men's fashion. Poole's still love to make their own silhouette: a natural shoulder line, chest drape, a nipped waist and some flair to the hip. We feel this gives an elegant, individual look. But we cannot ignore current trends and have become more diverse in our fabrics, style and construction.

Cloths have become much lighter in weight. These days we consider a winter suit to be a 11–14 oz (300–390 g), which is far lighter than the 14–18 oz (390–450 g) of not too many years ago. Cloths can now be had in featherweight 6.5 oz (180 g). Many fashion brands utilize similar cloths, but take away the natural characteristics by bonding a back layer to it. We still use the same tailoring techniques that have been used for over a hundred years, thus keeping the energy of the cloth.

We have been cutting jackets noticeably shorter and neater than in the past, although we always advise the client on what would be a proportioned cut for them. It's so easy to cut a short jacket, but when it's for a realistic 44–46-inch chest, the higher the hemline, the neater we have to go on the girth and that results in a boxy jacket … not an elegant look.

Glance in the window of any designer store and you'll see a slim-figured 36-inch mannequin adorned in a super-fitted jacket. Look at the rear of the mannequin, with inches of cloth pinned out, and perhaps you will realize that it's not a realistic silhouette for a man. But for sure the partner you're standing with expects us to be able to make you look like that. I would argue that because of this shift in cloth weight along with a less structured jacket, modern men's tailors have to be far more meticulous in their manufacture.

We see many of our clients travel less for business, whether because of concerns about carbon footprint or the tech behind video conferencing. In addition to our many international trunk shows, we have become far more approachable about visiting individuals around the world, whether that be Europe, Russia or the Middle East. These clients will likely visit London, but lead times can be reduced by personal visits. New bespoke business tends to come from tech companies, entrepreneurs and hedge funds. In Silicon Valley, where dressing down is the rule, new clients might order sports jackets to wear with jeans and sneakers, but there's an increasing demand for suits – albeit worn without ties.

With escalating costs involved in a trunk show and our small workforce, we are selective about seeking out new markets. We have seen an increase in Indian and Chinese clients and are considering trunk shows to help reduce lead times. We are astounded by the diversity of our client base. Of course the majority of our customers are forty- to seventy-year-old lawyers, bankers, architects, designers and accountants. But recently we have seen an increase in younger clients, many of whom visit the showroom in jeans, flip-flops and a T-shirt; very different from the debonair chap in a three-piece and handmade shoes.

The new tech/media clientele do have an appreciation for finer things – shoes, watches, gadgets – and realize that there is a place for bespoke tailoring in their wardrobes. They'll certainly need a dining suit from the creator; they'll likely want a velvet smoking jacket, worn with an open-necked shirt and jeans; a few suits, because they can actually look very cool in them; and some unstructured jackets just so they can look a little different from the other guys in HQ. We're seeing these clients ordering suits in linen/silk mixes, corduroys and vibrant tweeds: suiting fabrics that are far more adventurous than grey herringbones!

Poole's has recently partnered in limited edition co-designed collaborations with Adidas and Canada Goose – brands that have depth and heritage that complement Henry Poole. The Adidas NMD made using our Churchill grey chalk-stripe House Cloth was available only in Europe and sold out the first morning, but that didn't stop enquiries from all over the world. The W1 Canada Goose down blazer inspired by the hand-sewn quilting inside classic Poole's evening tails was available worldwide, but it was particularly pleasing that it created interest around us in China. The collaborations have brought young people to us in Savile Row who appreciate that our garments are still cut and tailored on the premises. It is extremely important to expose our brand to a demographic that perhaps would not have come across us.

It is perhaps difficult for an individual to realize how they will feel in a bespoke garment but what we do is impossible to replicate in ready-to-wear, be that designer or high street. I guarantee that the man who arrives at a restaurant in a beautifully cut overcoat and a fantastic suit will command far more respect and admiration than the man nobody notices in the waterproof, breathable, light-weight down jacket. This is not about being flashy, it's about feeling confident and special. Bespoke gives a feeling of sophistication and confidence on a completely different level from the immediate gratification purchase. Even in this day and age, 'good things come to those who wait' is still a very relevant phrase.

CEREMONIAL TAILORING

KEITH LEVETT, DIRECTOR

Henry Poole & Co has held the Royal Warrant as livery tailor to every British monarch from Queen Victoria in 1869 to Queen Elizabeth II today. But the company's authority on ceremonial tailoring really dates back to 1843. Towards the end of his life, James Poole was solicited by the Lord Chamberlain's Department to modernize the uniform worn by civilians attending court.

Using the best black silk velvet, James Poole cut a tailcoat, waistcoat and breeches that echoed the lines of the formal evening wear that was beginning to emerge as a separate order of dress at this time. Shrewdly, he retained the magnificent cut-steel buttons, shoe buckles and swords from Georgian court dress and, for good measure, appeased the older generation going to court by tidying up the cut of the former style and cutting it in the same crisp silk velvet. Thus, two subtly different types of civil uniform emerged: Old Style and New Style Velvet Court Dress. The latter was immediately popular and made in very significant numbers right up until the outbreak of World War II, when the requirement for gentlemen to wear such sumptuous uniforms ended. Old Style survives as the official dress of the High Sheriff and of certain members of the judiciary today.

Historically, Poole's produced virtually every conceivable variety of ceremonial uniform, notably military, court, diplomatic, ministerial and livery. When we opened a dedicated Livery Department in 1875, fifty to seventy craftspeople worked a seven-day week, such was the demand. Today the call for such magnificent finery is inevitably diminished, but the company still has excellent knowledge of the purpose and function of these uniforms and of the manner in which they ought to be cut and made. We continue to produce state and other dress livery worn in the British royal household and mews. In addition, the company still produces many of the traditional uniforms worn by the Lieutenancy and those of the High Sheriffs in England and Wales.

Most of the ceremonial uniforms still made by Henry Poole & Co were designed a century or more ago and as such have little reference to modern-day tailoring. That the company is still able to produce such clothing is perhaps remarkable in itself. However, because we understand historically how such uniforms developed and were cut and crafted, we are able to maintain the same high standards of workmanship required when replacing historical livery or other garments. As livery tailors to HM The Queen it is not uncommon to be called upon to replace garments that were cut in this house as far back as the 1870s, not because they are worn out, but because modern bodies will simply not fit into them.

Our attitude is simple: formal ceremonial uniforms of whatever character should, as far as possible, be crafted to the same standards as those they replace; to do anything less would be to create carnival costume. The state and other livery garments made under Royal Warrant are built to last, and have to be. Carriage livery endures a fair amount of wear and tear in service and horses have scant appreciation of history or fine tailoring.

An eye for detail is extremely important when cutting and making ceremonial dress. The correct patterns of gold or silver braid in the correct widths – some of them varying only by one sixteenth of an inch – is all-important and can make all the difference between stately and tawdry. All too often one sees uniforms, military or otherwise, cut from substandard cloth and laced with whatever happened to be on the shelf and looking one stage removed from theatre costume. Poole doesn't do that. Poole does it correctly, or not at all. Today, virtually all our superfine uniform cloths, gold lace and buttons are made to order following exacting specifications gleaned and understood through decades of experience to ensure that new ceremonial garments are true to those they replace.

I joined Poole's in 1989, having developed a fascination with historic military and ceremonial dress at an early age. The blue, white and gold of the naval officers' uniforms of Nelson's time seemed particularly beautiful. Much later, I would write to trustees of various national collections for access to study historic garments, learning much about the development of cut and tailoring techniques at any given period as well as something of the characters of the men who wore these exceptional garments. The task of making livery demands skill and dedication. A coachman's full state livery, for example, requires upwards of 45 metres (50 yards) of gold lace to be hand-sewn on to each coat and waistcoat.

The Royal Warrant has been likened to a peerage for trade. Those companies in possession of one form part of an elite group whose quality of manufacture, knowledge and reliability set them apart. A warrant from the Crown confirms the integrity of the company and, while we never trade directly off it, its very presence above our name acts as an assurance to would-be customers that our product is the best of British.

Right: Black velvet court dress tailcoat with distinctive cut-steel buttons in the cutting rooms.

THE BIRTH OF THE DINNER JACKET

In 1865, the Prince of Wales (the future King Edward VII), known to his family as 'Bertie', asked his tailor and friend Henry Poole to cut a short celestial-blue evening coat to be worn for informal dinners at Sandringham, his private estate in Norfolk. This garment, modelled on day dress but cut in evening cloth, was the blueprint for what we now know in Britain as the dinner jacket. Evening dress designed especially for individual royal residences was still in commission from the Hanoverian dynasty. The dark-blue tailcoats with red facings still worn by royal males at Windsor Castle date back to the reign of King George III. The Prince of Wales's Norfolk estate was bought in 1862 and the red-brick mansion house built as a retreat from the sartorial protocol of court. So we can presume Bertie's dinner jacket was cut for comfort and as a release from the tailcoats, breeches, orders and decorations worn when the Prince dined in public.

In the etymology of British bespoke tailoring, it is notoriously difficult to map how a particular garment evolved over and above the certainty that its origins will be found in equestrian or military attire. Despite the best efforts of the author and of livery director Keith Levett, no photograph of the Prince of Wales wearing the prototype dinner jacket at Sandringham could be found in the Royal Archives at Windsor. This is hardly surprising. Even the Princess of Wales, a keen amateur photographer who might conceivably photograph her husband at dinner, did not wield her camera until the 1880s. Fortunately, we have the Prince of Wales's ledger entry in the Poole Archive to precisely date the construction of the first dinner jacket as 1865.

A more contentious question is how and when Henry Poole's dinner jacket crossed the Atlantic and became known as the tuxedo. The story upheld by New York's Tuxedo Club, founded in 1886 by Pierre Lorillard, is as follows. Tuxedo Club member and financier James Brown Potter sailed for England in 1886 with his beautiful wife, Cora. On being introduced to the Prince of Wales, whose notoriously wandering eye fell upon Cora, the Potters were invited to Sandringham for a weekend dine-and-sleep. Potter, not knowing the form for an informal evening in the company of British royalty, asked his tailor, Henry Poole, what he should wear. Poole answered with no little confidence that a short celestial-blue evening coat was generally considered appropriate.

Thus James Potter ordered a dinner jacket from Poole's and returned to New York with it, where he introduced the dinner jacket to fellow Tuxedo Club members. The story is persuasive. Cora Potter was certainly pretty enough to enflame the Prince of Wales's lust, and Potter did return to America. Cora did not. Like the Prince's mistress Lillie Langtry, Mrs Brown-Potter (as she was billed) went on to become one of the first society ladies to

Opposite: Classic one-button barathea dinner jacket.

pursue a successful career on the West End stage. Cora's divorce from Potter in 1900 is well documented. Sadly for the sake of a good story, there is no record of James Potter's being a customer of Henry Poole in 1886 or any other year.

However, the founding fathers of the Tuxedo Club, Messrs William Waldorf Astor, Robert Goelet, Ogden Mills and Pierre Lorillard himself, are all well-documented Poole's men in the 1860s. It is likely that these social peacocks copied the Prince of Wales's dinner jacket when visiting their tailor and brought the jacket back to America. It is also likely that these chaps attended a bachelor party at Delmonico's in Manhattan wearing their dinner jackets and this was the moment New Yorkers christened the garment a tuxedo.

Another rather colourful character in the Henry Poole family who lays claim to introducing the dinner jacket to America is Evander Berry Wall, 'King of the Dudes', who is alleged to have worn a short dinner jacket to a formal event in Saratoga in 1887, postdating Lorillard and his tuxedo chums. Wall was a prolific Poole's customer from 1881 to 1935 and the tailor was credited in newspaper articles dated 1885 as Berry Wall's 'suit designer by special permission'. Wall earned his 'King of the Dudes' moniker in 1888 when he won a sartorial duel in Saratoga Springs against a fellow dandy by parading forty outfits in one day, all cut by Henry Poole. The lack of a connection between Wall and the Tuxedo Club, however, seems to scupper his claim.

HENRY POOLE & CO ROYAL WARRANTS OF APPOINTMENT

1858: HIM Emperor Napoleon III of the French

1863: HRH The Prince of Wales (King Edward VII)

1868: HRH The Duke of Edinburgh

1868: HRH The Crown Prince of Prussia

1869: HM Queen Victoria

1869: HM King Leopold II of the Belgians

1869: HRH The Crown Prince of Denmark

1870: HRH The Prince of Teck

1870: HRH Prince Christian of Schleswig-Holstein

1870: The Khedive of Egypt

1871: HRH Prince Oscar of Sweden and Norway

1871: HM King Amadeus I of Spain

1871: Prince Louis of Hesse

1874: HRH Crown Prince Alexander of Russia (HIM Emperor Alexander III)

1874: HIM Emperor Pedro II of Brazil

1875: HIM Emperor Alexander II of Russia

1877: HM The King of the Hellenes

1878: HRH Crown Prince Rudolf of Austria

1879: HM King Umberto I of Italy

1879: HIM Emperor Wilhelm I of Germany

1881: HIM Emperor Alexander III of Russia

1891: HG The Duke of Genoa

1891: HG Friedrich, Grossherzog of Baden

1892: HG The Duke of Aosta

1892: HRH Prince Emanuel of Savoy

1892: HIM The Shah of Persia

1893: HM The King of Denmark

1902: HM King Edward VII of Great Britain, Emperor of India

1903: HRH Prince Albrecht of Prussia

1905: HH The Maharaja Gaekwar of Baroda

1906: HIM The Shah of Persia

1910: The Khedive of Egypt

1911: HM Dowager Queen Alexandra of Great Britain, Dowager Empress of India

1922: HRH The Prince of Wales (King Edward VIII)

1923: The Imperial Household of Japan

1928: HM King George V of Great Britain, Emperor of India

1936: HM King Boris III of the Bulgarians

1940: HM King George VI of Great Britain, Emperor of India

1959: HIM Emperor Haile Selassie of Ethiopia

1976: HM Queen Elizabeth II of Great Britain

HONOURABLE MENTIONS

THE EXTENDED HENRY POOLE & CO HALL OF FAME*

1846–1850
Thomas Cubitt (Architect)
HRH Prince Jérôme Bonaparte (Ex-King of
  Westphalia)
Baron Meyer Amschel de Rothschild (Politician)
Baron Lionel de Rothschild (Banker/Philanthropist)
James Hamilton, 1st Duke of Abercorn (MP and
  Lord Lieutenant of Ireland)
James 'Jem' Mason (Grand National Jockey)

1850–1860
Sir Robert Peel (Prime Minister/Founder of
  Metropolitan Police)
Baron James de Rothschild (Politician/Philanthropist)
HIM Empress Eugénie of the French (Wife of
  Emperor Napoleon III)
William Russell, 8th Duke of Bedford (Politician)
HRH Grand Duke Charles of Saxe-Weimar (Ruler)
Junius Morgan (Banker)
Henry Paget, 2nd Marquess of Anglesey (Politician/
  Lord Chamberlain of the Household)
Francis D'Arcy-Osborne, 7th Duke of Leeds
  (Politician)
Henry Fitzroy, 5th Duke of Grafton (Politician)
HIH Grand Duchess Maria Alexandrovna of Russia
  (Wife of HRH Prince Alfred, Duke of Edinburgh)
HG Louise, Duchess of Manchester and Duchess
  of Devonshire (Society Hostess/Wife of the
  7th Duke of Manchester and 8th Duke of
  Devonshire)
HH Princess Pauline von Metternich (Socialite/
  'The Coco Monkey')

1860–1870
Prince Charles de Sagan (French Dandy)
Prince Nicholas Troubetskoy (Chamberlain of
  Russian Imperial Court)
HRH Grand Duke Michael Nikolaevich of Russia
  (Son of Tsar Nicholas I)
Henry Somerset, 9th Duke of Beaufort (Aide-de-
  Camp to Queen Victoria)
Prince Boris Galitzine (Physicist)

Antoine, 10th Duc de Grammont (Diplomat)
Prince Pierre Soltykoff (Russian Collector of Clocks
  and Watches)
HG William Drogo Montagu, 7th Duke of
  Manchester (MP)
William Hamilton, 11th Duke of Hamilton and 8th
  Duke of Brandon (Premier Peer of Scotland)
HRH Prince Adalbert of Prussia (Admiral)
HRH Grand Duke Frederic of Baden (Sovereign
  Duke)
Prince Richard Metternich (Austrian Diplomat)
Field Marshal Prince Henry Bariatinsky (Russian
  General)
George Sutherland-Leveson-Gower, 3rd Duke of
  Sutherland (MP)
HRH Prince Mustafa Pasha of Egypt (Ottoman-
  Egyptian Prince)
John Beresford, 5th Marquess of Waterford (MP/
  Master of the Buckhounds)
Sir Edward Bulwer-Lytton (Poet/Playwright)
Le Prince de la Tour Auvergne (Minister of Foreign
  Affairs for Emperor Napoleon III)
George Spencer-Churchill, 8th Duke of
  Marlborough (British Peer)
Francis, Duke of Teck (Queen Mary's Father)
John Douglas, 9th Marquess of Queensbury
  (Nemesis of Oscar Wilde)
John Campbell, 9th Duke of Argyll (Governor
  General of Canada)
HRH Prince Christian of Holstein (Husband of
  Princess Helena of the United Kingdom)
HM King Luis I of Portugal (Monarch)
Louis Comfort Tiffany (American Jeweller)
Sir Edwin Landseer (Artist)
Alexander Duff, 1st Duke of Fife (Married to
  Princess Louise of Great Britain)
HRH Frederick William, Grand Duke of
  Mecklenburgh-Strelitz (Ruling Grand Duke)
HRH Duke of Edinburgh (Queen Victoria's Son)
James Brudenell, 7th Earl of Cardigan (Commander
  of the Light Brigade)
Henry Petty-Fitzmaurice, 5th Marquis of Lansdowne

(Fifth Governor General of Canada)
William Holman Hunt (Artist)
HIM Empress Maria Feodorovna of Russia
(Dowager Empress)
HIM Empress Frederick of Germany (British
Princess Royal)
HM Queen Victoria (Queen of Great Britain and
Empress of India)
HRH Princess Helena of England (Daughter of
Queen Victoria)
HIH Prince Imperial of the French (Son of Emperor
Napoleon III of the French)

1870–1880

Lord Randolph Churchill (Politician/Father of
Winston Churchill)
Carlo Pellegrini (*Vanity Fair* Caricaturist)
Lord Arthur Somerset (Equerry to the Prince
of Wales)
Prince Louis de Lichtenstein (Social Reformer/
'the Red Prince')
Sir Coutts Lindsay (Watercolour Artist)
HRH Prince Arthur, 1st Duke of Connaught
and Strathearn (Son of Queen Victoria/Tenth
Governor General of Canada)
HIH Grand Duke Vladimir Alexandrovich of Russia
(Son of Emperor Alexander II of Russia)
Sir William Gull (Surgeon to Queen Victoria)
HH Prince Frederick Lobkowicz (Bohemian Noble)
George, 4th Marquis of Cholmondeley (Lord Great
Chamberlin of England)
HRH Louis IV, Grand Duke of Hesse and by Rhine
(German Ruler)
HH Prince William of Württemburg (German
Royal Prince)
HM Queen Marie Henriette of the Belgians
(Queen Consort)

1880–1890

HH Prince Alexander of Bulgaria (Royal Prince)
HH Nawab Nazim of Bengal (Bangladeshi Ruler)
Evander Berry Wall (American Dandy/'King of the
Dudes')
Arthur Wellesley, 2nd Duke of Wellington (Soldier/
Politician/Master of the Horse)
HRH Prince Frederick William of Hesse-Kassel
(Elector of Hesse)
HH The Maharaja of Mysore (Indian Ruler)
HIH Grand Duke Vladimir of Russia (Son of
Emperor Alexander II)

HIH Grand Duke Sergei Alexandreovich of Russia
(Son of Emperor Alexander II)
Sir Arthur Sullivan (Composer/Gilbert and Sullivan)
John Thynne, 4th Marquis of Bath (Diplomat)
Andrew Carnegie (Industrialist/Philanthropist)
Henry Wellesley, 3rd Duke of Wellington (MP)
HH The Maharaja of Cooch Behar (Indian Ruler)
Col Hon Oliver Montagu (Royal Equerry)
Lord Napier (Viceroy of India)
HRH The Prince of Naples (Future King Victor
Emanuel II of Italy)
HRH Prince Albert of Prussia (Field Marshal/Regent
of Brunswick)
HM Queen Olga of the Hellenes (Queen Consort)

1890–1900

HRH Hereditary Grand Duke Alphonse of
Luxembourg (Ruler)
Charles Spencer-Churchill, 9th Duke of
Marlborough (Soldier)
Sir George Sitwell (British Aristocrat)
HH The Raj Kumar of Cooch Behar (Queen
Consort)
King Lewanika of Barotseland (Monarch)
HH Prince Aga Khan (Spiritual Leader)
Motilal Nehru (Indian Statesman)
HRH Prince Danilo of Montenegro (Crown Prince/
Soldier)
Prince Vladimir Orlov (Adviser to Tsar Nicholas II)
Cornelius Vanderbilt (Financier/Philanthropist)
HRH George, Prince of Wales (Future Monarch)
HM Queen Alexandra (Queen Consort)
HH The Maharaja of Gujarat (Indian Ruler)
HH The Maharaja of Tajore (Indian Ruler)
Payne Whitney (Financier)
HIH Grand Duchess Elizabeth of Russia (Grand
Duchess/Nun)
HRH Princess Victoria of Wales (British Royal
Princess)
HRH The Duchess of Teck (Mother of Queen Mary)

1900–1910

Henri de Toulouse-Lautrec (Post-Impressionist
Artist)
HH The Maharaja of Alwar (Indian Ruler)
HIM Emperor Taisho of Japan (Monarch)
Alfred Harmsworth, 1st Lord Northcliffe (Press
Baron)
HM King Chulalongkorn Rama V of Siam (King
of Thailand)

Consuelo, Duchess of Marlborough (American
	Heiress)
HIH The Emperor of Abyssinia (Monarch)

1910–1920
Victor Cavendish, 9th Duke of Devonshire (MP/
	Eleventh Governor General of Canada)
General Sir Dighton Probyn (Soldier/Equerry to
	Dowager Queen Alexandra)
HRH Prince Felix Yusupov (Murderer of Rasputin)

1920–1930
Hon Anthony Asquith (Film Director)
John Spencer-Churchill, 10th Duke of Marlborough
	(Soldier)
David Beatty, Admiral of the Fleet, 1st Earl Beatty
	(Sailor)
HG The 11th Duke of Bedford (Soldier/MP)
Marcel Boussac (Founder of Christian Dior)
Major HH The Maharaja of Jodhpur (Indian Ruler)
HH The Maharaja of Kolharpur (Indian Ruler)
HIM The Crown Prince of Japan (Emperor
	Hirohito)
HH The Maharaja of Kapurthala (Indian Ruler)
HH The Maharaja of Jaipur (Indian Ruler)
HE Shigeru Yoshida (Prime Minister of Japan)

1930–1940
HH Prince Kyril of Bulgaria (Prince Regent of
	Bulgaria)
HH The Prince of Bikaner (Indian Ruler)
Lionel Barrymore (Actor)
HH The Maharaja of Dhgarbanga (Indian Ruler)
HH The Maharaja of Alwar (Indian Ruler)
Hastings Russell, 12th Duke of Bedford (Far Right
	Politician/Ornithologist)
HH The Sultan of Muscat and Oman (Monarch)
HH The Raja of Nilgiri (Ruler)
HH The Maharaja of Patiala (Indian Ruler)

1940–1950
HM King George VI (Monarch)
HIM The Empress of Ethiopia (Queen Consort)
HIH The Crown Prince of Ethiopia (Heir to the
	Throne)
Lord Redesdale (Father of the Mitford Sisters)
Frank Lloyd Wright (Architect)
HH Prince Stanislas Radziwill (Husband of Princess
	Lee Radziwill née Bouvier)
Rt Hon Sir Alan Lascelles (Royal Equerry)

HH The Maharaja of Bhopal (Indian Ruler)
HH The Khabaka of Buganda (Ugandan Ruler)
Rt Hon Neville Chamberlain (Prime Minister)
HH Prince Mukarram Jan of Hyderabad (Indian
	Prince)
HM The Nawab of Hyderabad (Indian Honorary
	Ruler)
HRH The Duke of Windsor (Ex-King Edward VIII)

1950–1960
Robert Mitchum (Actor)
HE Prime Minister H. S. Imru of Ethiopia
	(Politician)
Sir Ernest Fisk (English/Australian Entrepreneur)
HIH Crown Prince Akihito of Japan (Future
	Emperor)
HRH Crown Prince Faisal of Saudia Arabia (Future
	Ruler)
HE C. Douglas Dillon (American Ambassador)
Esmond Harmsworth, 2nd Viscount Rothermere
	(Press Baron)
HM Queen Elizabeth II of Great Britain (Monarch)

* *In a bid to reduce the extended Hall of Fame to a
manageable length only those entries in the Oxford
Dictionary of National Biography, subjects in the
National Portrait Gallery collection and/or individual
Wikipedia profiles have been included.*

ACKNOWLEDGMENTS

I first named Poole's chairman Angus Cundey the godfather of Savile Row in 2006. To this I would add guardian and friend for steering this book to completion. Of the Poole's family, I would particularly like to thank Simon Cundey, Alex Cooke and Richard Craig, who have supported my work in the archives at Poole's for well over a decade with great patience and kindness. The restoration of the Poole's ledgers and the evolution of the book was very much a joint effort with Keith Levett. This is my sixth Thames & Hudson book with Lucas Dietrich, so we must be doing something right. *Henry Poole* is my fifth book art-directed by Pete Dawson at Grade Design, who it is a pleasure and a privilege to work with every time. This is the third title that Andy Barnham has shot as principal photographer and, on this occasion, he was nothing short of heroic. This is my first Thames & Hudson book edited by Kirsty Seymour-Ure, who negotiated a royal flush of crowned heads in record time and improved this manuscript considerably. My research for the historical profiles was carried out at the London Library and my thanks to Lara Mingay for the gift of membership.

JAMES SHERWOOD

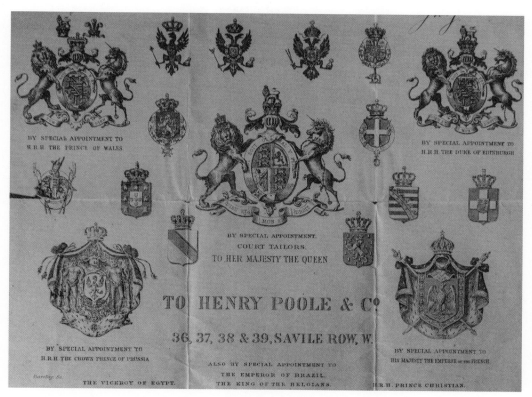

Detail of Poole's 1884 letterhead displaying the provenance of twenty-two of the firm's Royal Warrants.

CAPTIONS TO GALLERIES

Page 1: The Henry Poole & Co showroom at No. 15 Savile Row in 2019.

Page 2: HM Queen Elizabeth II rides out in the Irish State Coach in 2015. The Coachman wears State Livery tailored by Henry Poole & Co.

Page 3: Director Keith Levett sews a state cypher onto a coachman's full state livery in 2011.

Page 4: Cutter Daniel McDonald (above) and under-cutter Charles Button (below).

Page 5: Above: Director Thomas Pendry (left) and cutter William Smith (right); below: Head cutter and managing director Alex Cooke.

Pages 6–7: Poole's showroom gallery of illustrious customers: (left to right) King Edward VII, Winston Churchill, Prince Francis of Teck and Napoleon, Prince Imperial of the French.

Page 8: Henry Poole & Co. ambassador model and designer David Gandy.

Page 10: Detail from a coat tailored in Poole's stock grey 10/11oz flannel.

Pages 88–89: The palatial façade of Nos 36–39 Savile Row that was home to Henry Poole from 1846 until its demolition in 1961.

Page 90: The design of British royal coachmen's state livery can be traced back to the early years of Queen Victoria's reign and has remained virtually unchanged.

Page 91: Detail of a Henry Poole & Co Privy Council tailcoat made for the 6th Earl of Clarendon, Chamberlain to King George VI, *c.* 1931. The intricate gold bullion embroidery was so lavish that it could take up to four months to complete.

Page 92: Howard Cundey, proprietor of Poole's from 1883 to 1927, photographed *c.* 1903 when he wed Mabel Houle.

Page 93: Howard Cundey's grandson, the present chairman of Henry Poole & Co, Angus Cundey MBE (2015).

Page 94: Detail of a bespoke forest-green silk velvet smoking jacket with silk facings and frogging.

Page 95: Two ledgers contain more than 1,000 gilt livery buttons struck for Poole's royal and aristocratic customers. The crowned eagle is the cipher of Emperor Napoleon III made between 1852 and 1870.

Page 196: Double-breasted stock model for display tailored in midnight-blue birdseye.

Page 197: *Top left.* Model David Gandy wears a blazer tailored in Henry Poole House Check. The cloth was first woven as a tweed in 1989 by Harrisons of Edinburgh and reconsidered in lighter 11/12 oz (300/340 g) lambswool in 2014. *Top right.* Adidas Global Senior Production Manager Patrick Reinhardt wears a blue barathea dinner jacket with silk peak lapels. *Below left.* Land Rover Design Director Gerry McGovern wears a two-piece suit tailored in 'Churchill House Cloth' grey chalk-stripe flannel. *Below right.* Then US Secretary of State John Kerry and British Foreign Secretary William Hague both tailored by Henry Poole (2013).

Page 198: The façade of Poole's at No. 15 Savile Row, where the firm has resided since 1982.

Page 199: The showroom and cutting boards at No. 15 Savile Row. Select cabinets, chairs, Royal Warrants and Napoleon III's eagle are 19th-century antique pieces from the Nos 36–39 Savile Row shop.

Page 200: Seventh-generation Henry Poole & Co managing director Simon Cundey.

Page 201: Director Keith Levett, who is a world-class authority on ceremonial tailoring.

Page 202: Window display stock model of the 'Churchill House Cloth' grey chalk-stripe flannel coat and vest before the baste stitches have been removed.

Page 203: *Above.* Adidas Originals x Henry Poole 2017 remix of the Adidas Originals NMD featuring the Churchill chalk-stripe flannel. *Below.* In 2019 Poole's and Canada Goose collaborated on the co-designed W1 Blazer made in red, navy and graphite flannel for men and women. The quilted goose-down lining brought together 19th-century tailoring techniques and 21st-century performance wear.

ILLUSTRATION CREDITS

All photography is by Andy Barnham unless otherwise stated below.

2: Ian Gavan - WPA Pool/Getty Images; 3: Dan Kitwood/Getty Images; 4–7: Henry Poole & Co; 8: Richard Hardcastle; 13: Henry Poole & Co; 15: Dan Kitwood/Getty Images; 19: Paul Popper/Popperfoto/Getty Images; 23: Capt. Horton /IWM/Getty Images; 28: Henry Poole & Co; 32: DEA/G. Dagli Orti/De Agostini/Getty Images; 34: Universal History Archive/Getty Images; 37: The Art Collector/Print Collector/Getty Images; 40: Keystone-France/Gamma-Keystone/Getty Images; 42: Chris Hellier/Corbis/Getty Images; 45: Henry Guttmann/Hulton Archive/Getty Images; 47: Fine Art Images/Heritage Images/Getty Images; 50: Imagno/Getty Images; 52: ullstein bild/Getty Images; 54, 64: Universal History Archive/UIG/Getty Images; 66: Time Life Pictures/Mansell/The LIFE Picture Collection/Getty Images; 68: Library of Congress, Washington, D.C.; 71: Hulton Archive/Getty Images; 72: Culture Club/Getty Images; 75: Time Life Pictures/Mansell/The LIFE Picture Collection/Getty Images; 77: Bettmann/Getty Images; 81: Marie Hansen/The LIFE Picture Collection/Getty Images; 83: J. A. Hampton/Topical Press Agency/Getty Images; 88–89: Henry Poole & Co; 90: Tim Graham/Getty Images; 91: Henry Poole & Co; 93: Henry Poole & Co; 104: Time Life Pictures/Mansell/The LIFE Picture Collection/Getty Images; 107: W. & D. Downey/Getty Images; 109: Picture Post/Hulton Archive/Getty Images; 111: Hulton Archive/Getty Images; 113: Library of Congress/Corbis/VCG/Getty Images; 115: Bettmann/Getty Images; 118, 121: Hulton Archive/Getty Images; 124: ullstein bild/Getty Images; 127: Photo 12/Alamy Stock Photo; 133: Keystone-France/Gamma-Rapho/Getty Images; 136: The Print Collector/Getty Images; 139: Hulton Archive/Getty Images; 141: The Print Collector/Getty Images; 145: Josef Albert/ullstein bild/Getty Images; 147: DEA/Biblioteca Ambrosiana/Getty Images; 150: Three Lions/Getty Images; 153: Library of Congress, Washington, D.C.; 156, 159: George Rinhart/Corbis/Getty Images; 163: Keystone-France/Gamma-Keystone/Getty Images; 169: Henry Poole & Co; 173: London Stereoscopic Company/Getty Images; 175: Time Life Pictures/Mansell/The LIFE Picture Collection/Getty Images; 178: Hulton Archive/Getty Images; 180: The Print Collector/Getty Images; 182: Photo12/UIG/Getty Images; 186: London Stereoscopic Company/Getty Images; 189: Fine Art Images/Heritage Images/Getty Images; 191: Granger Historical Picture Archive/Alamy Stock Photo; 194: Bettmann/Getty Images; 197 top left: Richard Hardcastle; 197 bottom left: Gerry McGovern; 197 top right: Henry Poole & Co; 197 bottom right: Ben Stansall/AFP/Getty Images; 198, 200–201: Henry Poole & Co; 203 top: Henry Poole & Co; 203 bottom: Canada Goose; 206: Henry Poole & Co; 209: Jack English/Working Title/Kobal/REX/Shutterstock; 213: W. & D. Downey/Getty Images; 214: Baron/Hulton Archive/Getty Images; 219: Library of Congress/Corbis/VCG/Getty Images; 221: Popperfoto/Getty Images; 224: Hulton Archive/Getty Images; 227: The Print Collector/Getty Images; 230: Hulton Archive/Getty Images; 233: Mary Evans Picture Library; 234: Mick Sinclair/Alamy Stock Photo; 237: Rex Hardy Jr./The LIFE Picture Collection/Getty Images; 239: Henry Poole & Co

INDEX

Page numbers in *italic* refer to the illustrations

ABOUT THE AUTHORS

Author and broadcaster James Sherwood has been working with the tailors of Savile Row on exhibitions, books and television series since 2006. This book, his sixth published by Thames & Hudson, is the culmination of a decade-long project to restore and catalogue Henry Poole & Co's customer ledgers.

Simon Cundey joined his family's firm Henry Poole & Co in 1987, after studying at the London College of Fashion. He took on the US market as chief marketing officer in 1985 and is now joint managing director and the co-owner of the firm with his father, Angus Cundey. He also serves on the Livery of the Merchant Taylors and chairs the Golden Shears Awards – the Oscars of the tailoring industry.

Alex Cooke is joint managing director and head cutter at Henry Poole & Co Originally trained as a designer womenswear pattern cutter, he now drafts and designs for discerning clients in the Henry Poole cutting room, as well as making many visits to the US, Japan and the Middle East.

Keith Levett began his apprenticeship with Henry Poole & Co in 1989, learning both tailoring and cutting before gravitating towards ceremonial and other specialist tailoring. A director since 2013, he is responsible for maintaining the company's Warrant of Appointment to Her Majesty the Queen.

For the Cundey family

First published in the United Kingdom in 2019 by Thames & Hudson Ltd,
181A High Holborn, London WC1V 7QX

Henry Poole & Co.: The First Tailor of Savile Row © 2019 Thames & Hudson Ltd, London
Text © 2019 James Sherwood
Foreword © 2019 Simon Cundey
'Savile Row Today' © 2019 Alex Cooke
'Ceremonial Tailoring' © 2019 Keith Levett
All images © the copyright holders, please see the illustration credits list on page 251.

Designed by Peter Dawson, gradedesign.com

British Library Cataloguing-in-Publication Data
A catalogue record for this book is available from the British Library

ISBN 978-0-500-021958

Printed and bound in China by Toppan Leefung Printing Limited

To find out about all our publications, please visit **www.thamesandhudson.com**.
There you can subscribe to our e-newsletter, browse or download our current catalogue,
and buy any titles that are in print.

R 450

R 451

R 452

R 453

R 454

R 460

R 461

R 462

R 463

R 464